JOHN BACH McMASTER

John Bach McMaster,

John Bach McMaster

AMERICAN HISTORIAN

By

ERIC F. GOLDMAN

1971

OCTAGON BOOKS

New York

Reprinted 1971
by special arrangement with Eric F. Goldman

OCTAGON BOOKS
A DIVISION OF FARRAR, STRAUS & GIROUX, INC.
19 Union Square West
New York, N. Y. 10003

LIBRARY OF CONGRESS CATALOG CARD NUMBER: 73-154664

ISBN-0-374-93179-8

Printed in U.S.A. by
NOBLE OFFSET PRINTERS, INC.
NEW YORK 3, N. Y.

TO

MY GALLANT FATHER

Preface to the Octagon Edition

THE REPUBLICATION of a book written many years ago inevi-
tably provokes a moment of reflection. I was attracted to the
project of a biography of John Bach McMaster and an analysis
of his writings because it was he who first based a major American historical work on the highly evocative conception, a
"history of the people." He made a considerable place for himself in the annals of American culture by telling the story of
the United States less in terms of celebrated politicians, generals, and entrepreneurs than of the workaday lives of ordinary
men and women. But McMaster was a decidedly conservative
gentleman of the turn-of-the-century vintage. Despite the Jeffersonian and populistic connotations of the phrase, "the people,"
his overall historical interpretation turned out to be one which
was more than acceptable to the plush corporate figures looking
out from the windows of the Union League Clubs of the nation.
The multi-volume *History of the People of the United States,*
full as it was of plain people doing plain things, cast a firm vote
for that President of the advantaged or at least of the secure,
William McKinley.

By the time I began research for this book at the close of the
1930's, the idea of "history of the people," now frequently called
"social history," was being widely applied and was acquiring
sharply different overtones. A new generation of historians did
their own interpreting and the result in many cases was a
strong vote for Franklin Roosevelt. In recent years, a good deal
of the social history has carried an impact that would have
discomfited McMaster even more. It expresses the interests and
aspirations of groups well below the chief beneficiaries of New
Dealism in their income and status, who were just so many
undeserving outcastes in the eyes of a sound Republican of
the early 1900's.

All of this represents a somewhat less than perfect world. What about The Truth without regard to the author's own ideological bent—the achievement of The Truth which for so long had been said to be the prime justification for writing history? Some practitioners of the historian's craft still believe that they can arrive at such Truth, or come quite close to it. However, many of my generation have assumed that historians are very human human beings, and that no matter how much they should try, no matter how arduously they do try, what they see in the past will be influenced by their view of the present and their vision of the future. Certainly what has happened to the conception of a "history of the people" from McMaster's day to the present does nothing to gainsay the assumption.

Yet to state that a historian must to some degree be a prisoner of his prepossessions is hardly to dismiss the value of his work. Whatever his limitations, the able and dedicated craftsman continues to ferret out fresh facts of significance, to listen to the message of factuality, to wrest from his pile of file cards a sense of the past which alone can give a civilization moorings. The very fact that he writes in part out of his own attitudes and feelings, conscious or unconscious, helps give him the drive to carry out his long and lonely task.

McMaster's *History of the People* may have voted for McKinley. It also brought to the fore a mass of forgotten material, widened the scope of what was considered the proper subject-matter of history, played a part in breaking open new paths of historical research and thinking. If he did not offer The Truth, he did present his own array of truths, arranged according to his own best lights, which resulted in a reconstruction of the American experience that had both substance and juice.

E. F. G.

Princeton, New Jersey
April 24, 1971

Acknowledgments

THIS BIOGRAPHY of John Bach McMaster has been made possible by the generous coöperation of his family. The historian's son, Dr. Philip D. McMaster, of the Rockefeller Institute for Medical Research, has extended to me every possible facility for using the mass of correspondence which his father left behind. The historian's sister, Mrs. Samuel G. Metcalf, placed at my disposal additional materials in her possession, and both Mrs. Metcalf and Mrs. Philip D. McMaster gave me the benefit of their reminiscences. By all members of the McMaster family I was left entirely free to use and interpret the materials as my historical sense dictated.

I did most of the work on this volume at the Johns Hopkins University and the book owes a great deal to the patient interest and discriminating criticism of colleagues in the Hopkins Department of History—Charles A. Beard, Kent Roberts Greenfield, W. Stull Holt, Frederic C. Lane, and Sidney Painter. Miss Lilly Lavarello, secretary of the History Department, could not have given more care to the typescript had it been her own. It would be embarrassing for them and for me if I tried to express the gratitude I feel to these genuine friends.

Chapter III is better for the suggestions of Professor Thomas J. Wertenbaker, of Princeton University; Chapter VI, for the suggestions of Dr. Richard Thursfield, of the Department of Education, Johns Hopkins. I also want to thank the men and women listed in the bibliography, who aided me in various ways in collecting McMaster materials.

Acknowledgments are due to the following publishers for the permissions they granted to use quotations from the books listed after their names: American Book Company, McMaster, *School History of the United States;* D. Appleton-Century Company, McMaster, *History of the People of the United States* and *With the Fathers;* Houghton Mifflin Company, McMaster, *Benjamin Franklin as a Man of Letters;* Little, Brown and Company, Lloyd C. Griscom, *Diplomatically Speaking;* The Macmillan Company, Charles H. Firth, ed., Thomas B. Macaulay, *History of England.*

E.F.G.

Princeton University
October 5, 1942

Contents

ACKNOWLEDGMENTS   vii

CHAPTER   PAGE

    I. "I WILL"   1

    II. YOUNG MAN IN A HURRY   14

    III. VOLUME ONE   31

    IV. SETTLING DOWN   50

    V. PROFESSOR AND PUBLICIST   61

    VI. PEOPLE'S HISTORIAN OF THE PEOPLE   79

    VII. THE HISTORY OF THE PEOPLE   105

    VIII. AS THE PATRIARCH   145

APPENDIX

    I.   159

    II.   160

    III.   161

    IV.   162

LIST OF McMASTER'S PRINTED WRITINGS AND
    SPEECHES   179

BIBLIOGRAPHY   185

INDEX   187

Illustrations

JOHN BACH McMASTER   *frontispiece*

McMASTER CARICATURES HIMSELF IN A LET-
  TER TO MISS STEVENSON   *facing page* 44

UNIVERSITY OF PENNSYLVANIA HISTORIANS
  ABOUT 1895   *facing page* 66

JOHN BACH McMASTER

CHAPTER I

"I Will"

When the *History of the People of the United States* became an overnight success in 1883, readers all over the country wanted to know who John Bach McMaster was.[1] The author was of little assistance, then or later. Indeed, he commanded his fiancée never to "tell anything about me on the peril of your life. I want the book but not myself 'to go down to posterity' as the saying is. I should like above all things to be the one man who wrote a book and never had anything more said about him than could be found in a biographical dictionary."[2] For a person seeking such seclusion, McMaster had written the wrong kind of history. His work was too different from its predecessors, too manifest in successors, too drenched in the individuality of its author. No synthesis of America's past, unless it be the audacious pages of Charles and Mary Beard, more persistently provokes the question, What kind of person wrote that kind of book?

The answer is so simple another book seems necessary to give it specific meaning. This historian of the people was, above all, one of "the people"—one of the middle classes which he associated with that term. New England families gave Henry Adams and Edward Channing names laden with distinction. Before James Ford Rhodes turned to history, iron ore had made him rich and Mark Hanna had become his brother-in-law. James Schouler was, quite consciously, of the *genus Harvardiensum*. But McMaster was

[1] An editor of *The Critic*, in a letter representative of many others, told McMaster, "We receive a great many inquiries as to who the new historian is but our information is of the most limited order." J. Gilder to McMaster, March 19, 1883, MS, McMaster Papers. For a description of these papers, see the bibliography at the close of this book. Unless otherwise identified, all manuscript sources used in this book may be found in the McMaster Papers.

[2] McMaster to Gertrude Stevenson, April 8, 1883, MS.

I

simply McMaster, of Brooklyn and the public schools. His very different history came after formative experiences very little different from those of thousands of other Americans.

Early in these experiences was first-hand knowledge of a heritage intertwined with the workaday past of the United States. During visits to the home of his grandfather, Robert Bach, young McMaster learned the business saga of that enterprising Londoner. In the year of Washington's Farewell Address, Bach had arrived in New York City as the apprentice of an importer of medical supplies. Before long, Bach was able to take over the business and set up what he boasted was "the finest shop in the city, all in the English style."[3] To gain a ready supply of imports, Bach established relations with the well-known Samuel Solomon, of Liverpool, whose *Guide to Health* was already in its fifty-third edition and whose "Cordial Balm of Gilead" was a national institution in England. Soon all along the northern seaboard agents of Bach sold the book and the balm, and the business expanded into a major pharmaceutical supply house. Later it was joined with others to become the giant McKesson and Robbins, Inc.

Bach took a bride from across the ocean, Margaret Cowan, of Newry, Ireland. In a Brooklyn that was a pleasant village of about six thousand people, on a spot where now stands one end of the Brooklyn Bridge, he built a capacious house of brick and marble and surrounded it with a large and luxuriant garden. Life was rich and varied in the Bach home, particularly in its cultural contacts across the ocean. The boys went to college in England, and the girls entertained young men like Thomas Crawford, the Italian-trained sculptor who was to do the figure of Freedom which stands on the dome of the Capitol. "Are you coming to Italy again," Crawford inquired of a friend in a letter which reached its destination by being addressed simply, "Frederic W. Philip, somewhere in New York or Brooklyn." "Or are you married, and consequently D—d.

---

[3] McMaster, "First Memoirs," p. 1, MS. All statements in Chap. I, unless otherwise supported, come from McMaster's "First Memoirs" or "Second Memoirs." These manuscripts are described in the bibliography.

Come to us and be happy my lad—."[4] But Philip had already chosen to be "D—d" and was married to Julia Anna Matilda Bach. The sudden death of the promising young artist widowed Julia Anna four months after the marriage. Five years later, in 1845, she married James McMaster.

The past of the McMaster family invited John's attention to other segments of American life. Both grandparents on this side were natives of Ballston Spa, near Saratoga Springs, New York. In the girlhood of grandmother Elizabeth Watrous, the settlement was frontier; her father, the pastor of the community, died in an Indian raid. By the time Miss Watrous grew to womanhood, people were beginning to flock to the Spa for the mineral waters and to trample over her grounds on the way to the adjacent spring. Curiously enough, she married first one and then the other of the twin Scottish boys, the McMasters. Twice widowed, she helped to support her sons by what a guidebook of the day called "a private boarding house. . . . Those who are fond of a retired situation, will be much gratified at this place, and withal will find a hospitable hostess, and very excellent accommodations, at a moderate price."[5] John remembered his grandmother only as a charming old lady nearing ninety, spectacles pushed up on her forehead, vigorously hobbling about on crutches.

The boy knew far more, and far more exciting things about his father. What John did not learn for himself dribbled down to him through the reminiscences of his mother. Before his marriage, James McMaster had packed merchandise on a mule and traded with Indians and half-breeds in villages stretching from Mexico City to Vera Cruz. Then this Yankee adventurer went to New Orleans, where he and his brother set up a banking house. Though the business prospered, James McMaster withdrew from the partnership in the late forties and struck out for even bigger stakes. He bought

[4] Thomas Crawford to Frederic W. Philip, Sept. 28, 1840, MS. This letter is in the possession of Mrs. Samuel G. Metcalf, John Bach McMaster's sister.

[5] Gideon M. Davison, *The Fashionable Tour: A Guide to Travellers visiting the Middle and Northern States and the Provinces of Canada* (Saratoga Springs, 1830), pp. 155-56.

the Oak Lawn, a plantation adjoining the lands of the future Confederate general, Pierre Beauregard.[6] There, on fields stretching back seven miles from the lower Mississippi, McMaster made a success of the growing of cane and its manufacture into sugar. His wife, Julia Anna, brought a touch of Yorker respectability to the French-speaking slaves. By affection and by promises of gifts, she succeeded in bringing about a number of *ex post facto* marriages only to find that the Negroes soon lapsed back into their free-lance ways.[7]

While making his living as a planter, James McMaster seems to have remained a Yankee in everything else, and he frequently returned to his native state for long visits. The couple's second child was born and died at Oak Lawn; after this tragedy, Mrs. McMaster never went south again.[8] John himself was born in the Brooklyn home of grandfather Bach on June 29, 1852. He had scarcely passed from swaddling clothes when his father sold the plantation on the installment plan, the payments to be made each year after the sugar was produced. Perhaps Oak Lawn was proving unprofitable, as so many other plantations were in the fifties; perhaps James McMaster was moved by his chronic restlessness. Whatever the impulse, selling on these terms ended by practically giving away the plantation, for few payments had been made when the Civil War stopped them completely. John did not see Oak Lawn except as a visitor years later, but he knew something of plantation life in a personal way unique among major American historians of his period.

After selling the plantation, James McMaster settled with his family in New York City, if it may be said that he ever settled. Soon McMaster and some associates organized a petroleum refining

[6] The location of the McMaster plantation is shown on a sketch opposite p. 147 of Charles Ellet, *The Mississippi and Ohio Rivers*, Philadelphia, 1853.

[7] In this and the preceding two paragraphs a few details come from interviews with Mrs. Samuel G. Metcalf and with the historian's son, Dr. Philip D. McMaster.

[8] The McMaster children were, in the order of their birth, Robert Bach, Roland Bach, John Bach, and Mary. The second child died shortly after birth. Philip D. McMaster, "Summary of the McMaster Family," MS, McMaster Papers.

company which, together with other projects, gave the family a comfortable living through the Civil War and in the period immediately afterward. For a long time the McMasters lived on or near East Fourteenth Street. In time the street was to become "the Fifth Avenue as well as the Coney Island of New York's Ghetto," but in the sixties Fourteenth Street was a prosperous residential district.[9] Later the family followed New York City in its movement up Manhattan and took a house on East Sixtieth Street, South Side. Not far away was a beer garden popular with the predominantly German neighbors. Many a summer evening during the Franco-Prussian War John heard *Die Wacht Am Rhein* resounding above the clinking beer mugs. Other summers were spent in the rusticity of 120th Street and Second Avenue, where, for a period, the McMasters rented a summer residence that was surrounded by nearly an acre of flower beds, vegetable patches, and fruit trees.

Merely living in New York City lavished on the boy a never-ending variety of ordinary people doing ordinary things.[10] John watched the Irish workers attacking with brooms made of twigs the thick dust that settled between the cobblestones when it was not swirling in the eyes of pedestrians. He wandered along one of the few paved avenues, Broadway, where, south of Chambers Street, song sheets were offered for sale from clothespins attached to strings wound through the fence. He bumped along in horsecars so crowded that, in summer, men hung on by the handrails. In winter

. . . the foulness of the air inside was made fouler still by the wet, reeking straw laid on the floor to keep warm the feet of the travellers. . . .

. . . The Second Avenue horsecars went as far as 63rd Street, and a "bob-tail" car took you the rest of the way. This vehicle was built like an omnibus. You entered by a door in the rear. The seats were carpeted benches along the side, and a light wire ladder up the outside of the end of the car led to a seat on the roof, just as. in an Irish jaunting car.

[9] Helen Worden, *The Real New York* (Indianapolis, 1932), p. 179.
[10] The sections of McMaster's memoirs covering his boyhood activities in New York and his description of the city have been edited and published under the title, "Young John Bach McMaster: A Boyhood in New York City," *New York History* (1939), XX, 316-24.

The passengers sat back to back. On top at the front sat the driver of the one horse. If you went inside, until you paid your fare the door was promptly shut and held tight by a strap which passed along the inside of the roof to the driver's booth. At the upper end of the car, near the roof, was a round hole through which you thrust your money if you wished change. You received the change in a little paper envelope from which you took the exact fare and dropped it through a slot into a glass box. The driver peeked in to see that the entire fare was there and then by a rod opened the bottom of the glass box and the money fell into a wooden receptacle. When you wished to get out you reached up and pulled the strap which pulled the driver's foot. He "loosened" up and the door swung open. At 125th Street, the end of the line, the driver by means of a chain drew a large pin out of a socket. The horse turned around in a semicircle, turning the car on a pivot as he went, until he was once more in the track. Then the pin was dropped into another socket and the car was ready for the return trip.[11]

John's education kept him in the center of New York life, for his schooling was public schooling. For six years he attended Grammar School No. 40, a dismal pile of gray stone on Twentieth Street, between First and Second Avenues. The book learning received here did not leave the historian with any memories of admiration; in his reminiscences, he paused only to remark that the history texts were "beneath contempt."[12] But he had a great deal to say about the principal's disciplinary methods, of which John could speak from personal knowledge:

On snowy mornings, or on mornings after a snow fall, it was the custom for the students who arrived early to line up along the curbstone in front of the school house and snow-ball the later comers. You had to run the gauntlet, and having done so and been well pelted, you might take your place in the lines across the street. After such sport the boys would be in fine fettle, and, on gathering in the assembly room to hear the Bible read and sing, would not be as quiet as Scott [the principal] thought they should be. Thereupon he would open his desk, take out a rattan as thick as your finger, and go down one aisle between the desks

[11] Ibid., pp. 318, 319.
[12] "Second Memoirs," p. 37, MS.

and up another, slashing right and left furiously. There was nothing to do but put your arms on the desk and take what came to you on the back of your head or across your shoulders. If some nervous or inefficient teacher lost control of his class and the boys whispered or grew restless, the offenders were sent to take their seats on a long bench that ran along the side of the assembly room. When some dozen or more of the culprits were seated on the bench, Scott would take out his rattan, line up the boys, and give each four lashes across the right hand held out at arms length. They were no gentle blows as I well know. . . .[13]

A little before three o'clock one of the boys would take a long pole, lift the hats from the pegs on which they hung, and shoot them to their owners. Overcoats were taken down in the same way "and, if necessary, catapulted across the room."[14] Then for John, boyish boy that he was, the day would really begin.

There was his stamp collection, to be taken care of and increased by purchases from the folding tables placed along the fence on Broadway from Chambers Street eastward. There was always a new Beadle and Munro dime novel, to be carried around in the pocket and devoured at every chance. After McMaster became a distinguished literary man, he still refused to speak harshly of the little paper-back thrillers. "They were fairly well written," he maintained, "were full of adventure, generally with Indians, for the cowboy had not come into existence, and were no more to be despised than are the mystery and murder novels so popular to-day."[15] Though the McMaster family was not pinched, John took pride in earning the money for his stamps and books. In winter he shoveled snow from the sidewalks in front of his home. Year round he saved old newspapers, lugged them on foot down to Ann Street, and received about a quarter for as large a bundle as he could carry. There was the genuine McMaster touch of his father in John's most ambitious project. With the dime novels he had purchased,

[13] "Young McMaster," *New York History*, XX, 320. David B. Scott was the principal.
[14] *Ibid.*
[15] *Ibid.*, p. 321.

he started a circulating library. The borrower was required to deposit ten cents as security and paid a penny each time he took out a book.

These activities did not consume so much of John's time that he neglected that institute of urban American life, the vacant lot. His favorite was on Fourteenth Street and Second Avenue, a large area which offered a fence to guarantee home runs, and an unpaved space between the fence and the flagstone walk which was ideal for spinning tops and shooting marbles. In winter the most exciting sports were hitching sleds to passing horse sleighs, firing snowballs at each other and at the drivers of vehicles, and ice skating on the lakes in Central Park. Now and then one of the neighborhood girls would stage a party where, between raids on the ice cream and cake, the youngsters danced the Lancers and the Virginia Reel and played Forfeits, Clap-in-and-Clap-out, and Going to Jerusalem.

New York City was all the more a school in American ways because of the times. The presidential campaign of 1860, with its brilliant torchlight parades on Broadway and on Fifth Avenue, amazed and delighted John. The war itself was more exciting than the best of his dime novels. John was nine when the struggle began; too young to understand its horror, he was old enough to enjoy its glamour. The gigantic Sumter meeting in Union Square, the roar that went up when the flag which had waved during the bombardment was brought before the crowd, the fifers and drummers urging men to enlist, the burst of enthusiasm as fresh contingents of New England troops marched through the streets, the thrills and laughs and tears of a city in crisis—these things stirred the boy with a sense of tremendous and bewildering happenings. The bewilderment was not decreased when John's father took him to the White House for the traditional handshake with the President of the United States. As the two neared the head of the waiting line, Lincoln was approached by a farmer in a linen duster crinkled by his railway journey from New York State.

"Up where I come from," the sturdy patriot said, "we believe that God and Abraham Lincoln are going to save this country."

"My friend," the President smiled, "you are half right."[16]

At home John waged with his own hands the war which he did not understand. The Surgeon General of the United States had appealed for scraped lint to be used in the army hospitals, and the younger son joined the rest of the patriotic family in preparing the material. Shortly after specie payments were suspended in 1862, the government issued paper currency in denominations of five, ten, twenty-five, and fifty cents. This money was purchased in long, continuous sheets, which it was John's job to cut.

In school, as he remarked later, "patriotism was pumped into us."[17] Every morning after the reading of the Bible, war tunes were sung and the boys were required to memorize every line of them. In time they acquired a repertoire including *Hail Columbia, Marching Through Georgia, John Brown's Body, In My Prison Cell I Sit, We are Coming, Father Abraham,* and of course *The Battle Hymn of the Republic.* One Monday in July 1863, the students were suddenly summoned to the Assembly Room, where they were told to go directly home and to remain there until further notice. The boys were now to have a holiday made memorable by the famous New York draft riots:

When I and many of my schoolmates reached the corner of Second Avenue and 20th Street, we beheld a great crowd gathered at the corner of 21st Street where there was then an arsenal. Of course, we did not go home but stopped to see what was happening. . . . The building was defended by a few employees and police who fired on the mob and fled by the rear doors. The rioters then broke down the front door, set fire to the building, threw out its contents and greeted the firemen when they came with a shower of cobblestones torn up from the street.

On the following day, as there was no school, I went with some playmates to Union Square to see what might be going on there, and heard that the mob was attacking the home of Mayor Opdyke on lower Fifth Avenue. Thither we went and from a safe distance beheld the looting. Alarmed at the condition of affairs in New York as the rioting grew worse day by day, my . . . father sent us to Brooklyn to visit my aunt. On the way down Broadway in the South Ferry Omnibus we saw, running from one of the side streets near Bowling Green, a negro chased by a howling mob. As he ran a cobble stone struck him on the back of the head. He fell forward and the mob closed over him and in likelihood he was beaten to death.[18]

The tragic dénouement of the war complicated further John's tangle of impressions. He heard that someone had shot the man with whom he had shaken hands in the White House, and this plain person seemed to mean so much that the whole city put on crêpe for the funeral. John stood in wide-eyed wonder as troops marched the streets with muskets reversed, bands wailed forth doleful music, and grown men and women wept openly at the sight of the hearse.

In the year of Lincoln's assassination, 1865, McMaster graduated from grammar school and enrolled in the New York Free Academy, now the College of the City of New York. Here he completed the work of the Introductory Class—which served in place of high school as a bridge between elementary school and college—and the four-year college course. He could not have attended a college more closely associated with its surrounding society. Offering a free education, in buildings located in the center of the city, the City College attracted the sons of all economic groups. Without dormitories or campus, it was New York at college rather than a collegiate world of its own.[19]

The full influence of this human mixer was felt by McMaster, for he was exceedingly active in the college life. In time he headed the Phrenocosmian Society, one of the two major literary clubs in the school, and Delta Kappa Epsilon, a fraternity powerful in student politics. By vote of the seniors, he became both president of

[18] *Ibid.*, p. 324. George Opdyke was Mayor, 1862-63.

[19] This description of City College is based on Richard R. Bowker, "The College of the Past," in Philip J. Mosenthal and Charles F. Horne, eds., *The City College, Memories of Sixty Years* (New York, 1907), pp. 3-63, and on a letter to the author, dated July 23, 1938, from Mr. Lewis S. Burchard, of the class of '76.

his class and a member of Phi Beta Kappa.[20] Economic pressure at home made McMaster even less the cloistered student. During his junior year, another oil company tapped the main supply of the McMaster firm and the adventure collapsed. The man who had made money from half-breeds, banking, sugar, and oil knew how to keep his wife and children from actual poverty, but the family budget was so strained that the son felt he ought to earn at least enough to pay for his clothing. This he did by devoting every afternoon and some Saturdays and evenings to a lithograph machine which turned out duplicate exercises for the professors. McMaster's college record slumped so seriously that he repeated the junior year, but this was all part of an education which a Henry Adams never had.

At the college stage McMaster's interests and aptitudes seemed to center in the sciences. Though not an honor man at graduation, he had led his class twice in both physics and chemistry; his emerging talent in free-hand drawing had been applied chiefly to engineering problems and to illustrating experiments in physics.[21] The City College courses in history were under the direction of a professor of history and belles-lettres, who is remembered chiefly as a coin collector.[22] The texts were eight books of literary selections and one history, and that history was Marcius Willson's *Outlines of History*, a dry compendium which contained only occasional brief

[20] In January, 1872—McMaster's senior year—the City College chapter of Phi Beta Kappa voted to make eligible for membership not only the honor men of the year but also five students selected by the senior class. McMaster was one of those chosen by his class. Probably there was some controversy over the matter, for these nominees were not admitted until the next year. Then the rules were changed so as to make only honor men eligible in the future. For this information I am indebted to Dr. Martin Goldwasser, secretary of the City College chapter.

[21] *Merit Rolls of the College of the City of New York*, 1865-72. These published records show the standing of each student in individual courses and in the class as a whole. McMaster's physics notebooks, which were illustrated profusely, won him prizes in both his junior and senior years. "Second Memoirs," p. 24.

[22] Charles E. Anthon, whose prominence in the field of numismatics is given most emphasis in the *Dictionary of American Biography* account.

references to American history.[23] Such history interested McMaster little. He made no exceptional marks in the courses and did not bother to join the History Club organized in his junior year.[24] When McMaster was graduated in 1872, outward appearances indicated that he was a good scientist in the making.

But the appearances were outward only. The swirl of events in which McMaster matured had not left his mind entirely in the laboratory. Scarcely less exciting and even more bewildering were the Reconstruction years which rushed along while he was in college. The people of McMaster's own country, the men and women he had sat beside in the horsecar or seen riding through Central Park, seemed to have stopped one kind of fighting only to begin another. In his junior year at college, while the Radicals rode high in Washington, McMaster became intensely curious about all this furor. Why had the South seceded? Why had the neighbor of Oak Lawn, General Beauregard, led soldiers against neighbors from Fourteenth Street? Why did people disagree so violently about Reconstruction? What did slavery have to do with all these things? In his senior year, amid a whirl of college life, McMaster set about finding out.

First, and naturally enough, he borrowed from the City College library the recently published book of Horace Greeley, *The American Conflict*.[25] Reading this was satisfactory enough until McMaster came to the Missouri Compromise and learned for the first time that a large section of his United States had belonged to France. Immediately he wanted to know how France had acquired this land and why she sold it. Turning to the College library again, he found answers to his questions in Parkman's *La Salle and the Dis-*

[23] The history courses McMaster took are described in the *Nineteenth Annual Register of the College of the City of New York*, 1867-68, p. 17, and in the *Twentieth Annual Register . . .* , 1868-69, p. 37. The 1854 edition of Willson must have been the one used.

[24] McMaster's history marks may be found in the *Merit Rolls of the College of the City of New York*, 1867-69. The members of the History Club were listed in a student publication, *The Microcosm*, 1870-71, 1871-72.

[25] Two vols., Chicago, 1864-66.

covery of *the Great West* and the large-scale histories of the United States by Bancroft and Hildreth.[26]

Before McMaster finished these works, his reading had become something more than a quest for specific information. He was groping for the balanced drama of a people in growth, and particularly intriguing to him were the decades immediately before the crisis of his own time. Bancroft and Hildreth offered little except politics and wars and, between them, carried the story only to 1821. The compendiums which did go farther disgusted McMaster by their inadequacies. With astonishment he told himself that a satisfactory history of the American people simply had not been written.

Inviting as this conclusion was, McMaster did nothing about it during his busy last year of college. After graduation in 1872 he visited an aunt in Ballston Spa with vacation rather than history on his mind. Leisurely he rambled through her small library, came upon a copy of Macaulay's *History of England,* and settled in an armchair to read it. When he finished the famous third chapter, "The State of England in 1685," the mood of leisure was gone.[27] Surely life in the United States had been as interesting as England in 1685. Yet no history had been written by an American Macaulay.

"Why don't you do it?" McMaster reflected with a thrill of adventure that must have made the armchair a frigate racing through wind and water.

For a moment, but only for a moment, he hesitated at the thought that this was a gigantic undertaking for a boy of twenty. Then firmly, almost gaily, McMaster told himself, "I will."[28]

[26] Francis Parkman, *La Salle and the Discovery of the Great West,* Boston, 1869; George Bancroft, *A History of the United States from the Discovery of the Continent,* 10 vols., Boston, 1834-75; Richard Hildreth, *The History of the United States of America,* New York, 6 vols., 1849-52.

[27] Thomas B. Macaulay, *The History of England from the Accession of James the Second,* ed. Charles H. Firth (6 vols., London, 1913-15), I, Chap. III.

[28] "Second Memoirs," pp. 28-29, MS. See also "Diary," III, March 5, 1883, MS. This diary is described in the bibliography.

CHAPTER II

Young Man in a Hurry

THE vow of McMaster to write a great history had the easy finality associated with youth at twenty. He seemed determined to do it— unless he became more determined to do something else. Research for history demanded drudgery without quick glory and a regular source of income to support the writer before, and perhaps after, he published. McMaster had the restless ambition that does not like to wait. By the time he was graduated from college, he was poor and growing poorer. A year later the father died, apparently leaving behind him little except affectionate memories of an adventurer who had ventured too often.[1]

Anxious about the present and fumbling for his future, McMaster undertook no specialized training in history. It was important for him and for historiography that he did not. Since American historical scholarship was in its adolescence at this time, it was customary for students to seek advanced training and a Ph.D. in Europe, where they came under the influence of men concerned primarily with the history of political institutions.[2] In the United States European-trained teachers were beginning to make history a profession, and the attitude they brought to their university chairs

---

[1] "Second Memoirs," pp. 24-25, MS.

[2] Charles F. Thwing, *The American and the German University* (New York, 1928) and Andrew D. White, *European Schools of History and Politics* ("Johns Hopkins University Studies in Historical and Political Science," V, no. 12, Baltimore, 1887), *passim*. Typically, H. B. Adams wrote, "In Germany, I first learned the true method. . . . I first began to realize that government and law are the real forces which bind society and the world together" (*The Study and Teaching of History* [Richmond, 1898], p. 8). Even James Harvey Robinson, who in time was to call for a "New History," had come back from his German studies interested primarily in the history of constitutional law. Harry E. Barnes, "James Harvey Robinson," in Howard W. Odum, ed., *American Masters of Social Science* (New York, 1927), pp. 327-28.

strengthened the tradition of political history already established by Bancroft, Hildreth, and a host of lesser Americans.[3] The leader in the professionalization of American history, Herbert B. Adams, was a Ph.D. from Heidelberg. On the wall of his seminar room he placed the words, "History is past politics and politics present history."[4]

From this downpour of political history McMaster was sheltered by the umbrella of his ignorance. He never sat at a seminar table until he sat at the head of one. He made no trip abroad. During the years between McMaster's armchair vow and the publication of his first volume, he was so little in touch with the established historical world that he even failed to read Green's *Short History of the English People*—a widely discussed volume that might have been expected to attract him if any history did.[5] Very much the amateur, McMaster lived out in the world of Black Friday and the Crédit Mobilier, a world of raw grapple and grab in which every day's newspapers screamed out that politicians and warriors were not the whole story.[6]

During the winter following his vow (1872-73), McMaster merely dabbled in history. Much of his time was given to the duties connected with a teaching fellowship in English at the City College.[7] In spare moments, the frugal student penciled notes for his history in old copy books, on unused halves of letters, and on

[3] The founders of graduate instruction in history in the United States—Andrew D. White, C. K. Adams, H. B. Adams, Moses Coit Tyler, Henry Adams—had studied in European universities. This was also true of four of the five men who made up the first officers of the American Historical Association (all except the Treasurer), and of four of its first five presidents.

[4] A picture of the old seminar room is in the possession of Prof. Kent Roberts Greenfield, of Johns Hopkins.

[5] McMaster, "Diary," III, March 5, 1883, MS.

[6] On the connection between contemporary conditions and the broadening of the content of history, see the comments of Carl Becker, "Some Aspects of the Influence of Social Problems upon the Study and Writing of History," *Publications of the American Sociological Society* (1913), VII, 78-79.

[7] "Second Memoirs," pp. 24-25, MS. The official announcement of McMaster's appointment to the fellowship is in the *Twenty-fourth Annual Register of the College of the City of New York* (1872-73), p. 38.

the backs of envelopes and handbills.[8] At the end of this winter, McMaster was sure of only two things about his history. The book was to begin with the Treaty of Paris, for "that document put an end to Colonial dependence, and introduced a new comer into the great family of Nations." The first chapter, in obvious imitation of Macaulay's third chapter, would describe the general state of the United States in 1784.[9]

Making these plans did not mean that McMaster was ready to devote himself to history. Work in the applied sciences, with its promise of steady salaries and steady advancement, had strong attractions for this young man who had led his class in two sciences.[10] In the spring of 1873, McMaster accepted a position as Chief Clerk and Civil Assistant to Lieutenant Colonel George L. Gillespie, Corps of Engineers, United States Army.[11] Philip H. Sheridan, of Civil War fame, was writing his memoirs and had secured from Congress an appropriation for a topographical survey of the battle-fields at Winchester, Cedar Creek, and Waynesboro, Virginia. Under the direction of Gillespie, McMaster led one of the small surveying parties. He had not been at work two weeks when he felt the exuberance that comes with early experiences of independent living and authority over others.

If you could see us trudging down the back woods and over the fields [McMaster wrote his mother] you would imagine we were a party of topers out on a spree. Every one has a dirty shirt and ragged breeches, a

[8] McMaster to Gertrude Stevenson, March 4, 1883, MS.

[9] "Second Memoirs," pp. 28-29, MS.

[10] McMaster is sometimes said to have taken a C.E. or an M.A., or both degrees during his postgraduate work. There is no evidence in the official records of the College that he was awarded either degree. At the end of his postgraduate year, McMaster was given a diploma (*25th Ann. Reg. of C.C.N.Y.* [1873-74], p. 42), but this merely represented a year of study and teaching and was not a degree. Mr. Donald A. Roberts, secretary of the C.C.N.Y. Alumni Association, has generously checked this matter for me.

[11] The section of McMaster's memoirs describing his experiences while on the Sheridan project have been edited and published under the title, "Reliving History: John Bach McMaster as an Army Clerk," *Journal of the American Military Institute* (1940), IV, 127-28.

red face and a broad brim "sun down" with a tuft of "ha-ar" out of the top. . . . As for myself, I go along like a lord. I have one of the party to carry the instrument, and have nothing to do but to take a look through it and note the readings, and have succeeded so well that I consider myself an accomplished surveyor.[12]

Winchester's many relics of a momentous past refueled McMaster's interest in history.[13] Less than a decade past, three pitched battles and about seventy-five skirmishes had been fought within two miles of the town. The fields McMaster surveyed stood almost as the soldiers had left them; bullets, fragments of shells, and remnants of uniforms lay scattered among trees riddled by artillery fire.[14] First-hand stories of the battles came to him from inhabitants of the town and countryside.[15]

Living in Winchester kept McMaster close—too close for his taste—to some of the people. The town impressed him as one of "pigs" and "niggers," the latter being "the only animals" visible when he arrived.[16] McMaster's living quarters were in a rickety hotel where he drank out of handle-less cups, wiped his fingers on wet napkins, and slept between dirty sheets.

The view from the windows is one of surpassing beauty. It opens on the kitchen yard, in which are several unnamable outhouses, a swill tub and the nigger quarters. A little further on are a few houses, whose roofs seem to be weak in the back, whose walls have more cracks in them than bricks and whose bricks have more dirt in them than paint. When the wind comes from this quarter it is generally ladened with the balmy odor of "Afric's dusky race" or that of sundry ditches . . . if it were

---

[12] McMaster to his mother, Aug. 16, 1873, MS.

[13] "Summary of an Autobiographical Talk of McMaster," a manuscript used through the courtesy of Prof. Roy F. Nichols, of the University of Pennsylvania.

[14] McMaster to Robert M. McMaster (a brother), May 31, 1873, MS; "McMaster as an Army Clerk," *Jl. of the Am. Mil. Inst.*, IV, 127-28.

[15] This statement comes from notes taken by Dr. Albert Cook Myers on conversations he had with McMaster in the Franklin Inn Club, Philadelphia. Dr. Myers placed his notes on McMaster in a separate folder in the archives of the Franklin Inn Club.

[16] McMaster to his mother, May 21, 1873, MS.

not for occasional work in the office I *might* imagine myself in Paradise.[17]

In the dull routine of Winchester, a Methodist camp meeting was an event indeed, and McMaster followed the crowd to the tent. "I . . . went forth to 'get religion,' " he wrote his mother, "but like many others who go for wool I came back nearly shorn."[18]

The flashes of exuberance in McMaster's early letters from Winchester quickly gave way to sarcasm. The squalor of Winchester seems to ·have sharpened in McMaster the realization that the young man in a hurry was slowly getting nowhere. When his twenty-first birthday came, McMaster let the day slip by unobserved, and then wrote his mother,

I was not one of those fortunate ones who are born to sit in high places, wear purple and fine linen and create holydays [*sic*] for the great unwashed. . . . I had no broad acres or ancestral title with an unlimited bank account to support it. . . .[19]

After the survey of the battlefields was finished, McMaster was sent to Chicago, where the materials were to be made ready for Sheridan's use. The new scene brought no new cheer. Though McMaster prepared one of the topographical maps that appeared in Sheridan's *Memoirs*, his regular work was the monotonous writing and filing of letters for Gillespie.[20] After a day of this, McMaster went home to a boarding house, where the dinner hour was enlivened only by squabbles between the husband and the landlady,

an unusually small, exceedingly dumpy and particularly talkative young married lady, owning to some twenty summers, who dresses in a most becoming manner, does penance in a huge gold chair with a huge gold

[17] *Ibid.*, May 24, 1873 [?], MS.
[18] *Ibid.*, Aug. 26, 1873, MS.
[19] *Ibid.*, June 30, 1873, MS.
[20] "McMaster as an Army Clerk," *Jl. of the Am. Mil. Inst.*, IV, 128. His bored unhappiness is revealed in all his letters of the period. The map McMaster prepared appeared in the *Personal Memoirs of P. H. Sheridan* (2 vols., New York, 1888), II, 117.

cross, wears her hair on the top of her head and looks as happy as a small sun-flower about to run to seed.[21]

The occasional visits of Sheridan to the office left McMaster with an unpleasant picture even of the great. Years later he retained the memory of

a hot-tempered, ugly-faced, long-armed little Irishman. . . . I remember one of his outbreaks of ill temper. His headquarters were in the Western Union Telegraph Company's building, corner of Washington and La Salle streets. Electricity was obtained, in those days, from wet batteries, and those the telegraph company used were stored on the top floor. One day Sheridan went to the elevator and pressed the button, but the car passed on up without stopping. It was loaded with wet batteries for the top floor. Sheridan went into a rage and, having a book in his hand, smashed the glass in the elevator door. The superintendent of the building thereupon put up a wire netting so that the elevator boys could see the General and at once take him on board. Sheridan went into another passion, sent an orderly to tear out the wire, and told the superintendent he would move headquarters elsewhere. He was told, so the story runs, that his quarters were leased for a term which would not expire for several years, and that it did not make any difference if he did move. He calmed down and the wire net remained.[22]

In the spring of 1874 McMaster returned to a New York writhing under hard times. For three years he lived at his mother's home and squeezed out a living by tutoring students, among whom were the cousins of Theodore Roosevelt. "Now and then Teddy would appear on the scene," McMaster remembered, "and then all work stopped."[23] Much of McMaster's free time was spent satisfying his "strange urge to write."[24] Quickly he turned out two technical books for the *Van Nostrand Science Series,* and a scattering of shorter writings.[25] Then a reading of Henry Buckle's *History*

[21] McMaster to his mother, January 7, 27, 1874, MSS.
[22] "McMaster as an Army Clerk," *Jl. of the Am. Mil. Inst.,* IV, 128.
[23] "Second Memoirs," pp. 32-33, MS.
[24] *Ibid.,* p. 34, MS.
[25] The books for the Van Nostrand Series were *Bridge and Tunnel Centres* (New York, 1875) and *High Masonry Dams,* New York, 1876.

of Civilization in England joined the scientific and historical interests of McMaster to produce a manuscript entitled "The Struggle of Man with Nature."[26]

We have been greatly impressed [replied one publisher to whom McMaster sent the manuscript] by the amount of research displayed in the chapters sent to us, as well as by the force and wealth of illustration with which you support your generalizations. If we were permitted to criticise we would suggest that the book errs, perchance, on the side of profuseness.[27]

From the point of view of commercial sales, the book must have erred in other ways too, for it was rejected by all of the several publishers to whom it was sent. Discouraged, McMaster tore up the manuscript.[28]

If reading Buckle produced this immediate failure, it may well have contributed to McMaster's eventual success as a historian. Buckle's *History* started McMaster on wide readings that presumably included others of the science-minded thinkers who had such wide audiences in the seventies. This group directed attention to conditions surrounding institutions rather than to the institutions themselves.[29] In the preceding decade, ideas almost identical with those of Buckle had led the American chemist, John William Draper, to write history which minimized the importance of great men and explained civilization on both sides of the ocean in terms of geography and physiology.[30] The emphasis of science on non-

[26] "Second Memoirs," p. 24, MS. Buckle's influence is also plain in McMaster, "The Influence of Geographical Position on the Civilization of Egypt and Greece," *National Quarterly Review* (1876), XXIV, 29-52.

[27] Scribner, Armstrong, and Co. to McMaster, March 25, 1878, MS.

[28] "Second Memoirs," p. 34, MS.

[29] McMaster speaks of his readings in *ibid.* For interesting discussions of the connection between science-mindedness and the broadening content of history, see "Darwinism and History," in Harold Temperley, ed., *Selected Essays of J. B. Bury* (Cambridge, 1930), pp. 23-42; Carl Becker in the *Publications of the American Sociological Society*, VII, 77-78; Henri See, *Science et Philosophie de L'histoire*, Paris, 1933.

[30] Donald E. Emerson, "Hildreth, Draper, and 'Scientific History,'" in Eric F. Goldman, ed., *Historiography and Urbanization, Essays in American History in Honor of W. Stull Holt* (Baltimore, 1941), pp. 153-69.

political factors was not likely to be lost on engineer McMaster.[31]

If McMaster's extensive reading included much contemporary fiction, that reading could have directed him toward social history. Victorian realism was focusing attention on the common stuff of American life. A great artist, wrote the master of Victorian realism, William Dean Howells, is one with a talent "robust enough to front the everyday world and catch the charm of its work-worn, care-worn, brave, kindly face." Publishers' lists were including more and more fiction describing the workaday existence of Indiana Hoosiers, Carolina Tarheels, Mississippi Yahoos, and other local groups.[32] The author of *The Hoosier Schoolmaster* even planned to write a history of the people. Three years before McMaster's first volume appeared, Edward Eggleston informed his brother,

I am going to write a series of volumes which together shall constitute a History of Life in the United States—not a history of the United States, bear in mind, but a history of life there, the life of the people, the sources of their ideas and habits, the course of their development from beginnings.[33]

Not the United States but its people—much of the literature of the day rings with the tone of the McMaster's *History of the People*.

Unrestricted reading and writing came to an end for McMaster in January 1877, when he was appointed to the faculty of the newly established John C. Green School of Science at Princeton.[34] The position, in the form of an assistant professorship of engineering,

---

[31] When McMaster's first volume appeared, the *Book News* (1888, VII, 63) said that it attracted attention "as constituting a powerful bond between natural science and philosophical and sociological literature. . . ."

[32] Vernon L. Parrington, *Main Currents in American Thought* (3 vols., New York, 1927-30), III, 237-53. The Howells statement is quoted on p. 249.

[33] Quoted in George C. Eggleston, *The First of the Hoosiers* (Philadelphia, 1903), p. 363.

[34] Officially Princeton was called the College of New Jersey until 1896. The section of McMaster's memoirs covering his Princeton period has been edited and published under the title, "The Princeton Period of John Bach McMaster," *Proceedings of the New Jersey Historical Society* (1939), LVII, 214-30. For McMaster's appointment, see p. 216 and James McCosh to McMaster, Dec. 29, 1876, MS.

had been originally offered to Professor William H. Burr, of the Rensselaer Polytechnic Institute, but Burr declined. In his place he recommended McMaster, and the younger and less experienced man was made Instructor in Civil Engineering at a salary of $350 a term plus room and board in the college dormitories. McMaster's room, in the isolated heights of Witherspoon Hall, was two floors above the living quarters of an undergraduate then known only as Tommy Wilson.[35] After long experience with the boarding houses of Winchester and Chicago, nothing impressed McMaster more than

. . . the victuals. Oh mi. Think of having eatable things to eat and drinkable things to drink. Think of coffee that keeps you awake at night, and tea that actually grew in China. Of pie that is "flaky" and of meat that is not cold. In the morning my peaceful (not so peaceful lately in consequence of mince pies with brandy in them), slumbers are "broken" by the college bell which rings at 7 A.M. Therefore I "rise" and "lave" myself in a basin all over blue lovers and blue boats and blue cows, and coam [sic] my flowing mane in a glass that does full justice to the richness of my teutonic loveliness. Then I excavate my nails & wend my way to the breakfast room. No sooner do I appear at the door of the said room than I am met by a waiter in a black swallow tail coat and a white vest with ditto tie and ditto gloves who escorts me to a chair which is drawn out by a second waiter in ditto coat and ditto vest and ditto tie. I seat myself in the chair and am lost in the contemplation of a table cloth and napkins as "white as a sheet" when the said waiter appears with a silver (?) dish of g-r-a-p-e-s (read it slowly) in one hand, a blue glass bowl on a red napkin on a white plate in the other, which he sets down before me and then diving after a breakfast programme politely invites me to order. . . . Imagine yourself chewing grapes and trying to decide whether you'll have coffee or tea or chocolate to drink, and whether you'll have boiled chicken or chops done up in blue paper, or liver stew or beaf stake [sic] with mushrooms, or smelts or salmon, or omelet, or . . . eggs, or fish cakes, or—oh lord! to eat.

[35] Letter to the author, dated Feb. 8, 1940, from Mr. Henry Crew, a student in the Green School in McMaster's day.

. . . I have been trying for four breakfasts to get even with the bill of fare, but it's no use, no use.[36]

Yet McMaster was not happy at Princeton. Very early in his stay he came to feel that he was not accepted by the community. Most of the professors, McMaster told his mother, left him "sublimely alone," and his experiences with the younger set were even less fortunate.[37] Probably while in college, McMaster had "come to the conclusion that dancing is one of the 'necessaries of life' and . . . that I should like to take a few lessons just enough to learn to jump in the fashionable way."[38] If McMaster learned to jump in the fashionable way, it was not enough. Quiet, even shy, with sarcasm for most of his small talk, he was rarely sought after by the belles of the community. "He used to call at my mother's house," one of them remembered years later, "but no oftener than I could help." McMaster was savagely hurt, Princeton legend has it, when his proposal of marriage was turned down by a socially brilliant daughter of one of the professors.[39]

The University itself came to seem a very unpleasant place. "Teaching lunk-heads to survey farms, and rivers, and railroads," McMaster assured a friend, "is not so much fun as it looks."[40] In time, surveying annoyed McMaster so much that he made it the subject of one of the tart little ballads in which he occasionally worked off his indignation:

> And so the level next he tried
> But all he gained by that

[36] McMaster to his mother, Jan. 7, 1877, MS. McMaster often deliberately misspelled, according to Dr. Philip D. McMaster, in order to add to the amusing effect of his letters.

[37] *Ibid.*, Jan. 15, 1877, MS.

[38] *Ibid.*, Aug. 28 [no year], MS.

[39] This paragraph is based on interviews with William B. Scott, Professor Emeritus of Geology, and William F. Magie, Dean Emeritus of Princeton. Mr. Henry Crew, in his letter to the author of Feb 8, 1940, remarked that McMaster was "a much under-estimated man" at Princeton.

[40] McMaster to Gertrude Stevenson, March 18, 1883, MS.

Was to find out that he himself
And not the ground was flat.[41]

The listlessness and self-importance of the students, the rigmarole of academic routine, the daily immersion in a subject for which he had no great enthusiasm again provoked from McMaster the sarcasm of discontent.[42] Especially irritating were the freshmen,

. . . spry, slick, funny little boys just fresh from their mammas and their schools, and afflicted with a super abundance of saliva which they deposit on the floor, notwithstanding that I have warned them that a student who expectorates on the floor must not expect-to-rate high in his class. . . . [I teach them in old Dickinson Hall where] the echoes are something terrible . . . when a few days ago I went in the room suddenly and sort of slammed the big door, the echoes started up and proved a proposition taken up in recitation the day before.[43]

And then there was always President James McCosh and his faculty. McMaster's immediate superior was a professor who seems to have richly earned the reputation of a crank by such exploits as abandoning a project because someone spelled a word inaccurately in the plans.[44] Both McCosh and the faculty ruined themselves in McMaster's eyes when the President, arguing against the expulsion of a student, threatened to carry the matter to the Board of Trustees if the professors did not support him. "Would you believe it," McMaster exploded, "the old fogies took in their horns and backed down!! Everybody has to eat a peck of dirt, but some folks are not satisfied with anything under a cartload."[45] The religious atmosphere prevailing at Princeton disgusted McMaster. "In 1876," President McCosh later declared, "we had a deep religious revival. . . . Every student, indeed every member of the college, felt awed and subdued. It was estimated that upwards of one hundred were

[41] *Ibid.*, Sept. 12, 1880, MS.
[42] See especially *ibid.*, Sept. 16, 1882, MS.
[43] McMaster to his mother, Jan. 15, 1877, MS.
[44] Interview with Prof. W. B Scott. The head of the Civil Engineering Department was Charles McMillan.
[45] McMaster to Gertrude Stevenson, Oct. 1, 1882, MS.

converted."[46] McMaster was neither converted nor subdued. It was not only that the Princeton men were sect-conscious Presbyterians, he snorted; they were "time serving, money worshipping, Mammon-loving. . . ." When McMaster's turn to preside at chapel came, he picked for his Biblical reading the stern lines of the sixth chapter of Matthew "for their especial benefit, and I declare I do not see how they can ever read it or listen to it without feeling that there is something 'pussonell' in it. I will bet you two to one they never ask me to read again."[47]

McMaster's Princeton-phobia was an encouraging background for his reviving interest in history. Direct impetus to go on with the story of the people came from the centennial celebrations of 1876, which set the mind of the country to thinking of its past and thereby created a vast new market for history.[48] Now that being the American Macaulay seemed more surely than ever a thoroughfare to success, McMaster pushed ahead on his history during the summer vacation of 1877 and, as much as his teaching duties would permit, in the following winter. During this period he decided upon a terminal date. If the work was to open with the birth of the country, he mused, a good place to close was the end of the struggle that preserved the Union. Careful consideration caused McMaster to pull his closing date back to 1861, "for I had just sense enough to know that many a year would have to elapse, before anybody could write the history of reconstruction and of our relations with Great Britain." Five volumes seemed enough for the seventy-eight years from 1783 to 1861.[49]

[46] James McCosh, *Twenty Years of Princeton College* (New York, 1888), p. 54.

[47] McMaster to Gertrude Stevenson, Oct. 1, 1882, MS.

[48] For the impetus that came to McMaster from the Centennial, see "Second Memoirs," pp. 37-38. For the general influence of the Centennial on the writing of history, see A. Howard Clark, "What the United States Government has Done for History," *Annual Report of the American Historical Association for 1894* (Washington, 1895), p. 549; J. Franklin Jameson, *The American Revolution Considered as a Social Movement* (Princeton, 1926), pp. 1-3. *The Magazine of American History* dates from 1877.

[49] "Second Memoirs," pp. 37-39, MS.

At the end of the school year of 1878, McMaster once again laid aside his history. This time he accepted an offer, made by Arnold Guyot, the director of the E. M. Museum at Princeton, to lead a group of postgraduate students on a summer fossil-collecting expedition in the West.[50] Here was a chance to be on the move again, engaged in a new kind of work in a place which offered at least the attraction of being far from Princeton. The way McMaster jumped at the position indicates that, despite renewed interest in his history, he was not ready to give up other opportunities in order to get it done.

The party crossed the country on the Union Pacific Railroad, and in June 1878 arrived at Fort Bridger in southeastern Wyoming. "General Sherman when he was here," McCosh wrote from Princeton, "did not anticipate any difficulties from the Indians. But if you find there is danger you must retreat immediately."[51] The instruction never had to be followed. Long uneventful hours in the saddle, often through country of stunning beauty, brought the party to the gnarled Bad Lands where their work was to be done. Then came day after day of

. . . climbing up & down the shale bluffs in search of fish. To do this scientifically you first pick out a good, steep straight up & down bluff; then you lay hands on your hammer & chisel & begin the ascent with all fours. When you have gone on this way for half an hour you will probably reach a "shelf" where you sit down & look about you. If Fortune favors you, half an hours work with your hammer & chisel will bring out a thin shale with a black chocolate looking streak about 1/16 of an inch thick running across it. This is the fish. You take your bowie knife, pry open the shale & there is your fish. This you keep up all day, cutting out shales, pulling big pieces of the bank down on you, & filling

[50] This expedition is described in "McMaster's Princeton Period," *Proceedings of the New Jersey Historical Society,* LVII, 217-24, and by one of the graduate students who made the trip, William B. Scott, in *Some Memories of a Palaeontologist* (Princeton, 1939), pp. 76-82. See also Robert B. McMaster to J. B. McMaster, May 23, 1878, MS.

[51] James McCosh to McMaster, July 8, 1878, MS. McMaster carried with him a letter from General Sherman to the "Commanding Officers on the Plains" (June 19, 1878, MS), instructing the army men to extend to the party "assistance if they . . . need it."

your eyes with dirt—& when evening comes you put your trust in Providence & begin the descent. This is the kind of work we have in store for us all summer. But it gives us mighty appetites. Only last evening I got away with seven tin cups of soup & two peaches & was then far, far behind . . . [some of the others]. *Damn* the mosquitoes.[52]

It was thus with McMaster during the whole of the expedition. Though interested in the work, he did not seem interested enough to feel content. No scientific enthusiasm soaked the acid from his letters. For William B. Scott and Henry F. Osborn, two of the five postgraduates, the expedition was practically the beginning of distinguished careers as paleontologists. Osborn alone gleaned five technical articles from the findings of the party.[53] But McMaster, the chief of the expedition, merely appended one scientific study to the report of Osborn and then presented a paper before the American Geographical Society that reads more like the work of a historian than of a paleontologist.[54] Opening with an observation from his favorite Macaulay, McMaster had not advanced a page before he talked of the rôle of fossils "when the history of civilization comes to be written, as it is to be hoped someday it will be. . . ."[55] Four of the twenty-one pages were devoted to a sketch of "the influence which fossil bones have exerted over the human mind at every stage of the long march from ignorance and barbarism to the highest degree of knowledge and refinement."[56] The findings of the expedition were presented in a Macaulay-like restoration of Wyoming's Cretaceous Age.[57]

The expedition was far more important to McMaster the his-

---

[52] McMaster to his mother and sister, June 20, 1878, MS.

[53] Henry F. Osborn, *Fifty-two Years of Research, Observation and Publication, 1877-1929* (New York, 1930), pp. 3-4, 56, 64, 66-67.

[54] Henry F. Osborn, *A Memoir upon Loxolophodon and Uintatherium . . . Accompanied by a Stratigraphical Report of the Bridger Beds in the Washakie Basin by John Bach McMaster* ("Contributions to the E. M. Museum of Geology and Archaeology of the College of New Jersey" [Princeton, 1881], I, no. 1); McMaster, "The 'Bad Lands' of Wyoming and their Fossil Remains," *Bulletin of the American Geographical Society* (1880), XII, 109-30.

[55] McMaster in the *Bulletin of the American Geographical Society*, XII, 109.

[56] *Ibid.*, pp. 110-13. The quotation is from pp. 109-10.

[57] *Ibid.*, pp. 123-30.

torian than to McMaster the scientist, for it brought him to a region
which presented a mute plea for social history. The non-political
aspects of frontier regions were by far the most striking; their
political institutions were patently influenced by their social conditions.[58] Long before McMaster's first volume appeared, Francis
Parkman had included in *The Old Régime in Canada* chapters on
"Marriage and Population," "The New Home," "Trade and Industry," and "Morals and Manners."[59] Theodore Roosevelt, certainly no social historian, was to give long sections to "habits of
thought and ways of living" in describing *The Winning of the
West,* and Hubert Howe Bancroft extracted from his many volumes
on the Far West a philosophy which minimized the rôle of great
men and emphasized "every species of social phenomena down to
the apparently most insignificant habits."[60] The Turner theory of
the democratizing rôle of the frontier may be applied to American
historiography as well as to American politics.

Alone among the men who were to write the major historical
syntheses of his generation, McMaster had first-hand contact with
this West. From the windows of the Union Pacific Railroad he saw
covered wagons bumping along the Overland Route; in Montana,
his party stopped to chat with an outfit that turned out to be the
entire population of a Wisconsin village seeking a less rigorous
climate in Oregon.[61] The cook of the expedition, a practical joker in
filthy buckskin pants, was but one of the Westerners whom Mc-
Master came to know intimately.[62] More intimate yet was his acquaintance with the terrors and toughening in store for the tender-

[58] On this point, see the comment of William A. Dunning, "A Generation of
American Historiography," *Ann. Rept. of the A.H.A. for 1917* (Washington,
1920), pp. 351-52.

[59] Boston, 1874, Chaps. XIII, XIV, XVII, XX.

[60] *The Works of Hubert Howe Bancroft* (39 vols., San Francisco, 1883-90),
XXXVIII, 84-85. The Roosevelt quotation is from *The Winning of the West*
(4 vols., New York, 1889-96), I, 101. For examples of his social history, see
ibid., I, Chap. V; III, Chap. I; IV, Chap. V.

[61] McMaster to his mother [no month and day], 1878, MS; W. B. Scott, *Some
Memories of a Palaeontologist,* p. 79.

[62] McMaster to his mother and sister, June 20, 1878, MS.

foot. Only by snatching up his rifle in the nick of time was McMaster saved from the fury of a she-cougar.[63] After a survey of himself in the jagged piece of glass which served as a mirror, he reported

. . . just two freckles joined by a hyphen over the nose and surrounded by a flaming background of red, on which grow seventeen scragly [*sic*] hairs which can't be said to form a whisker, but have sort of squatted down there to preempt ground for a whisker should one be needed, while what skin I have left has given me an idea of the force of the old English election cry, "*Peel* and *Repeal*"![64]

Day after day, in the mountains and on visits to town, McMaster lived among people who were building a new land in a way that doubtless made constitutions shrivel in significance. Sent to hunt fossils, McMaster found people. Again his interest in history was excited; more and more clearly than ever before, he thought in terms of ordinary men and women.[65]

But what did it all mean for McMaster's future—these constant stimuli to go on with his history of the people, these driftings to and away from the project? If he was to be the first American in the field, it was time for him to act. The encouraging influence of nationalism, scientific thinking, and realistic fiction did not surround McMaster alone. The idea of a history of the people was in the air of the United States, or at least that part of the air not enclosed by university walls. Before McMaster's first volume appeared, not only Eggleston but John Fiske was thinking of such a project. The latter, whose pen was as sensitive to public taste as any in the country, had opened negotiations with publishers for an American history modeled after John Richard Green's *Short History of the English People*.[66] When McMaster's first volume appeared, he

[63] Theodore Roosevelt, *The Wilderness Hunter* (2 vols., New York, 1893), II, 141-42.

[64] McMaster to Robert B. McMaster, July 21, 1878, MS.

[65] "Summary of an Autobiographical Talk of McMaster," a manuscript now in the possession of Prof. Roy F. Nichols, of the University of Pennsylvania.

[66] John S. Clark, *The Life and Letters of John Fiske* (2 vols., Boston, 1917), II, 220-21.

received a letter from Alexander Johnston which stated, "I had always intended to write just such a work in time myself."[67]

Almost certainly McMaster was not hurried by these projects, for there is no evidence that he knew of them. The drive came from within himself—the same drive that had carried him from one job to another in search of his future. McMaster was twenty-six now and approaching the years when wandering and wishing are not enough for young men in a hurry. Attempts to advance as a scientist had brought him little except irritation. The position to which he returned—instructing at Princeton—not only annoyed McMaster but pointed to a future that seemed bleak. The sect-conscious Presbyterian administration, he was sure, made it impossible for him to rise far in the college.[68] Winchester, Princeton, the Bad Lands—all of these experiences must have enlarged in McMaster's mind the delights and possibilities of turning his armchair vow into a reality.

After McMaster returned from the Bad Lands in September 1878, he pushed ahead on Volume I in a spirit he had never shown before. If new jobs were offered, he refused to accept them. He was even prepared to sacrifice the instructorship at Princeton, for he felt that when the volume appeared

. . . there will be some intimation that I had better keep to teaching engineering and not wander off to historical fields. In which case I shall simply hand the old gentleman my resignation and quit instanter. The day will be awful cold when I take sass from *that* old *gent*.[69]

The energy and single-mindedness which Rockefeller was giving to oil, and Carnegie to iron, McMaster now turned to history.

[67] Alexander Johnston to McMaster, April 30, 1883, MS.
[68] "Diary," III, June 21, 1883, MS.
[69] McMaster to Gertrude Stevenson, Oct. 1, 1882, MS.

CHAPTER III

Volume One

HAVING made up his mind to write the history, McMaster had to translate his vague ideas into the exacting specificness of words. A history of the people, yes; but just what did it mean to tell the story of the people from 1783 to 1789, the period to be covered by Volume I? Much had to be written, McMaster knew, of "wars, conspiracies, and rebellions; of presidents, of congresses, of embassies, of treaties. . . ."[1] Indeed, he was convinced that "when a people is building up a brand new form of government, politics is the next thing to life & that in our country in 1784 it was particularly so."[2] Yet McMaster was determined that his volumes, unlike their predecessors, would combine an "account of the acquisition of territory, the movement of population, the formation of new states in the west, the social, industrial, financial, political history of the country."[3] "Such a mingling of social with political history," McMaster bravely was to announce on the second page of his volume, "is necessary to a correct understanding of the peculiar circumstances under which our nation was formed and grew up."

In searching out material for this history of the people, McMaster often turned to the books others had written, but these alone, he came to feel, were not enough.[4] Bancroft and Hildreth could not be used as foundations because they had omitted too many significant bricks.[5] Few scholarly monographs were in print, for

[1] McMaster, *A History of the People of the United States, from the Revolution to the Civil War*, p. 1.
[2] McMaster to Gertrude Stevenson, April 4, 1883, MS.
[3] "Second Memoirs," pp. 1-2, MS.
[4] Almost one-third of the works referred to in Vol. I are secondary. William T. Hutchinson, "John Bach McMaster," in Hutchinson, ed., *The Marcus W. Jernegan Essays in American Historiography* (Chicago, 1937), p. 135.
[5] "Second Memoirs," p. 2, MS.

historians were just beginning to desert the telescope for the microscope. Biographies, state histories,. and memoirs existed in abundance, and McMaster had spent many hours of the fumbling years before 1878 taking notes from them. As he proceeded with his research, he reached the point where he declared that such works were "not reliable, that I must in every case go back to the original wherever the original could be had, and that all existing histories were false in dates and facts." Only sentiment prevented McMaster from burning most of the odd scraps that were the notepaper of his City College frugality.[6] "Newspapers, pamphlets, memoirs," he explained later, "books of travel, letters and lives of the great men of those days, manuscripts when they could be had, laws of the states and of the United States, whatever bore even remotely on my subject, were carefully examined."[7] Most striking of all McMaster's sources were the newspapers and pamphlets, to which more than a third of his citations in Volume I refer.[8] Even Bancroft had cited a newspaper or a pamphlet once in a while, Hildreth included both among his authorities, Draper and Von Holst used newspapers more than occasionally. Yet none of these men called upon newspapers and pamphlets as much as McMaster, and none of them used this type of source to write social history.[9]

In using newspapers or any other materials, McMaster labored under heavy handicaps. He was short both of funds and of time.[10] The richest scholar of 1878 had fewer opportunities for research than the poorest one of today. Bound to the Northeast by poverty

[6] McMaster to Gertrude Stevenson, March 4, 1883, MS.

[7] Eric F. Goldman, ed., "The Princeton Period of John Bach McMaster," *Proceedings of the New Jersey Historical Society* (1939), LVII, 224.

[8] Hutchinson in the *Jernegan Essays*, p. 135.

[9] For examples of Bancroft's use, see *A History of the United States, from the Discovery of the Continent* (10 vols., Boston, 1834-75), IV, 280, 352-54, 366; Richard Hildreth, *The History of the United States of America* (New York, 6 vols., 1849-52), VI, "Authorities" at end of volume; John W. Draper, *History of the American Civil War* (3 vols., New York, 1867-70), I, v, III, vi; Eric F. Goldman, "Hermann Eduard Von Holst: Plumed Knight of American Historiography," *Mississippi Valley Historical Review* (1937), XXIII, 528-29.

[10] McMaster to Gertrude Stevenson, March 4, 1883, MS.

and probably by provincialism, McMaster relied on individuals and on the few institutions for research scattered from Massachusetts to Washington, D.C. He borrowed manuscripts or other materials from George Bancroft, Oliver Wendell Holmes, and George H. Putnam, the publisher.[11] Long summer hours were spent in the Library of Congress where the librarian helped as much as he could in a place "that resembled nothing so much as an old fashioned second hand bookshop. The walls were lined with dusty books; they were heaped on long tables and stacked on the floor. As you went about, you walked along narrow lanes made by books piled shoulder high."[12] McMaster reveled in the coöperation of the American Antiquarian Society, in Worcester, Massachusetts, which turned him loose in the rooms where the newspapers were stored.[13]

It is a comment on the limits of organized scholarship in this period that McMaster spent more time in state historical societies than anywhere else. Though few in number and badly managed when compared with their modern counterparts, such institutions were still oases in a near desert.[14] The Massachusetts Historical Society, the grandfather of them all, showed the frank courtesy of a mellow old man. McMaster was told that the Society was at his service if what he wanted was not available elsewhere; otherwise, since he was not a member, he must do his research at the other places.[15] The Historical Society of Pennsylvania was squeezed in a little building which had been erected on the grounds of the Pennsylvania Hospital to house Benjamin West's painting, "Christ Healing the Sick," but it made up for its inadequacies by the qual-

[11] McMaster to O. B. Bruce, Feb. 12, 1883, MS.

[12] "McMaster's Princeton Period," *Proceedings of the New Jersey Historical Society*, LVII, 224-25.

[13] *Ibid.*, p. 227.

[14] Julian P. Boyd, "State and Local Historical Societies in the United States," *American Historical Review* (1934), XL, 11, 26. See also McMaster's remarks on historical societies in the *Pennsylvania Magazine of History and Biography* (1884), VIII, 190-93.

[15] "McMaster's Princeton Period," *Proceedings of the New Jersey Historical Society*, LVII, 227.

ity of its director, Frederick D. Stone. In him were combined a
mastery of his library and a strong sense of human decency. The
unknown McMaster could not have been given more help had he
been George Bancroft.[16]

Trying to work in other state historical societies provided Mc-
Master with experiences which he cherished all his life. If the Library of Congress resembled a second-hand bookshop, the New
Jersey Historical Society resembled a second-hand bookshop without a salesman. There McMaster was greeted by a note on the door
which said that the librarian was to be found at home. A trip to
the address revealed a courteous old gentleman with a bad case of
gout. McMaster was given the keys and carefully instructed to open
the door for no one unless he heard three sharp raps followed after
an interval by a fourth.[17]

Using the New York Historical Society required maneuvering
which might have been too much for a man who had not been
president of his fraternity and of his college class.

Immediately in front of the door at a desk sat a portly gentleman who
proved to be the librarian and a watchman without whose consent no
one could enter the library. After I had introduced myself and stated my
business, he said, "Non-members can only use the library if they bring a
card or note of introduction from a member."

"I have none," I said, whereupon he shook his head. I then asked
if I could see a list of the members. One was produced, but the only
name I recognized was that of General George B. McClellan. The
General was then Governor of New Jersey and as such was ex-officio

---

[16] *Ibid.*, p. 225; Hampton L. Carson, *A History of the Historical Society of
Pennsylvania* (2 vols., Philadelphia, 1940), I, 355-62, 439-40. The statements
concerning McMaster's relations with Stone are based on interviews with Drs.
Roland P. Falkner and Albert C. Myers.

[17] "McMaster's Princeton Period," *Proceedings of the New Jersey Historical
Society*, LVII, 225. The librarian of the Society was Martin R. Dennis. A friendly
chronicler of the Society wrote, "Mr. Dennis was in active business, and could not
give much time to the work, but he employed assistance largely at his own expense, so that the rooms were kept open regularly." William Nelson, "Fifty Years
of Historical Work in New Jersey," *Proceedings of the New Jersey Historical
Society*, 1895, 2d series, XIII, p. 253.

President of the Board of Trustees of the College of New Jersey, as Princeton University was then called. So back to Princeton I went, obtained from Doctor McCosh a letter of introduction to the General and presented it to McClellan at Trenton.

"You are," the General said, "writing history?" Then looking steadily at me for a half minute, he continued, "A history of the War?"

"No," was my answer, "That cannot be done until those who fought have written their memoirs."

To this he made no reply but wrote a note of introduction which was duly presented to the guardian at the door of the New York Historical Society library. The note was addressed to "John Austin Stevens, Librarian." On reading this, the gentleman at the desk laughed heartily and said, "Mr. Stevens died years ago and I don't know where to forward it. I don't know whether he went up or went down. But it is also addressed to the Librarian so I will open it," which he did, and having read it said, "An autograph note from General McClellan! It will do nicely for our collection of autographs. Well, Sir, what do you wish?" When I had named some books and newspapers, he asked, "Do you want them all today?" When told that I should like to spend many days in the library, he shook his head and replied, "Your introduction is good for but one day." Forced to be content with this, I named a certain newspaper, received it, and went to work.

About noon I heard him snap his watch repeatedly and soon he began walking about the room. A happy thought then occurred to me, and stepping up to him, I asked his company at lunch. There were some questions which could be answered then without intruding on his time.

"I'll go when that brother of mine returns," was the reply. On the return of the brother, we visited a restaurant of his selection, where he ate and drank whatsoever he liked. The hope that a good meal would have a mellowing effect was not vain, for, when closing time came and the borrowed volume was returned to the desk, he said, "You seem to be in earnest. You may come again tomorrow." I came on many a tomorrow, worked in the library for many weeks, found the librarian a very friendly gentleman and lunched with him often.[18]

[18] "McMaster's Princeton Period," *Proceedings of the New Jersey Historical Society*, LVII, 225-27. Apparently McMaster's memory has slipped in this anecdote. John Austin Stevens, librarian of the Society from 1876 to 1878, lived until 1910. Probably McMaster was speaking to Stevens and the note was addressed to an

McMaster's difficulties in getting to materials were the greater because of his extreme reticence in talking about his plans. Day after day he arrived early in the morning at the Historical Society of Pennsylvania, disappeared in the cluttered upstairs, and departed— all with a conspicuous minimum of words. The librarian later re- marked that he would have been able to help far more had he known what McMaster was writing. One evening as McMaster was leaving the library, after his book had been accepted for publica- tion, he said to Stone, "I've been writing a history, something like Green's. When it's out, I'll send you a copy."[19] Stone was among the first to learn that McMaster was preparing a history of the people, for no one was told before the completion of the manu- script.[20] His own brother was to pick up the printed work and re- mark, "Say, Mac, some fellow with the same name as yours has published a book."[21]

Urged on by ambition, slowed by the drags of teaching duties, McMaster pushed ahead on the lonely writing of Volume I. Once the first draft was completed, presumably in 1881, over a month and a half was given to redraftings.[22] Trying hard "to keep strictly to facts," he cut out many a favorite descriptive passage.[23] Finally the manuscript was ready, a huge pile of jerky handwriting which was to make over six hundred printed pages.[24]

Finding a publisher was a discouraging task for a man whose last effort had long since made its way to the city dump.[25] McMaster's

---

earlier librarian. For a list of the librarians, see Robert H. Kelby, *The New York Historical Society, 1804-1904* (New York, 1905), pp. 86-87.

[19] Interview with Dr. R. P. Falkner.

[20] "McMaster's Princeton Period," *Proceedings of New Jersey Historical Society,* LVII, 227. "I never knew a man as reticent," Prof. Scott said of McMaster's secrecy about the history. Interview with Prof. W. B. Scott.

[21] Interview with Dr. A. C. Myers.

[22] McMaster to Gertrude Stevenson, March 8, 1881, MS.

[23] "Diary," III, March 3, 1883, MS.

[24] Almost the entire manuscript is preserved and may be found among the Mc- Master Papers.

[25] The following paragraphs on the way Appleton came to publish the history are pieced together from "McMaster's Princeton Period," *Proceedings of the New Jersey Historical Society,* LVII, 227-28; Grant Overton, *Portrait of a Pub-*

one longhand manuscript of the history was too valuable to entrust to the mails. Instead he wrote letters to publishers, asking whether they would be interested in having him bring the manuscript to them. Usually they were not interested. No market, McMaster was assured, existed for the book. From another firm he learned that the field was already held by George Bancroft, whose main body of history, incidentally, stopped where McMaster began.[26] In desperation McMaster revealed his project to an old friend, William M. Sloane, a Princeton professor who had connections with the publishing house of Armstrong and Son. Sloane read the first chapter, was enthusiastic, and advised McMaster to see the head of the Armstrong firm. The hope was but the introduction to another disappointment. McMaster took his manuscript to this house only to be told that nothing could be done until Armstrong's return from Europe.

During this interim D. Appleton and Co. expressed a willingness to examine the manuscript. One summer day in 1881, McMaster again lugged his bundle of words to New York, and what happened after that is obscured in the fog that so often surrounds the pre-publication history of books. Apparently a regular reader—perhaps the same one who two years before had turned down Henry George's *Progress and Poverty*—considered the history "a good manuscript" but doubted whether it would sell well enough to warrant publication.[27] In the minds of several additional readers, the decision was weighted against McMaster because the firm was just bringing out the Centenary Edition of Bancroft's established work. Then the manuscript was submitted to a "very distinguished littérateur," who declared that on no account should it be published.[28]

---

lisher (New York, 1925), pp. 68-69; J. C. Derby, *Fifty Years Among Authors, Books and Publishers* (New York, 1884), pp. 188-89; and McMaster to Gertrude Stevenson, April 8, 1883, MS.

[26] The concluding volume of Bancroft's main work, published in 1874, carried the story only to the Treaty of Paris. In 1882 he published two additional volumes on the making of the Constitution.

[27] Henry George, Jr., *The Life of Henry George* (New York, 1901), p. 315.

[28] J. C. Derby, *Fifty Years Among Authors, Books and Publishers*, p. 188.

Still there was earnest discussion, still the firm could not reach the irrevocable decision, and the copy lay on Daniel Appleton's cluttered desk. Finally Appleton decided to take it to his country home and read it himself.

That evening the Appletons had several guests, who were enjoying a quiet evening browsing in books. After reading a portion of the manuscript to himself, Appleton suggested that he continue the reading out loud.

"Now don't do any such thing," objected Mrs. Appleton, who doubtless had learned that a firm hand was needed by a hostess with a publisher for a husband. "We are all interested in our books and don't want to hear you read from a manuscript."

"Permit me for one moment," Appleton challenged. "If I can't hold your attention I'll give up."

The moment was granted and Appleton read on and on without a murmur of discontent. After two hours he paused for a drink of water. Everybody pronounced the book most remarkable and most interesting, and the reading was continued far into the night.

In the morning, Appleton brought the manuscript back to the New York office. "We will publish the book," he ordered. "Find out where the author is." In a few days the author appeared and left with a contract.[29]

Though the book was now certain of publication, McMaster still did not shout out his triumph. Among the few people who heard the news was Miss Gertrude Stevenson, of Morristown, New Jersey. More and more, while his labors and his spleen belonged to Princeton, McMaster's heart took up residence in Morristown. He made frequent trips to the little New Jersey town, and long letters showed that the shy young man of the drawing-room was something of a gallant on paper. Now barbed, now whimsical, and always clever, the letters betrayed the McMaster that was struggling to be seen by the world as well as the development of a romance. A year before the book was accepted, Miss Stevenson was "Dear Miss

[29] *Ibid.*, p. 189.

Stevenson" and McMaster was "Sincerely and always your friend, John B. McMaster." Two years later, Miss Stevenson was "Zoe" or "Minnie," and McMaster, for reasons best known to the young lady, was "Heaptalk."

Miss Stevenson was kept fully informed during the trying period between the acceptance and the publication of the book. For more than a year the author and the publisher struggled over the title.[30] McMaster had put "The Great Republic" on his manuscript, but Daniel Appleton, pointing out that the title had already been used, thought something "quieter and more dignified" was wanted anyhow.[31] McMaster then proposed some quieter and more dignified titles, but Appleton was not satisfied.[32]

It would certainly be better [the publisher argued] if a title for your History could be obtained that indicated the special character of the work—the prominence of the life of the people over the mere political record. How then would this do?—*A Social and Political History of the United States.* A term somewhat broader than social is desirable—something that covers industrial and material as well as social and intellectual progress—but is there such a word? The success of the work will largely depend, we think, upon the recognition of the fact that it is a record not elsewhere given of the growth of all the various interests of the community. . . .[33]

But McMaster did not like the word "social," perhaps for reasons that later historians, having read a great deal of history called "social," can readily understand.[34] Since letters had failed, a conference was held in the Appleton office and the title, "The Republic of the United States from its Formation to the Civil War," was

[30] "Second Memoirs," p. 38, MS.

[31] Daniel Appleton to McMaster, Aug. 5, 1882, MS.

[32] McMaster proposed: "The American Republic: A History of the United States from the Revolution to the Civil War"; "The Rise and Growth of the Federal Union"; "A History of the United States from the Revolution to the Civil War"; "A History of," or simply "The Growth of the American Republic." Rough copy, McMaster to Daniel Appleton, Aug. 7, 15, 1882, MSS.

[33] Daniel Appleton to McMaster, Aug. 19, 1882, MS.

[34] Rough copy, McMaster to Daniel Appleton, Aug. 27, 1882, MS.

finally accepted by all parties. "Don't think much of it," McMaster reported to Miss Stevenson, "but it seems to be a last resort."[35]

At the time of the conference, William H. Appleton, the senior member of the firm, was abroad, and when he returned he re-opened the question by arguing as his son had done. "As Green's History of the *People* of England has been very successful," the author was told, "a similar title should be used for your book."[36] McMaster was probably the more amenable to this suggestion be-cause sometime late in these negotiations he had picked up a copy of the Constitution and been struck by the "We, the people of the United States" in the preamble. "That was what I wanted,"[37] he remembered many years later, but it was the publisher rather than the author who had been pushing for the title which epitomizes the fascination of the *History of the People of the United States*.

Other problems Miss Stevenson heard about took less time to settle. McMaster had planned no preface or table of contents.

Says the publisher a holding up his hands what no Table of Contents! Goodness,—gracious-grammany-King-George! You would not surely let your book go out without a Table of Contents? All right says the poor brown monkey a Table there shall be.[38]

And a table there was, one revealing to the glance of a casual book shopper what an extraordinary history this was. "Insecurity of the mails; use of ciphers," "House-maids," "Movement of the centre of population since 1789," "Presidential etiquette," "Rage for lot-teries"—no wonder Daniel Appleton, with his shrewd understand-ing of the book public, wanted a table of contents! McMaster's willingness to add a table of contents and change the title was a willingness to alter things outside the realm of history. When one of the Appleton editors argued that McMaster was too harsh on the Indians, that James Fenimore Cooper had approximated the truth more closely, the author would not budge:

[35] McMaster to Gertrude Stevenson, Sept. 10, 1882, MS.
[36] O. B. Bruce to McMaster, Dec. 8, 1882, MS.
[37] "Second Memoirs," p. 38, MS.
[38] McMaster to Gertrude Stevenson, March 11, 1883, MS.

I do not find anything to support this. Nobody can deny that the Indians of the Six Nations, the Indians Cooper knew were much above the Indians of the South. They lived in a cold climate they were human beings, and must therefore have been both physically and mentally as much above the Natchez and Chickesaws as the northern men of our time are above the southern. All the push, energy, mechanical skill business, wealth of the land lies north of the Potomac and the Ohio.[39]

Perhaps McMaster had discovered this enterprising North in the mirror. It was not enough, while Princeton still commanded most of his time, that he was completing the grinding labor of finally decided what he wanted to say in Volume I, of making sure that he was saying exactly that, and of getting the proofs corrected. Already he was pushing ahead on the second volume. Only McMaster could have been surprised that advertisements of the forthcoming *History of the People* left him feeling flat, that he found it difficult either to work on the second volume or to be idle, that in general he was in a state of "don't care."[40]

On March 3, 1883, the great day came. The expressman brought six copies of the freshly printed book in the dark green covers, and for an hour the author dawdled with his child. Moods of confidence, of unrealized opportunities crowded his mind:

I am greatly pleased with the way the printer and binder have done their work, and only hope mine is done so well. . . . No history which covers that time, not Hildreths, not Bancrofts, not Bryants [*sic*] can compare with it. But how far, how far from my ideal![41]

The next day, with his secret tucked away at home, McMaster went visiting and then he returned to it again. In the honest privacy of his room he compared parallel sections in his work and in Hil-

---

[39] *Ibid.*, Sept. 16, 1882, MS. McMaster's harsh description of the Indians is in the *History of the People*, I, 5-8.

[40] "Diary," III, Feb. 6, 1883; McMaster to Gertrude Stevenson, March 8, 1881, MSS.

[41] "Diary," III, March 3, 1883, MS.

dreth's. Yes, he liked his history still. "I cannot but think the book will succeed."[42]

Only with great timidity had Appleton's issued a first edition of 1,500 copies.[43] Before ten days passed, another edition was ordered to the presses and the author was being plagued for his second volume.[44] During the same short period the *Century Magazine*, which was running serially the opening chapters, rushed three editions to the newsstands.[45] By April 19, Appleton's had ordered a third edition of the volume; by May 22, a fourth.[46] Now it was clear that the book was, as Stone remarked,

. . . the chief event in the literary annals of the day. Few there were, we believe, who, when they first read its title, did not . . . exclaim: "What, another history of the United States!" "How can such a subject require five volumes for its treatment?" "To what proportions will our historical literature grow, if books are made at this rate?" "Who is John Bach McMaster?" We have watched with interest the change which has taken place, as the reading public have become acquainted with the book. The enthusiasm which it speedily excited overshadowed any attempt to damn it with faint praise, and the popularity it now enjoys equals that which it is customary to award only to works of fiction.[47]

Wherever men talked of books in the United States, they talked of McMaster's *History*. Peter Cooper, industrialist and Greenbacker, apparently overlooking what the *History* said about Greenbackers, recommended it right and left.[48] "I have read nothing else since I began it!" exclaimed the *New York Sun*'s Charles A.

[42] *Ibid.*, March 4, 1883, MS.

[43] "Diary," II, Jan. 9, 1892, MS. This entry is out of order in the "Diary."

[44] *Ibid.*, III, March 12, 1883, MS.

[45] McMaster to Gertrude Stevenson, March 11, 1883, MS.

[46] "Diary," III, April 19, 1883; O. B. Bruce to McMaster, May 22, 1883, MSS.

[47] Frederick D. Stone, "McMaster's History of the People of the United States," *Pennsylvania Magazine of History and Biography* (1883), VII, 206. The author of the unsigned review is identified in H. L. Carson, *A History of the Historical Society of Pennsylvania*, I, 427.

[48] McMaster to Gertrude Stevenson, May 19, 1883, MS. McMaster's harsh words about the Greenbackers are in the *History of the People*, I, 282.

Dana.[49] A friend who called on Justice Stephen J. Field, of the Supreme Court, found him immensely enjoying the work, and the two men spent the evening continuing the reading.[50] "Even J. G. Blaine has praised it," McMaster jubilantly wrote Miss Stevenson.[51] Some of the historians were inclined, as Jameson later confessed of himself, to view this strange new history "after the manner of a sagacious pointer examining a tortoise," but most of them came to like the engaging animal and to accept McMaster's volumes as the standard account of the period they covered.[52] Hermann Eduard Von Holst, being a German and enjoying an intimacy with the divine will, pronounced McMaster "manifestly an historian by the grace of God."[53] About a month and a half after the volume appeared, came the voice from Olympus:

At last Mr. Bancroft has been heard from. He has sent me a very neat letter, "welcoming" me into the field of historical labor in which he has spent so much of his life and hoping that all manner of success and &c. will attend me. He then ends with a civil request that when in Washington I will call upon him. All this is very kind and civil.[54]

McMaster's fame had become such that he could enjoy the unpleasantness of being lionized. Miss Stevenson, of course, heard about the graduate student from the Johns Hopkins University who had nothing to ask or to contribute "and so came and bored me for a whole afternoon."[55] She heard, and saw too in McMaster's self-caricature

---

[49] G. Overton, *Portrait of a Publisher*, p. 69.

[50] McMaster to Gertrude Stevenson, May 19, 1883, MS.

[51] *Ibid.*, March 25, 1883, MS.

[52] No historian published anything but an enthusiastic review of the history. Typical was Alexander Johnston's laudatory review in the *Nation* (1883), XXXVI, 279-80 (for Johnston's authorship of the unsigned review, see W. Stull Holt, ed., *Historical Scholarship in the United States, 1876-1901: As Revealed in the Correspondence of Herbert B. Adams* [Baltimore, 1938], p. 61). The Jameson quotation is printed in *Testimonial Dinner to John Bach McMaster . . . Letters Received* [Philadelphia, 1913].

[53] Von Holst was quoted in Henry A. Todd to McMaster, Dec. 27, 1883, MS.

[54] McMaster to Gertrude Stevenson, April 22, 1883, MS.

[55] *Ibid.*, May 23, 1883, MS.

what I look like. . . . I am not a particularly imposing man to look at. In fact I am rather under size. But I have a most remarkably shaped head. It would attract attention anywhere. "Except that it is not green it looks like a watermelon on a stalk"! How do I know all this? I read every word of it this morning in the Boston Herald . . . [I] think of hiring out for a scare crow.[56]

Since McMaster belonged to a generation that had not isolated history from literature, he was equally pleased by the attention that came from non-historical writers. No congratulation delighted him more than the praise from Charles Dudley Warner, a literary power of the day.[57]

While the enthusiasm mounted in most quarters, McMaster learned that writing a best seller brought boos as well as cheers. The larger part of the unfavorable criticism was minor, a matter of a petty mistake or a varying interpretation.[58] Even the enthusiastic Warner was sure McMaster had slipped by attributing the discovery of anesthetics to the wrong man. "For myself," McMaster generalized, "I do not care a fig who discovered it. But I do not want to do any man injustice especially when the world owes him so much."[59] The interpretation in the *History* which aroused most criticism was McMaster's low estimate of eighteenth-century American literature and art.[60] "Everyman," the weary author snapped to Miss Stevenson, "is entitled to his opinion even on *art*."[61] But as evidence of small errors and irritated readers mounted, McMaster wished he

. . . had put the publication off for another year. I think I could have

[56] *Ibid.*, July 22, 1883, MS.

[57] Charles D. Warner to McMaster, March 18, 1883; "Diary," III, March 19, 1883, MSS.

[58] Typical criticism of this sort may be found in the otherwise favorable reviews in the *Dial* (1883), III, 270-72, and in the *Atlantic Monthly* (1883), LII, 266-71.

[59] McMaster to Gertrude Stevenson, April 22, 1883, MS. McMaster attributed the discovery to Morton of Boston (*History of the People*, I, 30), but Warner was sure the credit belonged to Wells, of Hartford.

[60] *History of the People*, I, 74-83. Criticism of this section was so widespread that Stone (*Pennsylvania Magazine of History and Biography*, VII, 212-13) devoted part of his review to defending McMaster's position.

[61] McMaster to Gertrude Stevenson, April 29, 1883, MS.

I am not a particularly imposing man to look at. In fact I am rather under size. But I have a most remarkably shaped head. It would attract attention anywhere. "Except that it is not green it looks like a watermelon on a stalk"! How do I know all this? I read every word of it this morning in the Boston Sunday Herald. How are the mighty fallen! Hosannah yesterday. To day "a water-melon on

on a stalk!" Think of hiring out for a scare crow! Two more dinners since I saw you last. On Wednesday one of the members of the Antiquarian Society dropped in and asked me to come up and take a crack with him. I went, and saw a genuine library of Americana. Mr M⸺ has a hobby and therefore an interesting man. He takes books of any kind, and collects all manner of old prints, cuts autographs, anything that would be proper and binds them up with the book to serve as illustrations. Thus he has a copy of the declaration of Independence bound up with wood cuts and autograph letters of the signers. But what interested me most was a dozen or so of children's books printed

McMASTER CARICATURES HIMSELF IN A LETTER TO MISS STEVENSON

(See opposite page)

improved it a great deal, condensed, trimmed, and altered some statements which I fear are too strong. If I could only have afforded to hire some one who was a professed and regular "book slasher" to read it for me, I should, I know, have gotten rid of a good many crudities.[62]

The worst was yet to come. Several months later the *Boston Transcript* and the *New York Tribune* launched an attack which amounted to the charge that McMaster was a plagiarist. For this the *Boston Transcript* sharply rebuked him and the *Transcript* was mild compared to the *New York Tribune*.[63] Hot, screeching shots, McMaster called the *Tribune* attack; hot and screeching it was.[64] The wording of McMaster's opening paragraphs closely followed Macaulay's. In other places Macaulay had written "administer a rude justice with the rifle and the dagger"; McMaster wrote "administered a prompt and rude justice with the knife and the gun." Macaulay had written "Of others the numbers are so much diminished that men crowd to gaze at a specimen as at a Bengal tiger, or a Polar bear"; McMaster wrote, "An Indian in his paint and feathers is now a much rarer show than a Bengal tiger or a white bear from the Polar sea."[65] Imitation of this sort, the *Tribune* reviewer stormed, is "not easily distinguishable from theft."

Having denounced the similarities to Macaulay, the critic moved on to compare McMaster's volume and William C. Rives' *History of the Life and Times of James Madison*.[66] Indignantly he placed these selections from the two works in parallel columns of the paper:

[62] *Ibid.*, April 8, 1883, MS.

[63] Fred. A. Claflin in the *Boston Evening Transcript*, June 9, 1883; unsigned review in the *New York Tribune*, July 1, 1883. I have not been able to identify Claflin.

[64] McMaster to Gertrude Stevenson, July 17, 1883, MS.

[65] These parallel passages pointed out in the *Tribune* (here the *Tribune* was following the *Transcript*) may be found respectively in McMaster, *History of the People*, I, 140, 5 and in Macaulay, *The History of England from the Accession of James the Second*, ed. Charles H. Firth (6 vols., London, 1913-15), I, 274, 304. Similarities in language of the two men were also pointed out in the *Watchman-Examiner*, April 26, 1883.

[66] 3 vols., Boston, 1881.

McMASTER, I, 274-75

Benjamin Harrison was a bold, frank, outspoken man. He had all his life been active in the cause of liberty, and had, in the early movements of the revolution, borne a part marked with zeal and decision. A story is told of him which deserves to be narrated as it finely illustrates the character of the man. In the Congress of 1775, when the second petition to the King was under discussion, John Dickinson, who had the chief part in framing it, said that there was but one word in the paper he disapproved of, and that word was Congress. Scarcely had he said so when Harrison jumped to his feet and exclaimed: "There is but one word in the paper, Mr. President, which I approve, and that word is Congress." In the war he carried arms with distinction, rose to be colonel of a regiment of foot, had lately been Governor of Virginia, and had commenced the present session of the Legislature with an animated contest for the Speaker's chair.

Braxton, like Harrison, was early distinguished for the firmness and zeal with which he defended the rights of the colonies. No one had been more active in behalf of Henry's resolutions on the Stamp Act. Yet his popularity was for a time under a cloud. He

RIVES, II, 44-45

Colonel Harrison was a bold, frank man, and had been zealous and decided in all the early movements of the Revolution. When John Dickinson, in the Congress of 1775, expressed his self-complacency with regard to the second petition to the King, of which he was himself mainly the author, by saying there was but one word in the paper which he disapproved, and that was the word "Congress," it was Colonel Harrison who rose and said, "There is but one word in the paper, Mr. President, which I approve, and that word is Congress."

Mr. Braxton, though he had shown no want of firmness or zeal in maintaining the rights of America at all times, and was even among the champions of Mr. Henry's resolutions on the Stamp Act, had incurred a temporary loss of popularity by the scheme of government which he recommended to the Virginia Convention, under the signature of "A Native," in 1776. It was in consequence of the bad odor of that scheme, regarded with the more jealousy, perhaps, on account of the former residence of the author for a year or two in England, that he was soon afterwards pretermitted in the delegation to Congress.

had, while a Virginia delegate to Congress, recommended to the Virginia Convention of 1776 a plan of government under the signature of A Native. The scheme was coldly received. The author was believed to be much biased by his two years' residence in England, and soon after lost his seat in Congress.

But of the three, the political career of Meriwether Smith had been the most singular. He was a merchant, and believed to be quite familiar with public affairs. His pursuits, indeed, as a merchant, gave him great aptitude in the dispatch of business. But they were believed by his friends to have affected his political views as nothing else could. No man, as a delegate to Congress, ever went through so many stages of favor and of disfavor with his constituents. For his conduct on one occasion he was warmly thanked. For his conduct on another he was strongly censured. Several times he was subjected to charges and investigations, which, though ending indeed in a full acquittal, marked him out as an eccentric and impracticable character.

Mr. Meriwether Smith was much conversant in affairs, both public and private. His pursuits and connections as a merchant, while they gave him a greater aptitude for the conduct of business, were supposed, on some occasions, to impart a professional bias to his political views. As a Delegate in Congress, he underwent many vicissitudes of favor and disfavor with his constituents; at one time receiving their thanks, at another their censure, and in several instances subjected to charges and investigations which though terminating in exculpation, implied a certain degree of eccentricity and impracticableness in the character exposed to them.

"Surely common honesty, not to say common courtesy, should have led Mr. McMaster to give some sort of credit to Mr. Rives," the *Tribune* reviewer added, yet there was no mention of Rives in McMaster's footnotes.

After the explosion of the *Tribune*, the Rives matter quickly died out and the publishers showed concern only about the charges of imitation of Macaulay which came "from every quarter now. . . . Can you suggest what should be done, or name any others who could take up the gauntlet on your behalf?"[67] McMaster's policy was to say nothing:

That I have gotten some of Macaulay's sentences in the book is most true and most unfortunate. That I knew they were there. That I consciously put them there is false. To say this publicly would avail nothing. Many would not believe it.[68]

Worried and vexed, he consoled himself by varying attitudes. "I care not. I live with myself and not with my critics. When my conscience does not accuse me I am indifferent to the critics," McMaster told his diary one day.[69] At another time he wrote Miss Stevenson:

The way of the transgressor is hard and no mistake. I wish I were a hybernating beast of some kind and this was winter, and that I was snoring peacefully at the bottom of a deep deep hole with a stone over its mouth. "Those eyes! Those eyes!" said the murderer in Oliver Twist. "Those sentences! Those sentences!" say I. I can fancy just how a murderer must feel when he goes out into the light of day. I can see them painted on every barn, and every rock, and nailed to every sign post the country over. When I see two men talking on the street I know it is about those - - - lines . . . alas! alas! However did I come to do it.[70]

Worried moments like these were only moments. For every mention of the Macaulay sentences, there were heaps of ecstatic reviews; for every anxiety about the future, there were hundreds of assurances in the present. To the astonishment of everybody, except perhaps McMaster himself, the shy little engineering teacher had become a national literary figure. "Well, Mr. McMaster," exclaimed

[67] O. B. Bruce to McMaster, July 2, 1883, MS.
[68] "Diary," III, July 2, 1883, MS.
[69] *Ibid.*, July 1, 1883, MS.
[70] McMaster to Gertrude Stevenson, April 29, 1883, MS.

President McCosh, "Why did na ye tell us that ye were a great mon!"[71] If McMaster was inclined to dismiss the compliments as "taffy" in his letters to Miss Stevenson, he betrayed a sweet tooth by quoting long sections from the favorable reviews, and in time he hired two clipping agencies.[72] No wonder McMaster was jubilant. After a long period of unhappy ambition, he had arrived. By making the history of the people fascinating, McMaster had made himself.

[71] Ellis P. Oberholtzer, "John Bach McMaster," *Pennsylvania Magazine of History and Biography* (1933), LVII, 12.

[72] "Diary," II, Jan. 10, 1892; McMaster to Gertrude Stevenson, March 25, May 23, 1883, MSS.

CHAPTER IV

Settling Down

ONCE THE usual gossiping about the author of a best seller was under way, people began to ask why McMaster had not mentioned Princeton on his title-page. Asking was about all they could do, for the most they received from the author in the way of an answer was "Why should I?"[1] Why should he, indeed, with his opinion of Princeton! Far from feeling more reconciled to the University now that his book was a success, McMaster's irritation was increased by rumors that

... the "boss" [probably Professor Charles McMillan, head of the Civil Engineering Department] has been making some "low down" remarks about my taking "college time" [to write the *History*] which I have been so careful not to do. I shall tax him with them as soon as I can get them from a more reliable source, and unless he takes every one of them back, I shall go on a "strike." Anything for me but a "scientifically educated" man. Such men get into a rut invariably and are too small and narrow-minded to see over the wall of mud that shuts them in.[2]

Professor Sloane's efforts to have the Trustees set up a chair of American history and install McMaster in it were fruitless.[3]

Soon it became clear that finding a more congenial position would not be difficult. Two months after the appearance of Volume I McMaster heard that the University of Michigan was considering him for its department of history.[4] A little later a move was started to call him to the College of the City of New York, but already the

[1] McMaster to Gertrude Stevenson, Jan. 13, 1885, MS.
[2] *Ibid.*, March 11, 1883, MS.
[3] Because, according to Prof. Scott, Sloane "encountered that density and obtuseness which sometimes afflicts governing bodies. McMaster had been teaching engineering; why couldn't he stick to that? *Ne sutor ultra crepidam*; they remembered that much Latin." William B. Scott, *Some Memories of a Palaeontologist* (Princeton, 1939), p. 193.
[4] McMaster to Gertrude Stevenson, May 23, 1883, MS.

negotiations had been opened which were to fix McMaster at Philadelphia for the rest of his academic life.[5]

The offer was to come from the Wharton School of Finance and
Economy, a part of the University of Pennsylvania. This division
had been established in 1881 by Joseph Wharton, a Philadelphian
interested in a college curriculum that would prepare young men
for business.[6] For its first few years the Wharton School, with an
inadequate faculty and a seven-man student body, was known as the
Botany Bay of the campus. Recognizing the point of the jibe, Wharton and William Pepper, the provost of the University, planned to
strengthen the faculty of the School, and one of the new appoint-
ments was to be a professor of American history.[7] The position was
first offered to Herbert B. Adams, then director of the flourishing
historical school at the Johns Hopkins University. When Adams
declined, the Wharton School men became interested in McMaster
and Austin Scott, the Rutgers professor of history who had formerly
served as an assistant to George Bancroft.[8]

One evening in the spring of 1883, as McMaster worked at his
Princeton desk, he was visited by a stranger.

His name is Bolles [McMaster reported to Miss Stevenson], and [he]
is, of course, a Yankee. . . . They wanted a Prof. of American History,
and they want to know if I would come and sit in that chair. It was a
spick, span new one . . . and I was to be the first of a long line of famous
occupants. Says I, how much lecturing will I be expected to do? Says
he, we would like you to lecture nine hours a week. (Here I have been
doing six and sometimes seven and a half hours a day!) Says I What is
the, —the er—, the salary. Says he $2500. Says I, when I am elected
I will come.[9]

[5] For the C.C.N.Y. move, see R. R. Bowker to McMaster, June 26, 1883, MS.
[6] Edward P. Cheyney, *History of the University of Pennsylvania, 1740-1940*
(Philadelphia, 1940), p. 288.
[7] Letter from Dr. Albert S. Bolles to the author, May 20, 1939.
[8] Albert S. Bolles to Herbert B. Adams, June 6, 1883, in W. Stull Holt, ed.,
*Historical Scholarship in the United States, 1876-1901: As Revealed in the Corre-
spondence of Herbert B. Adams* (Baltimore, 1938), pp. 67-68.
[9] McMaster to Gertrude Stevenson, June 10, 1883, MS. Dr. Albert S. Bolles was

Professor Bolles went away very much interested in McMaster, particularly since it seemed doubtful if Scott could be drawn away from Rutgers:

With respect to Mr. McMaster the way is perfectly clear for us. His range of attainments is narrower than Dr. Scott's, but his knowledge of history in general and American history in particular is truly wonderful. He has read enormously and remembered everything. He began reading history when very young, and his devotion to the subject is as rare as it is beautiful. He is a quiet gentle sort of man; but underneath is a deep genuine enthusiasm which I am sure would be felt by every student who came under the shadow of his teaching. Then, too, his wide and just reputation is of no little worth to a collegiate institution. He has taught very efficiently at Princeton. . . . I think . . . that the tide among those who are the most deeply interested is setting toward Mr. McMaster.[10]

Shortly afterward the tide came in and McMaster was formally offered the position, one of the earliest professorships devoted exclusively to American history.[11] A chance to spend his whole working day as a historian, "to make the *History* fairly skip," to get away from hated Princeton—these were the things that danced through McMaster's mind as he wrote the news to Miss Stevenson.[12] On June 21, 1883, McMaster could tell his diary, "Left Princeton, Thank God forever."[13]

During his first year in Philadelphia McMaster lived at a hotel, but in 1884 he decided to save money by moving to a boarding house. Friends recommended the neighborhood of Spruce Street around Fifteenth Street,

---

one of the organizers of the Wharton School and its Professor of Mercantile Law and Banking.

[10] Albert S. Bolles to Herbert B. Adams, June 6, 1883, in W. S. Holt, ed., *Historical Scholarship in the United States*, p. 68.

[11] The appointment was approved by the Board of Trustees on July 3. "Minutes of the Board of Trustees of the University of Pennsylvania" (July 3, 1883), XII, 79, MS, University of Pennsylvania Archives. Cornell had established the first professorship of American history in 1881.

[12] McMaster to Gertrude Stevenson, June 10, 1883, MS.

[13] "Diary," III, June 21, 1883, MS.

. . . but how to find good quarters I did not know until a happy thought occurred to me. I went to the nearest butcher, told him what I wanted, and asked if he knew of a boarding housekeeper who bought his best meat. He laughed heartily, but gave the name of one. A grocer, after a good laugh, gave the same name. Whereupon I went to the house, 309 I think it was, South Fifteenth Street, secured a room and entered on a series of adventures the like of which surely never befell any other man in so short a time. The table was so good that several people not boarding in the house came in for meals. Among them was a man and his wife. As they were about to go home one evening after dinner, we heard the man fall and the wife scream and, rushing into the entry, found him dead on the floor from a stroke of apoplexy. A month or so after this experience, I was awakened one morning by what seemed to be the bleating of a goat in the bathroom which adjoined my bedroom. Only half awake I paid no heed to the sound, went to sleep, and at breakfast learned that one of the boarders, weary of life, had gone to the bathroom, hung his head over the tub and cut his throat. As happenings of this sort always come in threes, I wondered what the next would be and soon found out. Coming home on a certain evening after dark, I was met by the daughter of the landlady rushing down the stairs shouting, "My room is on fire. Call for help." Shutting the door quickly, I said, "No, no, don't call out, you'll have the whole town in here." Just as I spoke another boarder came in, and the young lady leading the way, we hurried to her room. It was the fashion in those days to have at windows red canton-flannel curtains hanging with the fluffy side out. In striking a match, the head had flown off and set fire to the curtains. When the blaze was out, we found under charred bits of canton-flannel a can of Platt's Astral Oil! Had it taken fire and exploded, every one of us would, at least, have been badly burned.[14]

Fortunately for McMaster's stability of mind, the young author received the social invitations that are a reward of success in his craft. Eagerly he accepted them. "My interest," McMaster told his diary, "is to be as much in good company as possible." When asked to sign a circular requesting Matthew Arnold to read some of his poetry during the Englishman's visit to Philadelphia, McMaster remarked, "Poetry! He cannot even read prose." Yet McMaster

[14] "Second Memoirs," pp. 60-61, MS.

added, "The names on the paper were good ones so I signed readily."[15] One dinner invitation brought McMaster around the table with Henry Irving, Ellen Terry, and Walt Whitman.[16] Another permitted him to meet Edward Eggleston, and McMaster found his co-pioneer in social history "a Hoosier and no mistake. Is proud of his broad tread shoes, his state, and his knowledge of western dialects and is a first rate talker and a good fellow to know."[17] At the Saturday Club of Philadelphia, McMaster

. . . was introduced to President C. A. Arthur. He had not much to say of course. But he has the rare nack [sic] of saying something pleasing. Noticed the ΦBK pin I wore and kindly proposed we should exchange the grip which we did. I watched him for a while after that and as each comer was brought up he seemed to try and say something pleasing. . . . When most of the guests had gone Kelly the life long Pennsylvania Congressman who was pretty full proceeded to make a fool of himself, and was ably assisted by a number of fellow congressmen.[18]

Exchanging grips with the President of the United States was a pleasant escape from the boarding house, but it was still an escape, and the existence of Miss Stevenson kept reminding McMaster that a more stable happiness was possible. The relationship between the couple was growing increasingly close, in work as well as in pleasures. McMaster would read to Miss Stevenson from the manuscript of Volume II, and she criticized everything from grammar to the propriety of printing oaths, even in quotations.[19]

Your suggestions about "indeed" and most of the other corrections have been accepted [McMaster would write when the discussion was being conducted on paper]. But I am not ready to go so far as you would in never using the same word or expression twice on a page. The Rhetorics support this view, but I say the Rhetorics be switched.[20]

[15] "Diary," III, Dec. 15, 1883, MS.

[16] McMaster to Gertrude Stevenson, Dec. 15, 1884, MS.

[17] *Ibid.*, Dec. 12, 1884, MS.

[18] "Diary," III, Dec. 22, 1883, MS. William D. ("Pig Iron") Kelly was a member of the House of Representatives from 1860 to 1890.

[19] "Diary," III, Sept. 2, 1883, MS.

[20] McMaster to Stevenson, Jan. 8, 1885, MS. For clarity, quotes not in McMaster's letter have been put around the word, *indeed*.

Miss Stevenson, prematurely assuming the burden of the academic wife, also read proof and helped in making the table of contents.[21] One summer evening, after four weeks of delightful vacationing in Maine, McMaster and Miss Stevenson "went for a last view of the sun. There as we sat on the rocks I asked M.G.S. to think over something which shall some day I hope bear fruit."[22]

With marriage in mind, McMaster strove desperately to increase his income.[23] He hurried off book reviews and articles for adult and children's publications—some of which he bluntly referred to as "pot boilers."[24] As part of the same pecuniary drive he jumped at an invitation from Warner to write a volume on Benjamin Franklin for the American Men of Letters series.[25] McMaster was sure the work could be made "most interesting . . . I mean to write a book that will outsell any three in the series."[26] But the publishers of the *History of the People* did not share McMaster's enthusiasm.

We have [Appleton wrote him] done more to give your first volume a good send off than for any other book for many years, and we cannot but feel that another book, from another house, can serve in many cases to gratify the curiosity that has been awakened, and which we have labored to intensify.[27]

This "queer letter" was answered by

. . . what I hope was a civil letter. told them they were quite mistaken and that they should have the second volume before I did anything

[21] *Ibid.*, Jan. 8, 1885, May 8, 1885, MSS.

[22] "Diary," III, Sept. 5, 1883, MS.

[23] See especially McMaster to Gertrude Stevenson, Feb. 28, 1886, MS.

[24] "Second Memoirs," p. 64, MS. McMaster felt that he did not have "any knack" for writing for children (McMaster to Gertrude Stevenson, Feb. 28, 1886, MS), and an editor of a children's magazine remarked about a contribution which he accepted, "The subject is probably treated too much as a mere record of history, thereby, in the lack of picturesqueness, making the account for our youthful readers, somewhat less interesting than if the peculiarities of life then had been indicated by characterizing incidents. . . ." Gerry Mason to McMaster, Aug. 5, 1884, MS.

[25] McMaster to Gertrude Stevenson, March 28, 1883, MS.

[26] "Diary," III, April 22, 1883, MS.

[27] Daniel Appleton to McMaster, April 27, 1883, MS.

else. If they think they can "bull doze" me they are mistaken. They have [given] the book splendid treatment, lavished money on advertisements, but everybody tells me, it is coming back to them fast. They have only the *money* in view. I have to bear all the criticisms.[28]

Having exploded off this irritation, McMaster went on writing furiously.

Occasionally this writing, which was fruitful both of money and of reputation, was interrupted by lecturing, which brought only assets in cash. McMaster was a bad lecturer. Audiences listening to him heard none of the comforting certainties of a Wilson, no Bryanesque evangelism, not even urbane chattings. The man who could be colorful and caustic on paper drew into himself when he stood before human beings. Shyly he faced the floor, and the words came slowly, almost inaudibly while he and his audience competed with each other to avoid fidgeting.[29] At one lecture, to cite McMaster the writer on McMaster the speaker, a

. . . poor little runt went dead asleep and had to be waked up by neighbors as she gave evident symptoms to a determination to snore. Then she bit her lips, punched her fingers and by a dozen such means kept awake and had her revenge! Twice! before I finished did *she* in turn rouse of a childlike slumber the neighbour who once awoke her! I am now fully convinced that my mission should be that of a lecturer to a hospital for the "nervously prostrate." In two hours I could have the whole tribe of them sound asleep.[30]

Four years the grind went on before McMaster could achieve his ambition of marriage. He had worked hard and now he was afraid he was not working hard enough. He had written a sucessful volume and now he had fits of discouragement that Volume II would fail to be as good.[31] He had fallen in love, and musty news-

[28] McMaster to Gertrude Stevenson, April 29, 1883, MS.

[29] This description of McMaster as a speaker is pieced together from interviews with Drs. R. P. Falkner and A. C. Myers and from James Monaghan, "John Bach McMaster, Pioneer," a manuscript used through the courtesy of the author.

[30] McMaster to Gertrude Stevenson, Feb. 19, 1884, MS. See also "Diary," III, Dec. 22, 1883, MS.

[31] "Diary," III, Dec. 16, 1883, MS.

papers were poor competition for Miss Stevenson. Once in a while McMaster would push aside his books and quit. "No use going on when I have to kick myself to work."[32] But most of the time he drove on, beating down his restlessness by work that made him

... feel every vertebra up my back. Every finger I have is callous. When I come home I have to be over a barrel for an hour to get the crooks out of "me back." ... Wish I were a dude with a bang and an allowance a year.[33]

In the midst of McMaster's discouragement, bad luck—a particularly annoying type of bad luck—came to him. While doing research in the American Antiquarian Society he was in the habit of carrying his notes in a hand satchel. One day McMaster stopped in the bank on the way to the library and some "incarnate Devil," noting the bulging bag emerging from a bank, stole it from the room of the hotel in which the historian was staying.[34] The thief's chagrin could not have exceeded McMaster's, for the satchel contained two manuscript chapters of the *History* and a quantity of notes. One of the chapters was easily rewritten; the other, which became "Town and Country Life in 1800," was such a mass of detail that almost three months were required to reconstruct it. "The foul fiend take him," McMaster exploded, and years later, when asked how it felt to do the chapters over he could only sigh, "Did you ever eat cold mutton gravy?"[35] Soon after the theft, McMaster bought one of the newly invented typewriters and, it may be assumed, a quantity of duplicating paper.[36]

In 1885 Volume II came from the press, to be followed two years later by *Benjamin Franklin as a Man of Letters*. The *Benjamin Franklin* is one of the most interesting of McMaster's works, not only because it was the first detailed attempt to treat Franklin

[32] McMaster to Gertrude Stevenson, May 19, 1885 [?], MS.

[33] *Ibid.*, July 17, 1883, MS. See also "Diary," III, Sept. 6, 7, 1883, MS.

[34] "Diary," III, Sept. 8, 1883, MS.

[35] The first quotation is from *ibid.*; the second is from a letter of Dr. William H. Allen to the author, April 19, 1940.

[36] The typewriter began to be marketed about 1874, and some sort of duplicating paper had already been in use.

as an author but also because it contrasts so plainly one type of eighteenth-century Philadelphian with one type of nineteenth-century Philadelphian. Franklin's casual non-conformities—his phonetic spelling, his arguments for paper money, his illegitimate baby—were too much for McMaster.[37] The whole "candle-end-saving philosophy in which morality has no place" was shocking:

Nothing in his [Franklin's] whole career is more to be lamented than that a man of parts so great should, long after he had passed middle life, continue to write pieces so filthy that no editor has ever had the hardihood to print them. The substance of all he ever wrote is, Be honest, be truthful, be diligent in your calling; not because of the injunctions "Thou shalt not steal, thou shalt not bear false witness against thy neighbour;" but because honesty is the best policy; because in the long run idleness, knavery, wastefulness, lying, and fraud do not pay. . . .[38]

Yet the contemporary of Carnegie and Rockefeller, who was desperately anxious to make history pay, did not fail to add that, "low as such a motive may seem from a moral standpoint, it is, from a worldly standpoint, sound and good. Every man whose life the world calls successful has been actuated by it. . . .[39]

The fact that both the *Benjamin Franklin* and Volume II paid was tremendously important for McMaster.[40] Now, at long last, he felt he was standing on ground firm enough to support two people. On April 14, 1887, Miss Stevenson became Mrs. McMaster, and the birth of John Bach, Jr., and Philip David completed the family circle that McMaster delighted in calling "The Big Four." After several shifts of residence the McMasters settled at 2109 DeLancey Street—"within good social boundaries," as an old Philadelphian looked at it—and the charm of the wife created a home that made all other activities of her husband tangential.[41]

[37] *Benjamin Franklin as a Man of Letters*, pp. 279, 60-64, 44-45.
[38] *Ibid.*, p. 278.
[39] *Ibid.*, pp. 278-79.
[40] The sales records of both books are preserved among the McMaster Papers.
[41] The quotation is from Ellis P. Oberholtzer, "John Bach McMaster," *Pennsylvania Magazine of History and Biography* (1933), LVII, 17. Unless otherwise

McMaster was thirty-five when he married. The thin, reddish-blond hair had become thinner and darker. A moustache softened the spare lines of his face. But the large head on a small body—the Princeton boys called McMaster "the Tack"—was still the physical characteristic people noticed.[42] This, and the bright, twinkling eyes that twinkled more than ever now. For McMaster had arrived, and he knew it. A national reputation in a congenial field, an adequate income, a home and a family—the things for which he had struggled so long and so hard were now his.

The man the world saw and the man inside both began to change. The sarcasm of McMaster's earlier letters melts into a mild playfulness or a colorless brevity of statement. The furious rhythm of his working hours evens off to a steady industry. The McMaster of Philadelphia's salons becomes a homebody, never more happy than when working in his study or amusing the children with comical freehand drawings. Most public functions, learned and social, now seemed "pretentious." His few intimates delighted in the occasion when McMaster, surrounded by Philadelphia's most dignified patricians, contributed "Tch, tch, look at that young lady's legs!"[43]

Of all social activities, the Franklin Inn Club was McMaster's favorite. Secluded in a Philadelphia byway, with men like the artist, George Gibbs, and the historical novelist, S. Weir Mitchell, around its long table, the club was a luncheon center for good food and good talk. For thirty years McMaster came, always sitting in the same chair and always replacing his pipe in the same spot on the

---

footnoted, the facts in this paragraph and in the rest of the chapter come from interviews with Drs. H. Friedenwald, E. W. Mumford, and A. C. Myers, and from a letter of Prof. F. L. Paxson to the author, Sept. 17, 1934. The interpretation, of course, is my own.

[42] The information about the nickname comes from an interview with Prof. W. B. Scott. A member of the class of '91 described McMaster as "an emaciated skeleton of a man with a domelike head, totally bald except for a few reddish remnants of hair." Lloyd C. Griscom, *Diplomatically Speaking* (Boston, 1940), p. 18.

[43] Interview with Dr. A. C. Myers.

mantelpiece.[44] Once in a while the club would erupt into a play, and McMaster sometimes found himself swept along on the lava of their inspiration. In the "First performance on any stage of a serious, soul-stirring, sensational, scenic drama of real life, entitled *A Bachelor's Baby* or *Relentless Rudolph's Revenge*," McMaster became "A Versatile Disseminator of News," with the able co-operation of "A Hellenic Danseuse," "A Lady in Gray," and "Another Lady in Gray." In *A Midwinter Day Dream* the casting revealed an even finer touch. Historian Ellis P. Oberholtzer, paunchy and formal, became "Princess Madeleine, a saucy puss; a tricksy little sprite"; McMaster was "Cupid, the very latest idea in [the] way of a boy scout."[45] McMaster's rôles brought him in the plays late and took him out early, and nobody seemed to mind.

That McMaster was a bad actor is not surprising, for he was the kind of man who is never really at home except when he is at home. Ambition had forced him into the world, had forced him to be pleasant to strange people and to be witty at strange tables, but not even ambition could make him like it. Now that he had arrived, McMaster retired behind the uncommunicativeness that is often the screen of shy but confident men. His cronies at the Franklin Inn Club thought of him as a man who said little, and that little usually a playful pointing up of a world that insists upon caricaturing itself. His colleagues at the University knew McMaster as a man whom nobody knew, and as one whose correspondence was conducted on the principle that "most letters, if laid aside for several weeks, will answer themselves."[46] Only Mrs. McMaster would have believed that her husband had once been an indefatigable correspondent, an energetic dinner guest, a sarcastic wit. Little wonder. The others knew the McMaster who had settled down.

[44] McMaster was president of the club from 1914 to 1930, and honorary president from 1930 until his death.

[45] The playbills are preserved among the McMaster Papers.

[46] Interview with Prof. Edward P. Cheyney.

CHAPTER V

Professor and Publicist

THE THIRTY YEARS after McMaster settled in Philadelphia were a period of hard, varied labor that left him not a, but the historian of the American people, as the President of the United States put it.[1] The massive eight volumes of the *History* were only one of the achievements that gave McMaster national importance. Prominence also came from his activities as a university professor, from his widely read publications on current questions, and from three textbooks that were staples of the country's school system.

For more than three decades, from 1883 to 1919, McMaster taught American history in the University of Pennsylvania.[2] Connected with the Wharton School for his first eight years, he was shifted to the new School of American History in 1891.[3] This School, the first of its kind in the country, was partly the creation of McMaster. For some time he and Francis N. Thorpe, Professor of American Constitutional History, had been collecting a library of nearly fourteen thousand volumes concerning the history of American institutions. Probably Thorpe and McMaster expected that the same men who financed the purchase of the books would supply a large endowment for the School.[4] At any rate, McMaster wrote enthusiastically about

[1] Theodore Roosevelt, quoted in the *Washington Post*, Nov. 17, 1903.

[2] McMaster's active service ceased on June 12, 1919, and on April 12, 1920, he was officially made Professor Emeritus.

[3] The School was established on April 7, 1891. "Minutes of the Board of Trustees of the University of Pennsylvania" (April 7, 1891), XII, 581-85, MS. University of Pennsylvania Archives.

[4] Interview with Prof. E. P. Cheyney; *Philadelphia Public Ledger*, Sept. 26, 1891; C. C. Harrison to McMaster, April 5, 1895, MS; McMaster and Thorpe, "School of American History: General Plan of Organization, submitted to the Provost and the Board of Trustees," April 7, 1891, MS, McMaster Papers; *Report of the Provost of the University of Pennsylvania for the Three Years Ending October 1, 1892* (Philadelphia, 1893), p. 12.

. . . the collection of material for the study of the History of the United States in the broadest sense. . . . *This school is the Pioneer* in what soon must be a general movement and will always be the leader. No man who now attempts to write the history of our country can possibly own all the books and documents necessary for such work. They must be gathered by great libraries. Then why not by one great library having that for its sole purpose? He cannot even read all the books necessary for such a piece of work. Hundreds of individuals must work up small pieces of our own history for one man to use. Then why not have all this work done systematically under one head, at one University, in one School of History?[5]

McMaster and Thorpe became co-directors of the School of American History, which was organized to include courses in non-American history as well.[6] The new division of the University, the *Philadelphia Inquirer* was sure, would do much to enlighten the average American, whose idea of the past was that "We licked the British twice, then we licked Mexico, later we licked the South, and now, by Jove, we can lick any nation on earth."[7] But no adequate endowment was forthcoming, and the professors of non-American history were disgruntled.[8] After three years the School ceased to exist even on paper, and McMaster, like the other members of its faculty, was assigned to duty in the regular college and university.[9]

When McMaster began teaching history, his ideal was clear. Probably remembering the narrow instruction he had received at the College of the City of New York, McMaster aimed

. . . to encourage students not to take such estimates of men and such statements of events as are to be found in text books and histories, but,

[5] Undated memorandum of McMaster, MS, Univ. of Pa. Archives.
[6] McMaster and Thorpe, "School of American History," MS, Univ. of Pa. Archives. Thorpe was to be dean, while McMaster was to "give special direction to all studies in American Institutional History."
[7] *Philadelphia Inquirer*, Feb. 9, 1891. Many newspaper clippings about the School are preserved in the McMaster Papers.
[8] Interview with Prof. E. P. Cheyney.
[9] "Minutes of the Board of Trustees of the University of Pennsylvania" (Nov. 6, 1894), XIII, 238, MS, Univ. of Pa. Archives.

collecting their own materials to form their own opinions and to support them with reasons based on a personal knowledge of the sources of history.

In the back of McMaster's mind was the ambition to give the best American history course in the country.[10]

His ambition was decidedly greater than his pedagogical abilities.[11] The man who appeared a bad lecturer to audiences paying to hear him seemed even worse to boys who could not avoid the occasion. "Cold and impersonal as a piece of chalk" was the impression of one undergraduate—a pale, unimpressive figure, whose "eyes looked out through large round glasses, like an owl unused to light."[12] In a low, almost inaudible voice McMaster would drone on. Only the front rows heard everything he said, and they were reminded of the tourist guide reciting a well-learned piece. Even the inevitable whisperings and shufflings could not interrupt the machine-like flow. Once two undergraduates began to talk during the lecture. "Iturbide," the lecturer continued without the slightest inflection of voice, "who henceforth called himself Augustine the First—will those two boys leave the room—having no more use for Congress—I said leave the room—decided to dismiss it."[13] The boys no doubt left the room, for the historian, when in a disciplinary mood, could unleash a tongue that bit. "Will the gentlemen who are talking please leave the room," McMaster remarked in the course of one lecture. No one moved and then, from the midst of the next

[10] Rough copy, McMaster to William Pepper, Jan. 28, 1884, MS. McMaster may have removed from the final copy the expression of his "ardent desire" to give the best course.

[11] The paragraphs on McMaster as a teacher are based on interviews with Drs. E. P. Cheyney, R. P. Falkner, H. M. Friedenwald, W. E. Lingelbach, and A. C. Myers; on letters to the author from Drs. W. H. Allen (April 19, 1940), E. S. Corwin (Oct. 29, 1939), F. L. Paxson (Sept. 17, 1934), J. T. Young (May 3, 1938); and from the accounts of McMaster's teaching in Ellis P. Oberholtzer, "John Bach McMaster," *Pennsylvania Magazine of History and Biography* (1933), LVII, 14-15, and in James Monaghan, "John Bach McMaster, Pioneer," *passim*, a manuscript used through the courtesy of the author.

[12] J. Monaghan, "John Bach McMaster," p. 1, MS.

[13] *Ibid.*

paragraph, came, "Will those men talking who are not gentlemen leave the room."[14]

Usually McMaster did not concern himself too much about discipline, as he did not struggle long with dull or indifferent students. His mind was on getting the *History of the People* done; his patience was short.[15] McMaster's indifference toward written work is legendary. Some of his students cannot remember a time when they were quizzed. Another tells how McMaster

. . . entered the room where we were all assembled in readiness, and announced: "Your question, gentlemen, is to write the history of the United States from 1800 to 1814." Then he looked at us owlishly and went home, leaving us entirely to ourselves.

Professor McMaster returned at noon to find us working like beavers, our copies of his *History of the United States* [*sic*] propped before us. Without comment he collected our papers. During the luncheon intermission we concluded that he never intended to open them and equipped ourselves for the afternoon session with bits of sealing wax. After another four hours of summarizing his book, we rolled up our abstracts, tied them with the prescribed red ribbon, and unobtrusively dropped a gob of wax on the knot.

Professor McMaster gathered in the scrolls, his face still expressionless. As he put them in his briefcase, he remarked in his precise fashion, "Gentlemen, I have a feeling that at least this examination may have accomplished something in the way of teaching you a little American history."

The whole class was marked excellent; the highest grade attainable. When my paper came back, I inspected it curiously; the seal was intact.[16]

Notes on McMaster's lectures were frequently inchoate, for he was easily led away from his theme by designed or perfectly sincere questions. An inquiry from the class "was often sufficient to

[14] Interview with Dr. R. P. Falkner.

[15] Even in his first year at the University, McMaster noted in his "Diary" (III, Dec. 19, 1883, MS) that he must see the Provost "to talk over the matter of giving up the Freshmen. I must get rid of them. The book drags beyond all endurance. I must work sixteen hours a day during the vacation." See also *ibid.*, April 27, 1883, MS.

[16] Lloyd C. Griscom, *Diplomatically Speaking* (Boston, 1940), pp. 18-19.

precipitate a monograph."[17] One year three of McMaster's pupils appointed themselves a committee to consult with him about "his faults as a teacher." The Professor listened sympathetically, promised to change his methods, and in a short while was teaching just as he had always done. The conference produced a more tangible result the following year when McMaster wrote a syllabus for his course which was required reading, brought an expense to the students, and did not solve the major difficulty.[18]

The trouble was with the method, not with the material McMaster had to offer. The information stored up in his Macaulay-like memory was prodigious, and the man was a peripatetic bibliography. "You'll get there this," he would say, and the *there* was often the page as well as the book.[19] It was something of a game—to the few students who considered such things games—to discover a legislative act which the Professor could not trace in detail from its appearance in Congress to the President's signature. Nor was the material political and military chronicle. Chockful of social history, McMaster's course was as much ahead of the usual college survey as his *History of the People* was ahead of its contemporaries.[20] Some of the homework McMaster assigned emphasized his progressiveness. Frequently he would have the students use the census to make maps showing what McMaster called "the three fingers of population expansion." For at least one pupil these exercises provided an explanation of the regional difference in trans-Appalachian America—why, for example, the people of northern and southern Ohio seemed so different.[21]

The student who benefited in this way was a better-than-average one, and McMaster was decidedly a good student's teacher. The

[17] Letter from Prof. E. S. Corwin to the author, Oct. 29, 1939.

[18] This story was told to me by Mr. E. W. Mumford, formerly secretary of the University. Messrs. Mumford, S. M. Lindsay, and J. L. Stewart were the "committee."

[19] Interview with Dr. A. C. Myers.

[20] See, for example, McMaster's approach to the Revolutionary period in the syllabus, *Political History of the United States*, pp. 1-10.

[21] Interview with Mr. E. W. Mumford.

caviar of erudition, smothered in the onions of bad presentation, will be appreciated only by connoisseurs. Naturally McMaster was more successful in graduate than in undergraduate teaching.[22] Put him at the head of a seminar table, give him interested students, and then his method of leaving students largely to their own salvation was far more likely to send them to academic heaven than to academic perdition. On one occasion a graduate student made a decidedly bad report on his decidedly bad research.

McMaster stopped him & proceeded to ask him whether he had seen this, that & the other thing, getting a negative answer each time. Thereupon Professor McMaster left the room, & was gone more than half an hour. He then returned with a page, each carrying a huge arm-full of books, including several volumes of Niles [*sic*] Register, the Register of Debates, Executive Reports, etc., and deposited the entire cargo in front of the unfortunate student. This was done without remark of any kind,—the student never showed up again.[23]

Other students did show up again, and these remember that their master's interest in good work was as great as his contempt for poor work. Quietly, without deserving the reputation of a great teacher, McMaster sent out from his seminar many men whose names were to become eminent in the scholarly world. Among the professional scholars who studied under McMaster are E. C. Barker, H. E. Bolton, E. P. Cheyney, E. S. Corwin, H. M. Friedenwald, E. R. Johnson, S. M. Lindsay, W. E. Lingelbach, E. P. Oberholtzer, F. L. Paxson, W. T. Root, W. R. Shepherd, W. W. Sweet, C. H. Van Tyne, and J. T. Young.[24]

In the general routine of University life, McMaster was more

[22] Like most of McMaster's students, Dr. James T. Young (letter to the author, May 3, 1938), says, "His classes were endured but not appreciated [by undergraduates]. . . . His graduate students were often enthusiastic."

[23] Letter from Prof. E. S. Corwin to the author, Oct. 29, 1939.

[24] Partial lists of McMaster's students may be found in "John Bach McMaster, Historian of the American People," *American Review of Reviews* (1913), XLVIII, 681, and in William T. Hutchinson, "John Bach McMaster," in Hutchinson, ed., *The Marcus W. Jernegan Essays in American Historiography* (Chicago, 1937), p. 125, note 9.

UNIVERSITY OF PENNSYLVANIA HISTORIANS ABOUT 1895
Dana Carleton Munro
Edward Potts Cheyney - John Bach McMaster - James Harvey Robinson

conspicuous than active. The famous historian was always writing another volume of the *History*.[25] McMaster represented the University when geography suggested it, made a speech for the University when the proprieties demanded it, and once served as a Presidential ghost-writer when McKinley consented to speak at a campus function if the speech were written for him.[26] McMaster was enough of a faculty man to be elected one of the vice-presidents of the Faculty Club when it was organized in 1898, and by this time he was consulted by the administrative officers of the University as the senior member of the History Department.[27] As such McMaster wrote the letter asking Frederick Jackson Turner whether he would be interested in a "professorship [at Pennsylvania] of what might be called American Constitutional and Institutional History."[28] But McMaster remained to most of his colleagues what he had been when he came—"a man of mystery"—and he was so little concerned with administrative duties that he frequently ignored committee assignments.[29]

One of McMaster's few administrative activities is made interesting by its association with Woodrow Wilson. The departure of Robert E. Thompson in 1892 emphasized the fact that Pennsylvania was losing many of its big names. "I am a Quaker," the Dean

[25] Most friends of McMaster tend to agree with Prof. Paxson in his assertion that McMaster "plunged into a thirty-five year job while a young man, and sacrificed all irrelevancies to the completion of his project." Letter from Prof. F. L. Paxson to the author, Sept. 17, 1934.

[26] For example, McMaster's address at the University celebration of Washington's birthday (Jesse Y. Burk to McMaster, March 5, 1895), MS, and McMaster's representing the University at the King Alfred Celebration while in England (*ibid.*, Aug. 22, 1901, MS). For the McKinley speech, see Oberholtzer in the *Pennsylvania Magazine of History and Biography*, LVII, 20.

[27] For the Faculty Club office, see *Philadelphia Public Ledger*, May 19, 1898; for typical letters treating McMaster as the key man in the Department, see Provost C. C. Harrison's letters to McMaster, Feb. 4, May 27, June 1, 1897, MSS.

[28] McMaster to Turner, April 9, 1897, MS. Turner accepted the invitation to visit Pennsylvania (C. Emory McMichael to McMaster, April 21, 1897, MS), but apparently the negotiations stopped there.

[29] Interviews with Profs. E. P. Cheyney and W. E. Lingelbach. The quoted phrase comes from E. Cheyney, *History of the University of Pennsylvania*, p. 289.

of the Dental School told the Provost, "and I have a concern about this."[30] The concern was shared by other faculty men, and a strong sentiment within the University called for the appointment of Wilson, then a professor at Princeton, as dean of the Pennsylvania Law School. The Provost, having been told by "several of Professor Wilson's friends . . . that one of his great interests would be a scholarly Law School, where he might deliver lectures," asked Mc-Master to sound out the political scientist.[31] McMaster went to Princeton to see the man who, as he once remarked, "could talk about potatoes and make it sound like Holy Writ."[32] The historian could only report that Wilson had his eye on the presidency of Princeton and was not interested in the Pennsylvania overture.[33]

While negotiating about Wilson's career, McMaster had to

[30] Interview with Dr. R. P. Falkner. Some of these faculty losses are explained in E. Cheyney, *History of the University of Pennsylvania*, pp. 291-95. The Dean of the Dental School who made the remark quoted was probably James Truman.

[31] Interview with Dr. R. P. Falkner and C. C. Harrison to McMaster, Dec. 14, 1895, MS.

[32] The remark of McMaster was quoted to me by Dr. A. C. Myers.

[33] Interviews with Drs. P. D. McMaster and R. P. Falkner. When Amherst was considering Wilson for its president, E. Winchester Donald, a member of Amherst's Board of Trustees, wrote McMaster (Feb. 17, 1899, MS), "The Trustees of Amherst College are considering the name of Woodrow Wilson for the Presidency of the College. Until yesterday we were under the impression that a contract either expressed or implied, between Mr. Wilson and Mr. McCormick would make it impossible for Wilson to leave Princeton. Yesterday we learned that no contract to that effect existed, and the question arises whether Wilson would be likely to consider an election. Naturally we do not wish to elect a man who is unable or most unlikely to accept, and I was therefore charged to learn if possible whether Mr. Wilson is free to leave Princeton; and, further, if there is any known likelihood of his leaving if elected to a position of honor and influence, such as the Trustees of Amherst naturally regard their Presidency to be. Of course, I am asking a difficult question; one which, were I in your place, I should find it hard to answer; and yet it may well be that you are in a position to know whether Wilson regards his Chair at Princeton as a permanency." The publisher, D. C. Heath, an alumnus of Amherst, had also been urging the selection of Wilson in letters to H. B. Adams, a member of the Board of Trustees. W. Stull Holt, ed., *Historical Scholarship in the United States, 1876-1901: As Revealed in the Correspondence of Herbert B. Adams* (Baltimore, 1938), pp. 254-56.

answer similar questions concerning himself, for his prestige was high and rising. Probably most important among the academic invitations he received was an offer made within the same year to Woodrow Wilson—the presidency of the University of Illinois.[34] A man midway in the writing of a monumental history, a man not interested in administrative work would have been foolish to take the presidency of a state university, and McMaster no doubt knew it. It was also possible for him to say to his Provost, "The financial inducement . . . was naturally tempting, but I feel that the prospect of developing a great school of American history in connection with the University of Pennsylvania is too important an opportunity to be relinquished."[35] Nor did McMaster nibble at non-academic offerings ranging from the position of State Librarian of Pennsylvania to "a proposition for becoming closely identified with the management of a life insurance company in somewhat of an advisory capacity . . . ?"[36]

Any proposition made to McMaster had to meet the supreme test: did it intrude too much on the *History of the People?* Yet a variety of by-products could be drawn from research for the *History*, and McMaster, always concerned about making "ends . . . not only meet but overlap," did not ignore his opportunities.[37] For a person who was not at home on the platform, he addressed audiences frequently; his bibliography of books and newspaper and magazine articles has the steady march of a telephone directory. One of these books, a collection of documents edited by McMaster and Frederick D. Stone on a subsidy from the Historical Society of

[34] Francis M. McKay (a member of the Illinois Board of Trustees) to McMaster, Feb. 20, 1892, MS. For the Wilson offer, see Ray Stannard Baker, *Woodrow Wilson, Life and Letters* (8 vols., New York, 1927-39), II, 21-22. From the available material it is impossible to determine which man received the offer first.

[35] McMaster to William Pepper, in "Minutes of the Board of Trustees of the University of Pennsylvania" (June 4, 1892), XIII, 19, MS, Univ. of Pa. Archives.

[36] Interviews with Drs. P. D. McMaster and A. C. Myers; Samuel W. Pennypacker to McMaster, Jan. 24, 1903, MS; Oberholtzer in the *Pennsylvania Magazine of History and Biography*, LVII, 21. The quotation is from W. E. A. Wheeler to McMaster, Aug. 26, 1909, MS.

[37] "Diary," II, Jan. 12, 1892, MS.

Pennsylvania, was to aid in revising interpretations of the Constitution.[38] The lectures McMaster delivered before a midwestern chapter of the Daughters of the American Revolution turned into *The Acquisition of Political Social and Industrial Rights of Man in America*—the little book that was a pioneer in calling attention to the undemocratic political machinery of the early United States.[39]

The more McMaster was accepted as an authority on the past, the more his opinion was sought about the present and the future. He had not been in Philadelphia a decade before he was a University and a civic sage. Most appropriate was the plea McMaster made when city officials were contemplating changes in the street names of Philadelphia. "Some importance," the historian reminded them, "should be attached to the value of historic associations."[40] More revealing was the statement McMaster gave to the reporters when Andrew Carnegie established his ten-million-dollar trust for pensioning academic men:

I don't know any more about it than what I have read, but I don't like it. I don't believe in this scattering of Carnegie libraries over the country, as he has been doing in the last few years. It is not a good thing, and I don't like Mr. Carnegie's methods.

In the first place, I do not believe in pension systems in general, and I am especially opposed to them in the teaching profession. It would be practically the same thing as the police pensioning, and it could not help but lower the profession.

When one of us enters the teaching profession he does not do it with the expectation of making money; he has an entirely different end in view. This pension system would certainly lower our standard.

---

[38] McMaster and Frederick D. Stone, eds., *Pennsylvania and the Federal Constitution, 1787-88.* This book is cited frequently in Charles A. Beard, *An Economic Interpretation of the Constitution*, New York, 1913.

[39] Published in Cleveland, 1903. Apart from Vol. V of McMaster's own *History of the People*, this was the first book to give detailed emphasis to the point. J. Allen Smith, a leader in calling attention to the conservatism of The Fathers, used to assign this book to his classes at the University of Washington. Herman Rensing to McMaster, Aug. 9, 1910, MS.

[40] *Philadelphia Press*, April 8, 1897.

I believe that in this and in all professions, as in business, each man should stand on his own basis, and on that alone. Personally, I would not accept such a pension, but I think that it might prove acceptable to the majority of the profession. I am speaking only for myself. We have "Carnegie libraries" and "Carnegie heroes," now we are to have "Carnegie professors." I do not like it.[41]

Each man should stand on his own basis, and on that alone—McMaster was reading back to Carnegie Carnegie's own credo of individualism. Having invoked the doctrine against something he did not like, McMaster later added his name to a memorial asking the Carnegie Institution to underwrite scholarship![42] Probably both the historian and the steel magnate, in their shifting and often contradictory conception of individualism, were simply their America incarnate.

As time went on McMaster assumed in the life of the nation a position similar to, if less important than, his rôle in Philadelphia. More and more newspaper editors telegraphed for McMaster's opinion on domestic or international problems; more and more organizations besought him for speeches; more and more magazine editors asked for articles, particularly for historical treatments of current questions. Both S. S. McClure and the Hearst papers wanted to syndicate a regular commentary by McMaster.[43] The historian was a standby of Walter Hines Page, editor first of the *Forum* and then of the *Atlantic Monthly*. In a typical request, made shortly before the Bryan campaign of 1896, Page wrote McMaster:

I find that a good many men, men of balance and cheerfulness, who believe fully in the democratic form of government, are now more despondent about the safety of our democratic institutions than they ever were before. Say they: "During the period of the physical conquest of the continent, as in the period before that—the time of the Revolution—, likewise in the great emergency brought by slavery, democracy proved

---

[41] *New York Tribune*, April 29, 1905.

[42] *To the Trustees of the Carnegie Institution of Washington*, Dec. 10, 1909, a printed memorial among the McMaster Papers.

[43] S. S. McClure to McMaster, March 18, 1886; Rudolph Block to McMaster, Dec. 30, 1905, MSS.

equal to the strain. The mass of men could understand that England was oppressive—could at least understand that it was desirable to have home-rule in America; so later, the mass at least came to feel the necessity of preserving the Union. These were definite, simple, single, concrete propositions.

"But now," they go on, "something different and more complex is presented. Can the mass of men ever be brought or be brought in time to save us—to understand that the principle of *fiat* money, whether it be paper or silver, is so vicious and dangerous a principle that it has in it possibilities of the wrecking of our whole commercial, political & social structure? When we have at last come to a practical question of some complexity, is there hope that this, too, will turn out well in the hands of mere majority-rule?"

This is a pretty serious thing, of course; and, I fancy, that a great many very thoughtful men are wondering how near we may yet have to come to ruin, before Congressional majorities learn the lesson of financial experience.

Mere exposition and argument and explanation—we have had enough. But it occurs to me that it would be exceedingly interesting and instructive to have condensed within the space of a *Forum* article some of the most striking and instructive parallels in our history to the present situation—not going over the same ground exactly that you went over in your other *Forum* paper, but taking up such striking instances as there are of the ultimate triumph of the principle of majority-rule, after a period during which it seemed impossible to teach the majority what was right—to get a complex idea through their heads.

What continues to impress me as desirable and as instructive is the historical parrallel [*sic*] with our present condition—if there be parallels which can cheer us.

What would you say, if I asked you to be good enough to write such a paper by the 8th or 10th of March? "Yes," I hope. May I not hear at your earliest convenience?[44]

---

[44] Page to McMaster, Feb. 18, 1895, MS. On the same theme, S. S. McClure wrote McMaster (April 17, 1895, MS):

"My brother who is traveling in the West for the magazine and has just gone over the route from St. Paul to New Orleans, states that 'Coin's Financial School' is selling by the hundred thousand that newsdealers everywhere say there is no subject people want to be so thoroughly informed about as the Silver Question and the problems lying behind the Silver Question. He also states that

Page heard, at a convenience that was not very early, and in time McMaster summoned history before the *Forum* audience to answer affirmatively the question, "Is Sound Finance Possible under Popular Government?"[45] "One Year of Cleveland; The Record It Has Made," "How to Deal with a Filibustering Minority," "A Century of Constitutional Interpretation," "Cheaper Currency," "National Expansion," "The Third Term Tradition," "Liberty Loans of the Revolution"—a glance at McMaster's titles recall the major problems agitating Americans in his day. History, speaking through McMaster, spoke in general for the side of late nineteenth-century American conservatism, for the gold standard, high tariffs, a Monroe Doctrine with teeth, a militant expansionism.[46]

A strong foreign policy in particular gave McMaster the theme which made him a publicist of national importance. His first major statements came in support of Cleveland's belligerent application of the Monroe Doctrine to the Venezuelan difficulty of 1895. Invited by the editor of the *New York Times* to write a historical interpretation of the Doctrine's meaning, McMaster prepared over four thousand words which were spread across six columns of that newspaper's front page.[47]

Lord Salisbury asserts [McMaster summarized] that even if there was a Monroe Doctrine it could not apply to Venezuela because Great Britain is not attempting to colonize or to extend her system. But the Monroe Doctrine is not limited to these conditions. It distinctly declares that no nation of the Old World is to *oppress or in any other manner seek to control the destiny* of any nation in the New. The area now

---

the majority of the people are in favor of free silver and they are buying and absorbing misinformation rapidly.

It seems to me to be the duty of any magazine of large circulation to enter upon this subject and to disseminate the truth and to make the truth appear like the truth.

. . . I know that you are thoroughly familiar with all the various cheap money crazes that have swept over the country. It might be that you have time to write me an article."

[45] *Forum* (1895), XIX, 159-68.

[46] McMaster's attitudes are analyzed in Chap. VII.

[47] *New York Times*, Jan. 2, 1896.

claimed arbitrarily, and with no proof submitted, by Great Britain is one hundred and nine thousand square miles—an area which is exceeded by no States in the Union save Texas, California, and Montana; an area ninety times as large as Rhode Island, fifty-four times as large as Delaware, thirteen times as large as Massachusetts, and forty thousand square miles larger than the six New England States. Were we to lose so great a tract, were Great Britain to take from us New England and all New York east of Rochester, would she not be controlling our destiny? . . .

. . . when a European power rightfully or wrongfully attempts to acquire so immense an area as this, she does, in the language of Monroe, "control the destiny" of a nation; she does, in the language of Polk, "interfere with the independent action of nations on this continent"; she is, as Cass expressed it, "holding possession of that country"; she is seeking "to control its political destiny"; and we are bound, as Buchanan asserted, to resist "the attempt to deprive our neighboring republic of her territory, and the Monroe Doctrine does apply."[48]

Republished, quoted, or commented upon all over the country, reprinted in pamphlet form by the *New York Times* and pirated by a Philadelphia publisher, this article brought a flood of mail to DeLancey Street, including an invitation to debate the question before the Massachusetts Reform Club.[49] McMaster's remarks on this occasion gave the expansionist press another field day, even the *Daily Northwest News*, of Grand Rapids, North Dakota, arousing itself to greet him "over two thousand miles of space from the centre of North America."[50]

The Venezuela crisis was not liquidated before McMaster was thinking about Cuba.[51] As war fever rose, he announced a special

[48] The quotation is from McMaster, "The Monroe Doctrine," in *With the Fathers*, pp. 44-45, a revised version of the *New York Times* article which states McMaster's points more succinctly.

[49] McMaster, *The Venezuela Dispute* (New York, 1896) and *The Origin, Meaning and Application of the Monroe Doctrine* (Philadelphia, 1896). For the pirating and the general reception of the article, see "Second Memoirs," p. 70, MS.

[50] Quoted in *ibid.*, p. 71, MS. Among McMaster's opponents was Dr. Albert Bushnell Hart. McMaster's full remarks are quoted in the *Boston Herald*, Jan. 18, 1896.

[51] Henry Cabot Lodge to McMaster, Dec. 23, 1896, MS.

course in the University of Pennsylvania which would deal with the Cuban trouble, lectured on "Expansion" before a chapel full of cheering students, and volunteered his own services as an army engineer.[52] The reporters who flocked to McMaster's office caught the excited nationalism of the historian. One newspaper paraphrased him as having said:

. . . if the Spanish war has no other result than in awakening a love of country, it will still be a great benefit to us as a nation, for he [McMaster] asserts that the philosophy of history teaches that if a generation passes away in which there are no occasions to call for the patriotism of a people, it produces a laxity of national cohesions that is more destructive in its effects than war and all its attending horrors.[53]

The way in which the *Chester* (Pa.) *Republican* manipulated this statement supports—perhaps more than it should be supported— the thesis of Charles A. Beard that the Spanish-American War was used to quiet internal discontent.[54] Had the newspapers turned back to the first volume of the *History*, they would have seen that McMaster believed wars produced not only "national cohesion" but "intellectual activity . . . the evils of war [are] succeeded by the fruits of genius."[55] The war-mindedness of McMaster, his admiration of the fierce life, his delight in the savage paintings of

[52] *Philadelphia Times,* March 22, 1899; *Philadelphia Record,* April 29, 1898; *Philadelphia Press,* April 21, 1898.

[53] *Chester* (Pa.) *Republican,* April 23, 1898. McMaster was quoted as having made the same point in the *Philadelphia Record,* April 24, 1898.

[54] "That this [McMaster's statement] is a true statement of socialistic conditions [ran the *Chester Republican* editorial] is now evidenced, although only a month has elapsed since Congress declared a state of war existed between this government and that of Spain. The advocates of the wildest theories of governmental reforms which found their only basis in delusive reasoning, who, less than a year ago, were accorded patient hearings, find few that now hearken to their impassioned appeals, for the nobler emotions of the people are addressed by the call which has gone forth summoning the nation to arms in defense of its flag and in discharge of the mission, which, in the progress of civilization has fallen as a duty to this people to discharge." Mr. Beard's interpretation may be found in "Giddy Minds and Foreign Quarrels," *Harpers* (1939), CLXXIX, 337-51.

[55] *History of the People,* I, 77.

Remington which hung in his office, have suggested the theory of psychological compensation for a small body and an academic life.[56] Yet McMaster was not grandiloquent about his own possible rôle in war. Asked whether military experience would be good for a historian, he replied, "It would be, if the historian was not scared too much."[57]

McMaster never had a chance to show whether he would be scared or not, for the government did not call him to army service. Only in articles and speeches could the historian conduct his expansionist war. Most influential were McMaster's newspaper and magazine articles—particularly "Annexation and Universal Suffrage," published in the *Forum*, which became the starting point for editorials written in all parts of the country.[58] The historian's argument was always an interpretation of history. Expansion had been a constant and desirable policy of the United States. It had always been opposed by prophets of evil, but "happily for us, the expansionists prevailed."[59] To annex the regions acquired after the Spanish-American War without giving a vote to the natives, McMaster continued, was simply traditional American policy:

When our forefathers founded the Republic they announced to the world certain political doctrines often asserted, but never before applied. . . . It might reasonably be supposed that, having deliberately proclaimed these truths, the men of '76 would have instantly made use of them; that, being free to create such governments as they saw fit, they would have founded new commonwealths in which the equality of all men was fully recognized. Had they attempted to apply the new truths generally the whole social fabric would have gone to pieces. Happily they were not so applied. They were ideals to be lived up to and gradually attained; and the very men whose lips were constantly heard demanding the rights of man, the inalienable rights of man, went

---

[56] The theory is suggested in J. Monaghan, "John Bach McMaster," p. 2, a manuscript used through the courtesy of the author.

[57] *Philadelphia Press*, April 24, 1898.

[58] *Forum* (1898), XXVI, 393-402. Clippings of many of the editorials are preserved in the McMaster Papers.

[59] McMaster, "The Dread of Expansion," *Outlook* (1899), XLI, 161.

carefully to work and set up State governments in which the rights of man were very little regarded, in which manhood suffrage was ignored. . . .[60]

. . . .

We have an ideal form of government, but there is no ideal government in practise. . . . The Louisiana purchase was largely overrun by Indians. The peoples were polyglot. . . . For the last forty years they had been under the rule of Spain. It was decided that men who had had that experience had no conception of American government, and, therefore, it was folly to give them the widest benefits of the Constitution. From the debate in this Louisiana purchase it was established that territory acquired from foreign countries is not part of the United States, and, therefore, is not under the Constitution, but is the property of the United States.

. . . .

Territory acquired from anywhere can be governed in any way that Congress sees fit to govern it, and the principles of government to be observed there shall be the best of which the people are capable.[61]

Sourly a Democratic paper commented:

The imperialists need a theory and John Bach McMaster is hailed with delight as the man who has supplied it. It is a very simple theory—to set aside the Constitution. As Tim Campbell remarked confidentially to Saxton: "What is a little thing like the Constitution among friends?"[62]

McMaster the publicist was becoming a minor national institution, even if some of his devotees could identify him only as "a man down in Princeton—he's connected with an institution of learning there, the one that has a football team that beat Yale some weeks ago."[63] This mis-identification, as another newspaper justly remarked, was "a small matter in comparison with the fact that the Philadelphia professor is doing more to make the paths of the anti-

[60] "Annexation and Universal Suffrage," Forum (1898), XXVI, 393.
[61] Quoted in the Philadelphia Press, Nov. 10, 1898.
[62] Rochester Post Express, Dec. 13, 1898.
[63] Meriden (Conn.) Republican, Dec. 14, 1898. McMaster was also said to be at Princeton in the Boston Journal, Dec. 13, 1898.

imperialists difficult than any other college professor in the United States. . . ."[64] And the Philadelphia professor of history had behind his arguments for imperialism and the rest of his high Republican creed a force which no other type of publicist could command. Politically astute Henry Cabot Lodge had made the point exactly in his congratulations on McMaster's address before the Massachusetts Reform Club. "I trust you will permit me to express my gratification with your speech," the Senator wrote, "for you stand outside of active politics and speak with the authority of an historian."[65]

[64] *Philadelphia Press*, Dec. 16, 1898.
[65] Quoted in "Second Memoirs," p. 71, MS.

CHAPTER VI

People's Historian of the People

OF COURSE, publishers were after McMaster to write a textbook.[1]
It was not only that his name had the prestige which sells schoolbooks; the man was writing a different kind of history and might
be expected to write a different kind of history textbook. It was the
American Book Company, then rising rapidly in the educational
book field, which finally committed McMaster to a contract. This
firm had attracted the historian in 1894 by a proposal to prepare
a collection of stories from the history of Pennsylvania which would
serve as supplementary reading in the schools of that state.[2] Mc-
Master was interested, but in the course of conferences with Russell
Hinman, an editor of the American Book Company, he began thinking in broader terms about

. . . a regular school text-book of the history of the United States, in
which the middle colonies and the country to the westward should receive more adequate treatment than they do in most of the current textbooks prepared from the ultra New England standpoint.[3]

"The more I think over your plan . . . the better I like it . . . ,"
Hinman encouraged McMaster. "We can give . . . [the book] a
phenomenal sale."[4]

Apparently McMaster agreed to write the text with the understanding that the book was to be done about February 1896.[5] As

---

[1] William Beostanson, of the Anderson Book Co., to McMaster, July 11, 1883;
Ivison, Blakeman, and Co. to McMaster, Oct. 31, Dec. 8, 1888; Silver, Burdett,
and Co. to McMaster, March 8, 1894; William A. Merriman, of the Western
Publishing House to McMaster, May 7, 1897, MSS.
[2] Russell Hinman to McMaster, Sept. 26, 1894, MS.
[3] Ibid., Nov. 3, 1894, MS.
[4] Ibid., April 9, 1895, MS.
[5] Ibid., Jan. 31, 1895, MS.

February came and went and the manuscript was not finished, the publishers feverishly pressed McMaster to hurry. Hinman knew that texts somewhat similar to McMaster's were being prepared for other companies and was "dreadfully afraid that somebody will steal your thunder."[6] Moreover,

Chicago with its million or more inhabitants is about to change Histories, and unless we can get your History in shape before very many weeks that city will probably be lost to Fiske or somebody else for a number of years. If we can only get your book out in time I believe we can take the cake. *Verbum sap.*[7]

Exactly how McMaster reacted to this pressure is not ascertainable, but much of the correspondence from the American Book Company suggests that they would have liked to write him, as did an editor of the *Century Magazine:* "There seems to be someone in Philadelphia who is an admirable imitator of your handwriting, who, from time to time, writes to us promising that your manuscript will be delivered to us"![8]

The textbook manuscript was delivered the more slowly because, in the last stages of preparing it, McMaster became involved in the school history agitation of the Grand Army of the Republic.[9] After long-continued rumblings among the local units of the veterans, the national encampment of 1896 had set up a Committee on School Histories and placed it under the chairmanship of Judge A. O. Marsh, of Indiana.[10] McMaster, apparently seeking to sound out the situation, wrote Marsh and asked what kind of history of the

---

[6] *Ibid.*, Oct. 10, 1895, April 15, 1896, MSS. The quotation is from the second letter.

[7] *Ibid.*, March 13, 1897, MS. The book referred to is John Fiske, *A History of the United States for Schools*, Boston, 1894.

[8] R. U. Johnson to McMaster, Dec. 3, 1900, MS.

[9] Unfortunately correspondence concerning the following episode has not been preserved either by the G.A.R. or by the American Book Company.

[10] The most extensive account of the G.A.R. textbook agitation may be found in Marie L. Rulkotter, "Civil War Veterans in Politics," 1938, MS, University of Wisconsin Library, pp. 295-98, 362-69. Marsh was a judge of the 25th judicial circuit, Indiana.

Civil War would be satisfactory to the G.A.R.[11] He was told that

We recognize the difficulties in writing a history intended for general use in the public schools to preserve the law of proportion and yet give a good and clear account of the events of the Civil War. We who were soldiers in the Rebellion have the serious thought that the multitude of children and youth born since the war and the multitudes who have come to us from other lands are not receiving proper instruction as to that great event. We have no desire to have anything done to glorify war, nor do we want any bitter or partisan history written to stir up strife. We feel, however, that we have a right while we are still living to ask that the facts as nearly as they can be presented, as to the causes of the war, the narrative of its events and its results, shall be so given that the right of the battle for the preservation of the Union, for the maintainance [sic] of law, for the suppression of rebellion, and, the resulting destruction of the doctrine of state sovereignty, and slavery shall be shown.

In many of the school histories now in use one would think that there was no conflict between right and wrong, that the South was in a measure justified in the attempt at secession, that the southern people were peculiarly noble and chivalrous, and that the North gained the victory simply by brute force. Histories that glorify Robert E. Lee, Stonewall Jackson and Albert Sidney Johnson [sic], and apparently find no such noble characters in the list of Union generals, do not fairly represent the true sentiment. For example a history that will give a glowing description of Pickett's charge at Gettysburg, and finds no space for the mention even of General Hancock is certainly deficient. Histories that have the names like those of Early and Longstreet and yet fail even to mention men like Logan and Howard do not satisfy our conceptions of the right kind of a text book. We can see no wrong in a clearer statement of the causes of the rebellion. We take it for granted that any United States history would discuss the adoption of the constitution, with its relations to slavery and judicial interpretations in that line. Should there not be a reference to the whiskey rebellion in Pennsylvania to illustrate the right of the national authority; to Jackson's action as to nullification and the slavery question in general as one of

[11] What McMaster had written is indicated in A. O. Marsh to McMaster, Jan. 15, 1897, MS.

the great causes of the war? Some prominence should certainly be given to the Missouri compromise, Kansas and Nebraska troubles, John Brown, William Lloyd Garrison, the debate of Lincoln and Douglas, the growth of sectional spirit in the South and the deliberate preparation of southern leaders for the rebellion. Of course there would naturally be some account of Buchanan's administration, and the steps in the election and inauguration [*sic*] of Abraham Lincoln. We recognize the great difficulty in a brief narrative of the great events of the four years [*sic*] war and the difficulty in the selection of material that shall go into a reasonable compass. We believe, however, that at this period in the history of our country there is no impropriaty [*sic*] in giving enlarged space to the war because its results had so important a bearing on many of the leading questions of our time. We surely have an abundant supply of material for a very accurate presentation of war history, and it ought to be presented in a way to encourage patriotic devotion to our constitution and laws and to the cause of the Union. There must be some things that will not be pleasant to many of those who took part in the effort to destroy the Union. We hardly see how such a history could omit some reference to the treatment of Union prisoners in Southern prisons. This history also should seek the recognition of the work of the whole Union army in its various departments, and not simply glorify one army, for example, "The Army of the Potomac."

The amendments to the constitution, the questions of reconstruction, and the results of the war and its affects [*sic*], on civilization & free government should have due space. We recognize that this is no easy task for a historian. We shall be glad to cooperate with you if we can get a history that we can consistently endorse. The committee did not see its way clear to endorse any of the histories now in common use. I think a majority of the committee gave decided preference to the work of Prof. John Fiske. I wish we might have had your presence with us at the meeting of the committee. I believe the time is right for a real patriotic loyal history of the rebellion, written in a philosophical spirit, with a desire to present facts and at the same time in sympathy with the cause that triumphed because it was right.

We will welcome any further correspondence with you. We are sure that if the committee can see its way clear to endorse any book, that book is certain to have a greatly stimulated circulation. We will be glad to hear from you, also as to the probable time of the completion of your history and whether the committee might have the privilege of seeing as early as possible the portion of it that refers to the war.[12]

Early in 1897 McMaster took the initiative in arranging a meeting in Chicago between himself and representatives of the Committee.[13] When the historian arrived in Chicago with his nearly completed manuscript, the Committee had finished a session in Cleveland where they had "decided," as Marsh told a *Chicago Post* reporter, "what kind of history the school children ought to have in order to get the right view of the issues involved in the civil war." The Chairman and the Rev. Duncan C. Milner, of the Armour Mission, Chicago, formed a sub-committee appointed to look over McMaster's manuscript.

We meet with Professor McMasters [*sic*] to-day [Marsh continued in the *Post* interview] in order to see if his work meets our views, but I am not in a position to say whether it will be accepted until I have communicated with the whole committee. If favorable, the army will take every step necessary at its next encampment. Its influence is such as to warrant the adoption of such a history in most of the schools. . . . Professor McMasters [*sic*] is endeavoring to have his history correspond with our views, but I cannot say what we will do just now.

In the same newspaper article, McMaster was quoted as having said:

I want it understood beyond doubt that in this history the great southern generals in the civil war are not condoned. General Lee, for example, was a man of education and came from West Point. This military school is established to make soldiers who will stand by the government. If General Lee wished to destroy the government he had no business in West Point. I admit all the good things that are said of him personally, but he must be regarded as a man who sought to disrupt the government and countenance states in withdrawing from the union. No matter how great his generalship or his heroism, they should not blind the historian

[12] Duncan C. Milner (a Committee member to whom McMaster's letter to Marsh had been referred) to McMaster, Jan. 19, 1897, MS. The letter is dated 1896, but this must be a mistake.

[13] A. O. Marsh to McMaster, March 1, 15, 17, 24, 1897, MSS.

to the facts. The treatment of the questions which preceded and brought about the civil war is sustained in the same manner. . . .[14]

This *Post* article, reprinted widely, was almost universally interpreted to mean that McMaster was writing a text under the supervision of the G.A.R.[15] Is "your new History of the United States prepared for the Grand Army of [the] Republic suitable for school purposes?" wrote a member of a New Jersey school board in a letter typical of many others. "If so I am anxious to get our Board to adopt it as the standard School History of our County."[16] The impression that McMaster was writing a text under such conditions provoked a savage newspaper assault on him and on the G.A.R. "GARbled history . . . Cut-and-Dried History . . . a most serious and mercenary breach of our national peace," Southern newspapers stormed.[17] Here and there a Northern paper pleaded McMaster's case, but more typical was the *Chicago Journal* editorial:

Admitting the correctness of the principle upon which this book was prepared, it is evident at once that it was not carried far enough. The Grand Army of the Republic, having read the proof sheets to see that nothing occurred therein to hurt its feelings, they should have been extended at once to the confederate veterans. Palmer and Buckner might have been asked, in all propriety, to review them for the gold democrats, Bryan and Sewall for the silver democrats, Bryan and Watson for the populists, McKinley and Hobart for the gold republicans, and Teller and Dubois for the silver republicans. A committee of Chicago gentlemen should have been called upon to see that no injustice was done this city in a comparison with New York, and a committee of New York gentlemen should have been given the opportunity to prevent any favoritism toward Chicago. Both the California and the Florida orange growers' associations should have been consulted. . . .

In fine, Prof. McMaster should have abdicated entirely, and we

[14] *Chicago Post*, March 30, 1897.

[15] Many of the newspaper clippings concerning the relations between McMaster and the G.A.R. are preserved in the McMaster Papers.

[16] H. W. Straley to McMaster, April 8, 1897, MS.

[17] *Charleston News and Courier*, Aug. 20, 1897; *Norfolk Landmark*, Aug. 20, 1897; *Atlanta Constitution*, April 26, 1897.

should say that if he had a proper sense of pride he would do so now, and refuse to identify his name with such a work.[18]

Indignation over the alleged relationship of the G.A.R. and McMaster's book gave new life in all sections of the country to the suggestion that a joint North-South commission work out a history satisfactory to both regions.[19]

Meanwhile the situation was aggravated by a rambunctious Mr. Perkins, editor of an independent veteran's journal which had been conducting what admirers called "a redhot fight against the infamous, lying works that are being put in the hands of the school children of this country, miscalled histories of the United States."[20] Perkins also wanted to see the proofs. The American Book Company declined on the grounds that the manuscript was still under McMaster's control and then wrote the historian:

As a matter of fact we do not think it would be advantageous to have this book issued as being distinctly a Grant [sic] Army book. We shall be very glad to have their approval, but we want also the approval of many people who are not wholly in accord with their special aims. If therefore we can put Mr. Perkins off until the book is nearly ready for issuance, I think it will be desirable.[21]

But Mr. Perkins was a very hard man to put off. The next day he wrote directly to McMaster:

I am somewhat familiar with the matter and could very quickly come to a conclusion as to the usefulness, if any, of the Grand Army Record in aiding the publishers after the matter shall be finally turned over to them. The situation is before you. No reply is needed or expected unless you think one is demanded by your interests.[22]

McMaster seems to have concluded that his interests could get along without Perkins.

[18] *Chicago Journal,* Aug. 11, 1897. For an able defense of McMaster, see *Des Moines Leader,* Sept. 4, 1897.

[19] See the editorials quoted in "School Histories of the Civil War," *Literary Digest* (1897), XIV, 755-56.

[20] *Ohio Soldier,* quoted in *Grand Army Record* (1896), XI, 21. John M. Perkins was editor of the *Grand Army Record,* published in Boston.

[21] Henry H. Vail to McMaster, April 19, 1897, MS.

[22] John M. Perkins to McMaster, April 20, 1897, MS.

Having his interests get along in association with the G.A.R. Committee was troublesome enough, yet the publishers advised Mc-Master to take no public action. After a conference of American Book Company officials, Vice-President Henry H. Vail wrote to his author:

We should not think it advisable for you to authorize any publication denying that the manuscript you have in hand is not exactly what it was described in the Chicago papers.

On the other hand we see no reason why you should not to your personal friends and other correspondents state the exact truth regarding the matter, viz: that you had for a long time considered the advisability of preparing a history of the United States which should bring out more clearly the social and economic growth of the people and contain more matter that would appeal to the child's imagination and be useful in its future career; that it was your purpose to have this book teach a broad and liberal patriotism and state the exact truth regarding all the chief events of the nation's growth, giving to each its due weight, and to avoid sectionalism and partisanship; that after this manuscript was nearly complete and mostly in proof, you learned that the G.A.R. had appointed a committee for the examination of Histories of the United States, and that both this association and the Confederate Veterans of the South felt that the histories in ordinary use were unsatisfactory in their treatment of the Civil War; that this committee being appointed for the express purpose of examining books and manuscripts, offered you an opportunity for presenting your proofs to their perusal, and that their suggestions were valuable and in the exact line of your original idea.

The above, without contradicting any portion of the Chicago interview would enable any one to see that your course has been a dignified and proper one, and if by chance your letter should be used by some newspaper men, it would do no particular harm.[23]

No such statement reached the press, and, as the 1897 Encampment of the G.A.R. approached, Chairman Marsh asked McMaster for another look at the book.[24] The historian replied that it would be "a great pleasure" to send the proofs on, and added, "The suggestions

[23] Henry H. Vail to McMaster, April 21, 1897, MS.
[24] A. O. Marsh to McMaster, June 16, 1897, MS.

you were kind enough to make have all been used."[25] The publishers coöperated in hurrying the proof to Chicago.[26]

News of a second review of the book by the G.A.R. Committee goaded the hostile press to fresh attacks—attacks that were not softened by the failure of the Committee to endorse, or even mention the McMaster work in its report to the 1897 Encampment.[27] In a typical assault, the *New York World* proposed putting over McMaster's study: "History to let. Will be altered to suit customer," and a little later the *Des Moines Leader* could accurately say, "No school book in recent years has been the subject of such bitter controversy."[28] In the opinion of Vice-President Vail, the *World* editorial offered the proper occasion for McMaster to speak out. "The meeting of the G.A.R. has come and passed," he told McMaster, "and whatever this order has to do with your book has been done, and I think it is now time to make a formal statement. . . ."[29] Accepting the suggestion, McMaster made his statement through "The People's Forum" of the *New York World:*

> In The World of Sunday, Aug. 29, appeared some unwarranted charges of a very serious nature against my forthcoming school history which I trust you will do me the justice to correct by publishing the following statement:
>
> 1. No member or members of the G.A.R. ever applied to me to write a school history.
>
> 2. I have never "agreed to write the sort of school history" the G.A.R. wanted, nor has any "price" or consideration of any kind so to do ever been offered me by anybody.

[25] Rough copy, McMaster to A. O. Marsh, June 18, 1897, MS.

[26] Russell Hinman to McMaster, June 19, July 20, 1897, MSS.

[27] The report of the Committee may be found in the *Journal of the Thirty-First National Encampment of the Grand Army of the Republic . . . 1897*, pp. 231-38. The report may have been referring to McMaster's text when it said (p. 234), "One history that is regarded by the committee as in most respects an admirable book, teaches that the war was a sectional affair, when it declares, 'This battle (First Bull Run) began to teach the people at [*sic*] the North that they must not expect to make a speedy conquest of the South.' " McMaster (p. 388) makes this point, but not in these words.

[28] *New York World*, Aug. 29, 1897; *Des Moines Leader*, Sept. 4, 1897.

[29] Henry H. Vail to McMaster, Aug. 30, 1897, MS.

3. The book in question was not "written to order," and not one word has been inserted nor any statement changed at the dictation of anybody. When it is published I trust that those who do me the honor to read it will remember these facts and judge the book solely on its merits.[30]

While harassed by the G.A.R. controversy, McMaster was undergoing the usual trials of a textbook writer—the tussle over a title, the endless emendations which he or the publishers wanted, the proof sheets crowding his weary desk.[31] McMaster ran into special difficulties because, having signed a contract calling for a ten per cent royalty on the net price of the book, he interpreted this to mean that the royalty should be paid on all copies sold, no matter what the conditions of the sale.[32] In this contention McMaster was strongly backed by his lawyer brother, Robert B., who told the historian that he was too mild in pushing his claim. Telegraph the company, Robert urged, and tell them that the final proofs would not be returned until they capitulated.[33] McMaster sent the telegram[34] and, after the matter had been taken to the highest officials of the firm, he received a letter which discussed the whole process of textbook salesmanship:

It is not customary with us, or with any educational publishers, to pay a ten per cent. royalty on the introduction sales of common school books. The schoolbook business is very different from the general book trade in several particulars. In the general trade a new book is puffed and advertised and thirty or forty press copies given away when it is

[30] *New York World*, Sept. 8, 1897.

[31] For the title, McMaster suggested "A Short History of Our Country," but Hinman thought this was too close to the name of another recently published book (Hinman to McMaster, July 1, 1897, MS). McMaster then made three other suggestions—among them "A School History of the United States," which seemed best to Hinman and the agency managers to whom the suggestions were shown (*ibid.*, July 15, 1897, MS). This was the title adopted.

[32] The royalty provisions of the original contract and McMaster's interpretation of them are made plain in a letter from Russell Hinman to McMaster, June 14, 1897, MS.

[33] R. B. McMaster to J. B. McMaster, July 24, 1897, MS.

[34] Copy of telegram from McMaster to Russell Hinman, July 24, 1897, MS.

first issued, and its largest sale is usually attained in the first year or two after its publication, after which the sales drop off very materially. The profits on such books must be made, by both publisher and author, within a year or two of publication, and therefore a relatively high price is put upon the book.

In the schoolbook trade, however, the book is thoroughly advertised upon its appearance, and very nearly the whole of the first edition of perhaps five thousand copies is given away to schoolmen all over the United States. This, of course, brings a number of orders directly to our regular sales department, and such regular sales bear royalty from the start. But, in very many of the cities and larger towns throughout the country, competition is so sharp that, when a change of text-books is contemplated, the various educational publishers put agents on the ground to present the special merits of their books, and use all legitimate means in securing their adoption. The salaries and traveling expenses of this large force of agents are of course very heavy, and yet each publisher has to meet his agency expenses, and we believe it to be a very necessary expense of the business. The agents are not under control of the regular sales department, but of a separate department of the business called the *introduction department.* This department keeps its own separate accounts of the books ordered as an immediate result of the agents' active operations, and it is these books only that constitute introduction sales. All sales either for first use in a school or for subsequent use that come through our regular sales department constitute royalty-bearing sales.

Our experience, which is not different from that of any other educational publisher, shows that there is not one cent of profit on the first sales of books introduced by agents. The agents' salary and expense and the manufacturing cost of the books, and the worthless accounts that are often opened by agents, fully equal the amount received from introduction sales. But, a schoolbook once introduced, if it is a good one, remains in use for an indefinite number of years, almost always from three to five, very frequently from five to eight, and sometimes from eight to twelve, and therein is the great difference between the schoolbook and the general book trade. A schoolbook once introduced has an assured sale for a number of years. In several instances we are still paying large royalties to the grandchildren of our authors. We are making introductions every year, and for a number of years after publication the sale of a good book is constantly increasing, and frequently does not reach its largest circulation for ten years after publication, when it continues at very nearly its high tide of use for a number of years more. It is because of the assured sale of schoolbooks that they can be sold so much cheaper than other books. The price of your History will probably be $1.00, but in the general trade a profusely illustrated book with colored maps and five hundred pages in length, similar to your History, would have a price of between $1.50 and $2.00.

In the schoolbook field both the publisher and the author must be satisfied with less profit on each volume sold than in the general field; but, because of the permanence of the sale, and hence the number sold, the aggregate profit may be even greater.

You thus see that the educational publisher uses the same means as the general publisher—by advertising, reviews, and complimentary copies—to secure a regular sale upon the publication of the book, and upon this sale pays the author a royalty from the start; but, in addition, he has an introduction department, which the general publisher has not, and this department is both offensive and defensive, and secures not only greater but more permanent sales at the *sacrifice of any profit* to *either publisher or author* upon the *first sales that it* makes.

As to your fear that, under our contract, there would be no regular royalty-paying sales until two or three years after the publication of the book, I would say that, in all my experience, I have never known a successful common school book that didn't have regular royalty-paying sales the first year after publication. I feel so sure of this that we would be willing, if you desire it, to guarantee that the royalty on your book during 1898 shall aggregate at least $500.00. Frankly, I think it will aggregate more than that.

In view of all these facts, which we carefully considered before we approached you concerning this book, we do not feel that we can deviate in this matter from the terms we talked over and agreed upon in January, 1895, for these are much better than the terms upon which many of our books are published.[35]

But McMaster, urged on by his brother, stood his ground, and the company compromised by agreeing to a ten per cent royalty on one-half the net price of books sold as introductory copies.[36]

[35] Russell Hinman to McMaster, July 1, 1897, MS.
[36] *Ibid.*, Nov. 3, 1897, MS.

In September 1897, McMaster's *School History of the United States* was published, and the actual appearance of the book unleashed the critics again. "Masters, not McMasters should write history," the *St. Louis Post Dispatch* snapped in a criticism that probably recalled the G.A.R. controversy.[37] McMaster's acceptance of the story that Whitman saved Oregon brought down upon him almost two hundred typed pages of "The 'WHITMAN SAVED OREGON HUMBUG' . . . being a Correction of 28 Errors in Paragraph 359 of 'McMaster's School History of the United States,' endorsing the 'Whitman Saved Oregon' fake, together with some other errors on Oregon in other paragraphs of said 'School History.' "[38] A "Jeffersonian correspondent" complained about a clause which read, "As Jefferson happened to be chairman of the committee."[39] A paragraph that juxtaposed prosperity at the beginning of Cleveland's administration and panic at its end brought from Hinman the warning, "All the admirers of Cleveland throughout the country, and their name is legion, read here between the lines a slap at his administration." The Masons were disgruntled at another sentence.[40] From Kansas City, Missouri, a near-illiterate handwriting was to ask, "will you please tell me why you use a small N-, in spelling the proper word Negro?"[41] A salesman of the American Book Company, noticing the footnote in which McMaster cast doubt upon the discovery of America by Leif Ericsson, promptly advised his superiors:

The discovery of America by the Norsemen is believed in by our Norse population as they believe in their Bible. They teach it to their children, and in many of the schools scattered throughout Wisconsin, Minnesota, and the Dokatas [*sic*] printed leaflets containing an account

[37] *St. Louis Post Dispatch*, Sept. 7, 1897.
[38] The author was William I. Marshall, principal of the Lawndale School, Chicago, who apparently was making a life's work out of Whitman debunking. The long criticism was sent to McMaster through the A.B.C., sometime late in 1899. Marshall to McMaster, Dec. 23, 1899, MS.
[39] Russell Hinman to McMaster, Dec. 16, 1897, MS.
[40] *Ibid.*, Dec. 9, 1898, MS.
[41] Eddie M. Paris to McMaster, July 8, 1904, MS.

of the Norse discoveries are given to the children and really form a part of their study in History. As you know, in some counties in Minnesota, Wisconsin, and South Dakota, the population is almost entirely Norwegian, and the omission of the name of Leif Erikson and the further statement of the foot-note on p. 11 of the History will effectually shut the book out of all the schools controlled by this class of people. I wish Dr. McMaster would consent to change that note. . . . The powerful influence of the Norse in the northwestern states in all matters of education must not be estimated lightly. They are represented on every school board of any city of importance, and in small towns and villages the Boards of Education in numerous cases are made up of natives of Norway and Sweden. They hold positions of county superintendent, city superintendent, etc., and are altogether so influential that without entering into any discussion of Mr. McMaster's statement from an historical standpoint, I invite you to consider its effect simply from the view of dollars and cents.

"I think some modification of note advisable," Hinman wrote on the side of this letter.[42]

[42] Copy of a portion of an unidentified letter in the McMaster Papers. Another interesting comment came in a letter to McMaster, dated Aug. 23, 1900, from C. Ellsworth Carey, Department of Public Instruction, U. S. Military Government in the Philippines:

I was in Hawaii from '89 to '93 . . . , and I beg to correct a slight error in the text quoted [from p. 473 of the *School History*]. The marines from the Boston were landed the day before the revolution occurred, when the city was peaceful, and the Queen's government in full and undisputed authority. The Queen protested unavailingly against the landing of armed troops, this landing of armed marines with gatlings, & etc was virtually an act of war. As your history states this landing was according to an agreement between the conspirators, U.S. Minister Stevens and the Commander of the "Boston." And it is quite true that without the moral aid of this armed force quartered in the Opera House that the revolution of the next day never would have occurred. Within thirty minutes after the revolutionists had taken possession of the Government building, and while the greater part of the city was unaware that any thing had occurred, Minister Stevens drove to the Government House and officially recognized the half dozen revolutionists there as the de facto government. I was present in the room when this occurred.

Word was at once sent to the Queen that the revolutionists had been recognized by the United States Government and if she attacked revolutionists, the troops from the Boston would assist the new government. As the Queen had no able advisers, she took the feeble advice offered and abdicated. The American flag was not raised until some days later . . . . our history has one dark spot which will grow blacker and blacker as time reveals all the iniquities that cluster about the theft of the Hawaiian Kingdom.

Important, too, from the point of view of dollars and cents were the Catholics. They "are a hard class to satisfy," Hinman told his author, "but we always try to satisfy them as far as possible."[43] An occasional Catholic review classified McMaster among "the narrow bigots," but in general the Catholic reception was favorable.[44] Father T. J. O'Brien, Inspector of the Catholic schools of Brooklyn, typically described the *School History* as

. . . eminently fair, exceptionally well arranged, and, in the treatment of the growth and development of the Nation, superior to any other text-book of United States history with which I am familiar. I regret, however, to find that the Catholics who took an important part in Revolutionary history receive such scanty notice, in fact, no notice at all. The names of Pulaski, Kosciusko, and Rochambeau are not mentioned, and the name of the illustrious Lafayette occurs only once, in a footnote. . . .

I might also observe that, for the pupils of the Brooklyn schools, the Battle of Long Island is always of absorbing interest, and they would claim for it in a history more than four lines.[45]

The agent who had sent to Hinman the suggestions of Father O'Brien added:

Father O'Brien is endeavoring to bring about the adoption of a series of books for use in the Catholic Schools of Brooklyn, and a great deal will depend upon the recommendation made by him. Under the circumstances, you will readily see that we will gain quite an advantage if we can prevail upon Professor McMaster to accept the suggestions offered by Father O'Brien.[46]

---

[43] Russell Hinman to McMaster, Dec. 18, 1897, MS.

[44] The quoted phrase comes from an attack in the *New York Irish World*, July 29, 1899, which argued that McMaster had slighted Irish-American contributions to American civilization. The *Philadelphia Catholic Standard and Times* (Oct. 30, 1897) accused McMaster of "extreme delicacy in the description of the Know-Nothing movement."

[45] T. J. O'Brien to G. W. Schmitt, Dec. 1, 1897, a copy of which was enclosed with a letter from Russell Hinman to McMaster, Dec. 18, 1897, MS.

[46] Copy of a letter from G. W. Schmitt to [no first name] Greene, enclosed with a letter from Russell Hinman to McMaster, Dec. 18, 1897, MS.

Hinman, in turn, asked McMaster:

Do you think you could find space to name, however briefly, Pulaski, Kosciusko, and Rochambeau, and possibly say something more of the "illustrious Lafayette." I do not believe the Battle of Long Island should be padded for Brooklyn alone. We would have a large book if we gave a detailed description of every battle of the Revolution to satisfy the people now living in that locality.[47]

McMaster did find space to add a section on "Revolutionary Heroes," placing Pulaski and the illustrious Lafayette among the "heroes entitled to our grateful remembrance," and in later editions the footnote on page 11 began, "There is reason to believe that about the year 1000 A.D. the northeast coast of America was discovered by a Norse voyager named Leif Ericsson."[48] But these changes were the compliance of a harassed man, a man who was once so annoyed by demands for revisions that he exploded to his son, "Never be damn fool enough to write a textbook."[49]

The mood of vexation must have quickly passed, for the *School History* was widely praised. Despite the G.A.R. squabble, strongly favorable newspaper reviews are not hard to find; the influential *Journal of Education* and the *School Gazette* rhapsodized.[50] Important praise came quickly in the form of large sales which rocketed the *School History* to a place among the most important American texts of its day. Within five years after its publication, the little book had sold almost 400,000 copies and brought its author over twenty thousand dollars in royalties.[51] Though the *School History* was written for the grammar schools, it proved better suited to pupils of high school age.[52] Since many schools objected to using

[47] Russell Hinman to McMaster, Dec. 18, 1897, MS.

[48] *School History* (1912 ed.), p. 149.

[49] Interview with Dr. P. D. McMaster.

[50] *Journal of Education* (1897), XLVI, 329; *School Gazette* (Nov. 12, 1897), p. 13. For examples of enthusiastic newspaper reviews, see *New York Press*, Jan. 9, 1898, *Boston Herald*, March 5, 1898, *St. Paul Globe*, Feb. 6, 1898, and *Denver News*, Jan. 30, 1898.

[51] The American Book Co. vouchers reporting to McMaster on the sales and royalties of his textbooks are included among his papers.

[52] "Second Memoirs," p. 73, MS.

books by different authors in the different grades, Hinman warned McMaster that large sales for the *School History* could not be kept up unless the historian quickly produced elementary texts to go along with it.[53] No sooner had McMaster agreed to do this than the old struggle between him and the publishers was on again. By 1899 Hinman was writing McMaster about a letter from a Pennsylvania agent

. . . telling me definitely that he has come to the crossroads on the Elementary History, and plainly intimating that, unless your primary book is forthcoming at once, he will be unable to hold your larger book where it has already been introduced or to secure new holdings for it.

I *will* not make any promises concerning the little book until I have the manuscript in my hands. I sincerely trust that you are not ill, and, if not, that you will have some consideration for me as well as for your own interest by "getting a walk on you."[54]

Two years later McMaster published the *Primary History*—a variation of the *School History* for the first years of school; in 1907 came another variation for the intermediate grades, the *Brief History*. Before these three histories went the way of all textbooks, over 2,500,000 copies of them had been sold—largely, of course, in the North.[55] Thousands of children in the newly acquired dependencies learned about the past of the United States from a Spanish edition of the *School History*.[56]

Why was McMaster's *School History* so successful? Readability was especially attractive at a time when a committee of educators could declare dullness to be the "great and conspicuous failure" of school histories, and McMaster's text was thoroughly readable.[57]

---

[53] Russell Hinman to McMaster, Dec. 9, 1898, MS.

[54] *Ibid.*, May 18, 1899, MS.

[55] McMaster stated that the sales up to 1930 were: *School History*, 1,500,791; *Primary History*, 937,044; *Brief History*, 333,342. "Second Memoirs," pp. 74-75, MS.

[56] *Compendio de historia de los Estados Unidos* . . . tr. y adaptación por Marcos Moré del Solar (New York, 1902). In 1902, 5,044 copies of this edition were sold, and in most of the years up to 1929, quantities usually under 100 were sold.

[57] "Text-Books in American History," *Educational Review* (1898), XVI, 493.

He may have preserved the dreary black numbers on paragraphs; he did not break away entirely from the monotonous 1, 2, 3 listings; and McMaster was capable, as a textbook writer, of closing the story of the United States with "He [McKinley] was inaugurated on March 4, and immediately called a special session of Congress to revise the tariff, a work which ended in the enactment of the 'Dingley Tariff,' on July 24, 1897."[58] But the book as a whole is a continuously flowing narrative, not, as one educational journal commented in contrasting the *School History* with rivals, "an artificial . . . rack on which historical facts are strung like toys on a Christmas tree."[59] A student must have been uninterested, indeed, if he did not enjoy sections like the one beginning:

If you had lived in 1791 and started, say, from Boston, to go to Philadelphia to see the President and the great city where independence had been declared, you would very likely have begun by making your will, and bidding good-by to your friends. You would then have gone down to the office of the proprietor of the stagecoach, and secured a seat to New York. As the coach left but twice a week, you would have waited till the day came and would then have presented yourself, at three o'clock in the morning, at the tavern whence the coach started.[60]

Allen Thomas, author of another textbook popular in the nineties, spoke of his difficulties with school boards because of their " 'exuberant patriotism.' These demand war, bloodshed, bloody shirt etc. etc."[61] Such a situation hardly retarded the sales of McMaster's book. About twenty-four per cent of the *School History* is devoted to military history, and a committee of the American Association of University Women has accurately reported that, although McMaster "does not glorify war . . . [he] frankly encourages war as a necessary means of settling disputes. . . ."[62] McMaster's handling

This article is the 1898 report of the Standing Committee on Text-books of the New England History Teacher's Association.

[58] *A School History of the United States*, p. 476.
[59] *School Gazette* (Nov. 12, 1897), p. 13.
[60] *School History*, pp. 187-88.
[61] Allen Thomas to McMaster, Nov. 27, 1896, MS.
[62] *Report of the Committee on U. S. History Textbooks used in the Schools of*

of Anglo-American relations won commendation from the Hearst papers in the days of their most self-conscious patriotism.[63] The Civil War is fought once more in the *School History;* the South suffers a rhetorical Gettysburg and Andrew Johnson is impeached again.[64] In other ways, too, the business men, lawyers, and educators who controlled most of the school boards of the North were likely to find their conceptions of America's past mirrored in the *School History.* The material progress of the United States, in which Americans proved themselves "the most ingenious people the world has ever known," was "beyond all question, *the* event of the world's history during the nineteenth century."[65] This progress was "chiefly due to great corporations and great capitalists," though "many of them abused the power their wealth gave them."[66] A reader gets the impression that Hamiltonianism, from Hamilton's day to McKinley's, was the party of patriotism and good sense.[67]

The general plan of the *School History*, no less than its attitudes, gave it saleability. The *School Gazette* called McMaster's text "the most radical departure from beaten paths in American school history that has been made for many years," but this was the exag-

---

the United States (—, 1929), p. 13. For example, see McMaster's comment on Jefferson's peace policy (*School History*, p. 228) and on the Civil War (*ibid.*, p. 383). The Association for Peace Education ranked McMaster's *Brief History* fifth among twenty-four books examined for their militarism ("War in the Textbooks," *Nation* [1924], CXIX, 277). Among major rivals of the *School History*, only Eggleston's text gave appreciably more space to military history. See Appendix I.

[63] Bessie L. Pierce, *Public Opinion and the Teaching of History in the United States* (New York, 1926), p. 217. "The text is considered partisan when discussing causes of the wars in which the United States has engaged," reported the A.A.U.W.'s Committee (p. 13).

[64] *School History*, pp. 320-63, 378-431.

[65] *Ibid.*, pp. 6, 370.

[66] *Ibid.*, p. 464.

[67] For example, see McMaster's sections on the funding of the debt and the establishment of the first national bank (*School History*, pp. 201-02); on the Whiskey Rebellion (*ibid.*, pp. 203-04); on the period, 1790-1815, (*ibid.*, pp. 246-57); on the Owenite communities (*ibid.*, p. 291); on the Democrats and the second national bank (*ibid.*, pp. 305-12); and on politics since 1880 (*ibid.*, pp. 462-76).

geration of approval.[68] The *School History* was far more saleable than "a radical departure" would have been. It was neither radical nor conservative; where it was not conventional, it did things which other texts were soon to do or did a little more of what many rivals were already doing. At a time when the topical method and the use of source materials for high school teaching were winning increasing approval, the *School History* made a bow in the direction of both.[69] But the bow was only a bow and could scarcely have offended adherents of older ways of teaching. Simply in the course of carrying out his ideas of how to make history meaningful to youngsters, McMaster had written a text which sometimes used a topical method.[70] His attitude toward collateral readings, source or otherwise, was similarly disconnected from any extreme pedagogical theory. Having inserted occasional suggestions for further readings, McMaster remarked:

> To have loaded down the book with extended bibliographies would have been an easy matter, but quite unnecessary. The teacher will find in Channing and Hart's *Guide to the Study of American History* the best digested and arranged bibliography of the subject yet published, and cannot afford to be without it. If the student has time and disposition to read one half of the reference books cited in the footnotes of this history, he is most fortunate.[71]

The *School History* was more completely a part of the educational trend which was de-emphasizing the colonial period and centering attention on the industrial empire built in the East and the agricultural empire built in the West since Independence.[72] The

[68] *School Gazette* (Nov. 12, 1897), p. 13.

[69] For the trend toward the topical method and source readings, see Tyler Kepner, "The Influence of Textbooks Upon Method," *National Council for the Social Studies, Fifth Yearbook* (Philadelphia, 1935), pp. 168-72.

[70] Compare the *School History's* Table of Contents with McMaster's remarks on how to teach history in the *Annual Report of the American Historical Association . . . 1896* (Washington, 1897), I, 258-63. See also Tyler Kepner in the *National Council for the Social Studies, Fifth Yearbook*, p. 170.

[71] *School History*, p. 6.

[72] *Report of the Committee on Secondary School Studies* [Committee of Ten] *. . . of the National Educational Association* (Washington, 1893), p. 189; *The*

texts of Eggleston, Johnston, and Thomas were among the chief rivals with which the *School History* had to compete when it first appeared.[73] None of them gave less space to the period before 1783 than did the *School History*, for McMaster believed that the colonial era should receive no more attention in a general history than a man's childhood does in his biography.[74] That the author of the *History of the People* should pace the textbook trend toward social history is hardly surprising. Before he published the *School History*, McMaster had criticized the authors of texts who had failed to point out that

A knowledge of the industrial and economic condition of Europe and Great Britain . . . is necessary to a correct understanding of the period of colonization. . . . The economical, the industrial, the political condi-

Study of History in Schools, Report to the American Historical Association by The Committee of Seven (New York, 1899), pp. 74, 75-81.

[73] It is exceedingly difficult to determine what textbooks for high schools were most widely used in 1897. Charles Altschul (*The American Revolution in Our School Text-Books* [New York, 1917], p. 18) printed a list of the texts which he, after an intensive survey, determined to be most widely used around 1897. "Text-Books in American History" (*Educational Review* [1898], XVI, 494-502) has a list constructed to make it "representative of the general average of books now in use, particularly in New England. It will be found to comprise most of the recent and best-known manuals, together with some older and less valuable ones which, because either of their wide use or of their typical character, it seemed well to discuss" (pp. 480-81). Marie E. Carpenter, *The Treatment of the Negro in American History School Textbooks* (Menasha, Wis., 1941) is based on a list of books (pp. 130-37) the majority of which "appear to have been popular in their time" (p. 16). Dr. Carpenter has in most cases estimated the popularity of the books on her list. Apart from the *School History*, the only high school texts which appear on all three lists are: Edward Eggleston, *A History of the United States and its People* (New York, 1888); Alexander Johnston, *A History of the United States for Schools* (New York, 1897); and Allen C. Thomas, *A History of the United States* (New York, 1894).

[74] For McMaster's attitude toward colonial history for school children, see *School History*, p. 5, and his remarks in the *Ann. Rept. of the A.H.A. . . . 1896*, I, 260. For a comparison of the space given to various periods, see Appendix I. The Brief History, written for younger pupils, was deliberately designed to include more colonial history (see the brochure advertising it, which is in the McMaster Papers). The *Brief History* is analyzed in Rolla M. Tryon, *The Social Sciences as School Subjects* (New York, 1935), p. 200.

tions which slowly but surely brought [about the separation of England and the Colonies] . . . are passed over in silence, and the whole history of a hundred years of colonial life is misrepresented. . . . The federal constitution in particular is the only embodiment of the industrial and economic experience of the people. . . . The constitution was not as Mr. Gladstone says, "struck out," "in a given time." It grew out of business conditions; it was a business necessity; it was the product of the experience and daily life of a thoroughly practical people. . . . [The student should see the northerners who migrated west] engaged in a thousand forms of diversified industry, and the southern stream ignoring commerce and manufactures and devoting its energy to growing cotton and tobacco, and he should be made to see how from these two opposite economic tendencies grew in time two separate and distinct peoples . . . and when this has been made clear to him he will understand the Civil War. . . .[75]

While McMaster did not carry out this ambitious interpretation, which sounds like a preview of the Beards' *Rise of American Civilization*, his *School History* did go beyond its rivals in giving space to social history and far beyond them in integrating this social history with other aspects of the national past.[76] Largely in the sections of social history, McMaster succeeded in living up to his original promise of writing a textbook "in which the middle colonies and the country to the westward should receive more adequate treatment than they do in most of the current textbooks prepared from the ultra New England standpoint."[77] This also was timely,

---

[75] "The Social Function of United States History," *Fourth Yearbook of the National Herbart Society . . . 1898* (Chicago, 1898), pp. 27-30.

[76] For a comparison of the attention to social history, see Appendix I. Some other competitive texts are analyzed, on a slightly different basis, in Rolla M. Tryon, *The Social Sciences as School Subjects* (New York, 1935), p. 160. M. E. Carpenter (*The Treatment of the Negro in American History School Textbooks*, p. 72) found that, of the men writing texts in the nineteenth century, "no other author attempts to portray the economic and social aspects of slave life as well as did McMaster." Eggleston seems to have been the only one of the three rival authors who attempted to integrate his social history with the rest of the story. To see how much farther McMaster had gone, compare Eggleston on the growing hostility of the North and South (pp. 257-302) with McMaster (pp. 301-04).

[77] This is the letter cited in footnote 3. McMaster not only gives more space to

for the *School History* was published when politicians like Bryan and historians like Turner and Woodrow Wilson were making the country increasingly aware that it was something besides a North and a South.[78] In the *School History,* McMaster had produced the right book at the right time.

But in textbook writing, success fails quickly. About 1910, McMaster's sales began to drop off sharply because, as he remarked, by that time a host of other writers had carried much farther the things which had made his book.[79] The *School History,* with its industrial focus, helped to do for high school history something of what the Beard-Robinson text was to do for college history.[80] Appropriately enough, Robinson had been a colleague of McMaster at the University of Pennsylvania, and McMaster's historical writings was a factor in making the younger man dissatisfied with the old-style history.[81] If McMaster is always given a place in the history of American culture as the historian's historian of the people, he certainly deserves some place as the people's historian of the people.

In his own day, McMaster's textbooks did much to make his name a byword among Americans who had never heard of his bulky volumes. Now he belonged to the children as well as the adults, to the semi-literate as well as the readers of the *Forum* and the *Atlantic Monthly.* Day after day the letters came to his desk, in-

---

the Middle States and the West (see Appendix I). The *School History* is the only one of the four texts analyzed which consistently treats these regions as if they were of importance in themselves.

[78] This point is made more fully in Eric F. Goldman, "Middle States Regionalism and American Historiography: A Suggestion," in Goldman, ed., *Historiography and Urbanization: Essays in American History in Honor of W. Stull Holt* (Baltimore, 1941), pp. 211-20.

[79] "Second Memoirs," pp. 73-74, MS.

[80] Charles A. Beard and James H. Robinson, *The Development of Modern Europe* (2 vols., New York, 1907-08). For the type and influence of this work, see Harry E. Barnes, "James Harvey Robinson," in Howard W. Odum, ed. *American Masters of Social Science* (New York, 1927), pp. 389-40.

[81] *Ibid.,* pp. 328-30, 333-35, 360.

teresting letters, routine ones, or merely, as McMaster once said, the "idle questions of idle people":[82]

An elementary school . . . is contemplating securing an oil portrait of Abraham Lincoln. The question arises in the minds of the committee whether it should be copied from a photograph of Lincoln with or without the beard. . . .[83]

By his own request I have to-day proposed James Schouler for membership in the Institute of Arts and Letters. Would you have the great kindness to . . . second him? If you do or do not pray let me know, because he is getting sensitive, somewhat: personally I think very highly of him and his work, dry and deaf as he is in the flesh.[84]

I am interested in finding out when people began to bathe, as you will observe from the enclosed correspondence. I would like to have the information which it suggests to your mind. . . .[85]

Have you yet had sufficient opportunity to look into and consider the subject of editing Prescott's works . . . ? Professor Ripley of Harvard University has suggested that I write you in regard to material for a thesis on the Anthracite Coal Industry. . . . Could you give a lecture on the life of Benjamin Franklin in the great hall of Cooper Union . . . ?[86]

Would you accept me into your home as,—in a way—a son of yours . . . I am . . . seventeen years of age. . . . At present I work in the Danver's [Mass.] Public Library afternoons and earn on an average of $5.00 per month. Many times—as even now while I am writing—I feel a longing to be far—far away . . . after I have made a place for myself in the world you shall not be forgotten.[87]

I have been informed that you are a master socialist. Could you out-

[82] "Diary," II, Jan. 3, 1892, MS.
[83] Michael G. Heintz to McMaster, Dec. 28, 1916, MS.
[84] William M. Sloane to McMaster, Nov. 25, 1911, MS.
[85] John A. Lusk to McMaster, Sept. 17, 1923, MS.
[86] J. B. Lippincott to McMaster, June 5, 1901; Eliot Jones to McMaster, Jan. 13, 1909; copy, Henry W. Leipziger to McMaster, Nov. 22, 1905, MSS.
[87] Arthur R. Kelman to McMaster, April 8, 1911, MS.

line for me a method whereby I could so inform myself thoroughly in this science . . .?[88]

Have just finished your book, which Appleton sent me for review in our Calif. papers. . . . I was at J.H.U. with Shaw & Wilson—Dear old Dr. Adams & our Hist Seminar used to discuss you & your work, back in 1883 & 84—You & I were born in 1852—and how much we've seen in this busy, loving and advancing world of ours![89]

Will you please send me a profile photograph of yourself from the left side. . . .

This is a very urgent and important matter, and I wish you would have one taken soon, and send me one. I have a reason, (and a very good one) for wanting a profile photograph.

(As the Jews said to the evil spirit, "We adjure you by Jesus whom Paul preacheth." And the evil spirit answered and said, "Jesus I know, and Paul I know; but who are ye?")

. . . I have been fortunate in making some important discoveries in the study of Physiognomy, which I have made a life study, and intend to write a book about it. I am not pursuing any ambitions of my own, but I have a story to tell, and I would rather die right now than fail to tell it!

Please give this matter your attention in the interest of posterity, and "science." I would like to come and see you about it, but am working nights on the C B & Q Ry here and cannot get away. Want to finish my work before I am overtaken by the war.[90]

The New York World is now fighting the Battle for a free and untrammeled press in the United States should the Government succeed in establishing a precedent for the prosecution of Newspapers in the present case against the world what in your estimation would be the resulting danger to the freedom of the Press to Public Liberty Freedom of elections and the possibility of maintaining a vigorous opposition to the

[88] [?] Tinney (Port Kennedy, Pa.) to McMaster, May 14, 1917, MS.
[89] Charles H. Shinn (Northfork, Calif.) to McMaster, Dec. 16, 1898 [?], MS.
[90] A. C. Antram (Firth, Neb.) to McMaster, July 29, Aug. 31, Sept. 14, 1917, MSS.

dominant party we invite you to contribute your opinion on this matter by wire answer prepaid.[91]

Other men, caught in the snare of prominence, might have permitted their days to turn into endless letters and interviews and speeches and articles. But not McMaster. "You are no good at answering demands on your time," even his friends discovered.[92] Having said what he thought was worth saying, McMaster shut off not only his tongue and his typewriter but also his mind. If bombing a letter out of McMaster required a major offensive, it was scarcely less difficult to involve him in "the folly of getting excited over politics."[93] "The country is saved again," the little man would quizzically observe as his mind turned back to the next chapter of the *History of the People.*[94]

[91] Telegram, *New York World* to McMaster, Jan. 22, 1909, MS.

[92] William M. Sloane to McMaster, March 20, 1900, MS.

[93] McMaster to Gertrude Stevenson, Dec. 12, 1884, MS.

[94] The quotation is from Ellis P. Oberholtzer, "John Bach McMaster," *Pennsylvania Magazine of History and Biography* (1933), LVII, 22. This whole paragraph is based on Oberholtzer, *passim*, and on interviews with Messrs. George Gibbs, Edward P. Cheyney, and Edward W. Mumford.

CHAPTER VII

The History of the People

TURNED BACK to the *History of the People*—this had been the theme for the thirty years that were the heart of McMaster's life. Articles and speeches were produced, classes were taught, textbooks were written and revised, but the bulky green volumes continued to spread across the nation's bookshelf. Appleton and Company, like the American Book Company, made every effort to hurry McMaster, and with equal futility.[1] The plan for the *History*, far from contracting under the pressure of actual execution, extended from five to six, then to seven, and finally to eight volumes.[2] 1883, 1885, 1892, 1895, 1900, 1906, 1910, 1913—by the time the last volume was ready the bachelor who had first lugged the manuscript to New York was the father of a college graduate, Tommy Wilson, of the upstairs room in Witherspoon Hall, was President of the United States, and a delay had to be announced because the printer, now using linotype machines, could not find enough hand type.[3] But the *History of the People* was done at last, and few, then or now, could deny it a place among the monuments of American historiography.

Friends in Philadelphia thought the event deserved a celebration, and a celebration there was. S. Weir Mitchell, the Philadelphia doctor who had become an important historical novelist, sat at the head of the huge table in the Historical Society of Pennsylvania. At

[1] William Appleton took every opportunity to urge speed on McMaster (for example, William Appleton to McMaster, Oct. 31, 1890, Sept. 2, 1897, March 20, 1908, MSS). Appleton's most repeated argument was that the delays diminished interest in the *History*. Few of Appleton's letters seem to have been answered.

[2] Vols. I-III announced five vols. on the title page; Vol. IV, six volumes; Vol. V, seven volumes; Vol. VII, eight volumes.

[3] For the delay in printing, see William Appleton to McMaster, Dec. 17, 1912, MS. Hand type had been used for the first seven volumes. John Bach, Jr., graduated from the University of Pennsylvania in 1912.

each guest's place was a printed booklet containing 162 letters, written by people invited to the dinner, which represent as resounding a eulogy as any American historian has received.[4] How McMaster must have enjoyed seeing the name of Macaulay's nephew among the testimonials from across the ocean! Guglielmo Ferrero, in Turin, spoke his praise by writing significance into the dinner:

The historians, contributing to conserve the traditions, are the most useful architects of progress, as the world progresses but in conserving the best things created by previous generations. I am glad to see that the high classes of America fully realize how great and important is this social mission of the historian. . . .

Historians in the United States were represented by a group whose names read like a catalogue of the great and the rising in that day. "A revolution in our historical outlook . . . a really great historical work . . .," rang their praises, ". . . he has conferred a permanent benefit upon his country—greatly appreciated now, but sure to be more and more prized as time goes on."[5] Brooks Adams, critical scion of the critical House of Adams, declared the volumes " a model of everything that a history should be." Scarcely less sweeping were the praises of the literary world, spoken by Edward Bok, William Dean Howells, Walter Hines Page, Albert Shaw, Oswald Garrison Villard, and Barrett Wendell. Cultural-minded politicians and business men waxed enthusiastic; Theodore Roosevelt, about to leave for South America, paused to write that he was taking the last volume along. And, fitting climax, the words of the historian-president, Woodrow Wilson, who joined in "the universally accepted verdict concerning the interest and the quality of the great work. . . ." We do not know the thoughts that came to Mrs. McMaster as she, with her two sons and some friends, watched from

[4] *Testimonial Dinner to John Bach McMaster, LL.D., at the Historical Society of Pennsylvania, Philadelphia, November Twenty-Second, Nineteen Hundred and Thirteen, Letters Received* [Philadelphia, 1913]. The pages are not numbered, but the letters are alphabetically arranged.

[5] These phrases come, respectively, from the letters of Edward Channing, James Harvey Robinson, and Andrew D. White.

the gallery the national accolade for the man at whose side she had worked for more than two decades.[6] McMaster, of course, was deeply moved, but not so much that he lost his wry skepticism. The letters were of interest to him, he later remarked, chiefly because they showed "by direct statement, or by allusions that they had really read at least several of the volumes. I have always suspected that they were requested to do so by the Committee in charge of the dinner."[7]

What kind of history was this *History of the People*, so widely hailed in its own generation and still, according to the standard manual, a work to "be neglected by no student of the field it covers"?[8] McMaster has said little about his philosophy of history. Like most of his generation, he did not concern himself with interpretations of history; his presidential address before the American Historical Association was history, not historiography.[9] "It is not the business of a historian," McMaster was sure, "to be a philosopher."[10] No more frequently did he discuss the technique of reconstructing the past, and what little McMaster said on this subject is contradictory.[11] He had never been taught any rules of the craft, and his graduate teaching at the University of Pennsylvania included little drill in method.[12] Writing history, it would appear, was something you simply did—without theorizing about the matter any more than Carnegie theorized about the building of a steel trust.

Certain inferences concerning McMaster's method may be drawn

[6] "Second Memoirs," p. 99, MS.

[7] *Ibid.*, p. 98, MS.

[8] William H. Allison, *et al.*, eds., *A Guide to Historical Literature* (New York, 1931), p. 1019.

[9] "Old Standards of Public Morals," *Annual Report of the American Historical Association for the Year 1905* (2 vols., Washington, 1906-07), I, 57-70.

[10] Interview with Prof. E. P. Cheyney.

[11] The more important of McMaster's statements on this subject are collected in William T. Hutchinson, "John Bach McMaster," in Hutchinson, ed., *The Marcus W. Jernegan Essays in American Historiography* (Chicago, 1937), p. 135.

[12] Letters from Profs. F. L. Paxson (Sept. 17, 1934) and E. S. Corwin (Oct. 29, 1939) to the author.

from the selective analysis of the *History* which makes up Appendix IV. The volumes do not appear to be based on a comprehensive strategy of research which would inquire, first, what materials were the proper ones for a given segment of history, and then, where and how they could be used. In many places McMaster seems to have picked his sources simply by using what was in the library or libraries in which he was working at the time. In a section on the election of 1856, for example, all of McMaster's sources may be found in the Historical Society of Pennsylvania, many of them collected together within bound volumes, and do not represent the broad national picture that could have been obtained by going to other repositories as well. Other parts of the *History* have a structure clearly based on some one work. The key to Section B of Volume I (see Appendix IV) is Rives' *Life and Times of Madison;* to Section B of Volume V, *Niles' Register;* to Section A of Volume VIII, Commons' *Documentary History*.[13] By and large, in these sections, McMaster's order of events and interpretation come from the other work, and more than half of his footnotes are the same as footnotes in the other books or refer to material which is printed in the other books. With the exception of Rives, the other books are cited by McMaster somewhere in the sections based on them, but for a specific point. The reader is given no indication of the extent to which Rives, *Niles' Register,* and Commons were actually relied upon. In particular, there is no indication that many pamphlets and newspapers cited by McMaster were almost certainly used not in the original, but as they were quoted in other works.[14]

No matter what the source of his materials, McMaster used them with a conspicuous casualness about borrowing. The *New York*

---

[13] The section on the election of 1856 may be found in the *History of the People,* VIII, 264-76. Works mentioned by an abbreviated title in this chapter are identified fully in the bibliography included in Appendix IV.

[14] This is particularly striking in view of the statements usually made, for example, Lucy M. Salmon's *The Newspaper and the Historian* (New York, 1923), Preface, p. xliii: "In their use of newspapers and similar materials, McMaster and von Holst submitted them to all the critical tests necessary to determine their value for their own work. . . ."

Tribune reviewer of Volume I, who was so indignant at the Macaulay-like sentences and the three paragraphs copied from Rives, was spared literary apoplexy by having failed to check further. It was not simply that some of McMaster's phrases were Macaulay's and that the chapters of the two men on the "State of" their countries open with similar paragraphs.[15] In these chapters most of the topics discussed by Macaulay are also discussed by McMaster. The sequence of topics in the latter part of the chapters is almost identical, and both historians end on the same note—material and non-material progress:[16]

<table>
<tr><td>McMASTER, I, 98</td><td>MACAULAY, I, 417</td></tr>
<tr><td>It is pleasing to reflect that while our countrymen have been making such astonishing progress in all that administers to the comforts and conveniences of life, they have at the same time grown charitable and humane. There is indeed scarce a scrap of information bearing upon the subject extant which does not go to prove beyond question that the generation which witnessed the revolution was less merciful and tenderhearted than the generation which witnessed the civil war.</td><td>It is pleasing to reflect that the public mind of England has softened while it has ripened, and that we have, in the course of ages, become, not only a wiser, but also a kinder people. There is scarcely a page of the history or lighter literature of the seventeenth century which does not contain some proof that our ancestors were less humane than their posterity.</td></tr>
</table>

The check of two short sections in Volume I reveals close paraphrases from Rives other than the instance noted by the *Tribune* reviewer, and one close paraphrase of Edmund Quincy's *Life of Josiah Quincy:*[17]

[15] See *ante*, p. 45.

[16] Compare McMaster, *History of the People*, I, Chap. I, and Thomas B. Macaulay, *The History of England from the Accession of James the Second*, ed. Charles H. Firth (6 vols., London, 1913-15), I, Chap. III.

[17] The other close paraphrases from Rives are not the almost word-for-word copying of the instance pointed out by the *Tribune*, but all of them are as close as the example from Quincy given here and some of them are closer.

McMASTER, I, 13

There the houses of brick with Corinthian pilasters up the front, and columns of the same order supporting the porch, and handsome entrances to which led up a long flight of sandstone steps, stood back in little gardens dense with English elms and shrubs. Honeysuckles twined round the porch and high damask roses grew under the windows.

QUINCY, p. 36

It was a handsome edifice of three stories, the front ornamented with Corinthian pilasters; and pillars of the same order supported a porch, from which three flights of steps of red sandstone, and a broad walk of the same material, descended to Pearl Street. Honeysuckles were twined round the porch, and high damask rosebushes grew beneath the windows. . . . The grounds . . . were adorned by four English elms of full size and beauty. . . .

After Volume I, and perhaps because of the severe *Tribune* chastisement, the checking of selected passages reveals no similar close paraphrasing from secondary works.

In all the volumes analyzed, McMaster often took over the language of primary sources without quotation marks. In using memoirs, travel books, and newspapers, both for facts and for opinions, McMaster's technique was usually this:

McMASTER, V, 516

The party of the Administration, anxious to have a pretext to censure the Jackson majority, attempted to speak eternally on every subject that could be discussed, and had they not been stopped by the previous question, would have debated the bill till the end of the session, and thus abused the Jacksonians as enemies of the tariff.

New England Palladium, June 20, 1828

The Adams men, anxious to have a plausible pretext to censure the Jackson majority in Congress, evinced a disposition to speak without limit—aye eternally—on every subject that would admit of discussion; and had they not been stopped, they would have debated the tariff bill, until the termination of the session; and, then, they would have denounced the friends of General Jackson, as *enemies to the bill.*

In using speeches or letters, McMaster often followed the language still more closely without quotation marks:

McMASTER, I, 227-29

Adams now felt that American credit was indeed at stake, and, despite his ill-health and the rigors of the season, set off in January for Amsterdam. The trip, which may now be made under the most unfavorable circumstances and in the .worst of weather with comfort and with ease, was then beset with as many dangers as would be encountered in a journey through Siberia in the depth of winter. From London he *hastened* to Harwich. But at Harwich he was obliged to wait several days for fine weather before the packets put out to sea. The weather was bitter cold. The vessel pitched and rolled so terribly that fires could not be kept up in the cabin, and the sea ran so high that *three days* were consumed in going thirty-three leagues. When at last the windmills of Holland came in sight, the ice lay so thick along the shore that Helvoet could not be reached. The passengers were therefore landed on the island of Goree. Here boors' wagons were obtained to carry the baggage, and the whole party set out on foot

JOHN ADAMS TO FRANK-LIN, Jan. 24, 1784[18]

Desirous of doing all in my power to save Mr. Morris's bills, I determined to go to Amsterdam, and accordingly *set off* the beginning of this month from London in a season too rigorous for pleasure. At Harwich we were obliged to wait several days for fair weather, which, when it arrived, brought us little comfort, as it was very cold, and the wind exactly against us. The packets were obliged to put to sea, and I embarked in one of them. We were *more than three days* in advancing thirty-three leagues, with so unsteady a course, and such a tossing vessel, that we could not keep a fire, the weather very cold, and the passengers all very sea-sick. As we could not, on account of the great quantities of ice upon the coast, reach Helvoet, we were put on shore on the island of Goree, whence we got a boor's wagon to carry our baggage, and we walked *about six miles* to the town of Goree; *not finding ice-boats here,* we were obliged to go in open boors' wagons across the island to

[18] Printed in Charles F. Adams, ed., *The Works of John Adams* (10 vols., Boston, 1850-56), VIII, 170-71. The italics are not in the original and will be used for another purpose.

through the snow for the town of Goree, *six miles* distant. *There Adams expected to meet ice-boats,* but none were to be had, and he was again forced to travel in an open boor's wagon across the island to Midel-Harnis. At Midel-Harnis he was detained several days in the worst of lodgings till the ice-boats came to carry him over the little arm of the sea to Helvoet. The boats at length appeared, and he embarked amid the waste of ice which every day went in and out with the tide. Sometimes the little boat was rowed, sometimes pushed by boat-hooks between great blocks, and at others dragged over vast fields of ice which now and then gave way and let it down. Before the day closed, however, the little craft reached the opposite shore. And it was most fortunate, for the boat which immediately followed became wedged in the ice, was carried out to sea and brought in by the tide, and did not reach land till *fifteen hours* had been spent in the water. But even when a landing was effected Adams found himself on the dike some two miles from Helvoet. Once more a boor's wagon took him to the Brille, where the night was passed. In the morning another sheet of water filled with floating ice was crossed in the boats, but

Midel-Harnis. Here we were detained several days in very bad lodgings, unable to find boats to carry us over the arm of the sea to Helvoet. At length ice-boats appeared, and we embarked amidst a waste of ice which passed in and out every day with the tide; and, by the force of oars and boat-hooks, sometimes rowing in the water, and sometimes dragging on the ice, which would now and then break and let us down, in the course of the day we got over; and we thought ourselves lucky, as the last boat which passed got stuck in the ice, and was carried out with the tide and brought in again, so that it was out *from nine in the morning to one o'clock the next night* before it reached the opposite shore. We could not reach Helvoet, but landed on the dike about two miles from it, and took boors' wagons again for the Brille, which we reached at night. Next morning, we took ice-boats again to cross another water obstructed by ice as before, and then a third, the Maese, which we found sufficiently frozen to walk over. Another boor's wagon carried us to Delft, and from thence a coach to the Hague. After the rest *of a day or two,* I went to Amsterdam. . . .

I should look back with less chagrin upon the disagreeable pas-

when the Maese was reached it was so firmly frozen that he crossed it on foot. Thence he went on by wagon to Delft, and from Delft by coach to the Hague. *Two days later he entered Amsterdam, to find, as he pathetically expressed it, American credit dead, never to rise again.*

sage from London, if we had succeeded in obtaining the object of it; but I find I am here only to be a witness that *American credit in this Republic is dead never to rise again, at least until the United States shall all agree upon some plan of revenue, and make it certain that interest and principal will be paid.* . . .

But McMaster did not always follow the language of primary sources without quotation marks. Sometimes he changed the language or put quotation marks around the whole section used. Almost as frequently as he used the whole section without quotation marks, McMaster put the marks around one part and not around the rest:

McMASTER, VIII, 273-74

Robert J. Walker was sure there could be no peaceable secession. "How could it be peaceable?" he asked. "Who was to have the army, the navy, the national flag, the public treasure, the public lands, the Capitol?" War, civil war, would surely attend the separation, and when it was effected the financial and industrial ruin of the North would be overwhelming. There would be total non-intercourse, absolute prohibition of imports and exports. The trade of the South would find new channels, and three million men in the North would be thrown out of employment and, with their families, reduced to starvation. Northern steamboats and railroads would

WALKER, pp. 11-13

I have never believed in a peaceable dissolution of the Union. If the disaster comes, it will be attended by civil war, and the sword must be the umpire. How can it be peaceful? Who is to arbitrate between the North and the South? Who is to have the army, the navy, the national banner, the public treasure or revenue, the Capitol [*sic*] of the Union, the government archives, and how are we to divide the public lands and common territory . . . ! No, it will be war, civil war, of all others the most sanguinary and ferocious. . . . The financial and industrial ruin of the North would be great and overwhelming. . . . Now, by a dissolution of the Union and civil

no longer carry Southern passengers, Northern business houses with Southern customers would be forced to close, hundreds of vessels would lie idle at the wharves, commerce would perish, and credit decay.

war, there would be total non-intercourse between the North and the South, an absolute prohibition of all imports or exports, which would necessarily throw the trade of the South into other channels. This . . . would throw out of employment more than three millions of the people of the North, including the families connected with them, most of whom would be reduced to absolute indigence. . . . The Northern railroads, vessels and steamers would lose their freight and passengers, passing to and from the South; the Northern stores, connected with this trade, would be closed, the Northern vessels lie idle at the wharves. . . . Commerce would perish; credit would decay. . . .

It will be noticed that the section within the quotation marks is not exactly quoted. Rarely did McMaster quote exactly. Usually the wording or the punctuation was slightly changed; sometimes sections were omitted without any indication.[19] In one instance McMaster attributed to the same person things said by more than one person, and in another, he altered the whole style of language:

McMASTER, V, 156-57

"Judge," said the foreman of a jury that failed to agree, "this is the difficulty: The jury want to know whether what you told us

FORD, p. 85

"Why, judge, this *'ere* is the difficulty. The jury want to know whether that *ar* what you told us, when we first went out, was *raly*

[19] McMaster's practice of omitting from quotations without indication is the more confusing because sometimes he used dots to show omissions—for example, *History of the People*, footnote 2 of I, 51, and footnotes to II, 573.

when we first went out really was   the law, or whether it was *ony jist*
the law, or whether it was only   your notion."[20]
just your notion."

In most cases McMaster's loose handling of quotations did not change the meaning, but within the sections analyzed there are three instances where the sense was altered. Typical of these instances was the one in which the source had a toast reading, " 'Gen. Atchison—hoping that he may live to see Kansas a slave state, *in the Union or out of the Union*,' " while McMaster put it, " 'General Atchison—hoping that he may live to see Kansas a State in the Union, or out of the Union.' "[21]

Outside quotation marks, McMaster's *History* was no more exact. In one place or another, and sometimes more than once within the sections checked, McMaster said things that were not in his source, made statements that were a little different from the statements in the source, omitted things in a way that changed the picture, and generalized on the basis of one instance when contradictory instances were in his source. In the passage quoted on pages 111-13, McMaster's text differs seven times from its source. Most of the variations are trivial, but one of them changed an important point in an important way.[22] John Adams did not say that "American credit [is] dead, never to rise again." What he did say was that "American credit . . . is dead never to rise again, at least until the United States shall all agree upon some plan of revenue, and make it certain that interest and principal will be paid. . . ." Omitting facts in a way that changed the sense and drawing implications which could hardly be defended are the most frequent type of important inexactitude, as in these instances:

---

[20] A misprint in Ford—the repetition of the word "went"—has been removed.

[21] See Volume VIII, Section B, p. 270, in Appendix IV. The other two instances are explained in Appendix IV: Volume V, Section B, p. 508; Volume VIII, Section A, pp. 104-05.

[22] The variations are indicated by the italics. McMaster was sharply criticized for small errors in another section of the *History* in C. C. Pinckney, "A Question of Fact, Thomas Pinckney vs. J. B. McMaster," *Publications of the Southern History Association* (Washington, 1897), I, 253-58.

McMASTER, VIII, 264

A large body of volunteer militia, he said, had been called into service by the late acting governor. Employment of such troops was not authorized in his instructions unless requested by the commander of the military department in which Kansas lay. It was, therefore, ordered that they be discharged. . . .

GIHON, p. 126

"Proclamation.

"WHEREAS, A large number of volunteer militia have been called into the service of the Territory of Kansas, by authority of the late acting governor. . . .

"WHEREAS, The employment of militia is not authorized by my instructions from the general government, except upon requisition of the commander of the military department in which Kansas is embraced; and

"WHEREAS, An authorized regular force has been placed at my disposal, sufficient to insure the execution of the laws that may be obstructed by combinations too powerful to be suppressed by the ordinary course of judicial proceedings; now

"*Therefore*, I, JOHN W. GEARY, Governor of the Territory of Kansas, do issue this, my proclamation, declaring that the services of such volunteer militia are no longer required; and hereby order that they be immediately discharged. . . .

McMASTER, VIII, 271

Longfellow wrote that he had given up a trip to Europe that he might vote for Fremont.

LONGFELLOW, II, 282-83

I have just had a narrow escape of going there [to Europe] myself. . . . The state-rooms were engaged,—when this rap on the knee impeded all further move-

ments in that direction, and all the
mirage of white town and purple
hill has vanished quite away.

. . . .

Besides,—my vote in the au-
tumn! I have great respect for that
now, though I never cared about
it before!

. . . .

You must not think that our
not going to Europe is any great
disappointment to me. . . . The
undertaking was too formidable.
If I had gone at all, I should have
gone very reluctantly.

But McMaster could also make flat errors of a most serious nature.
In Volume VIII, about a page is devoted to the report of a Massachusetts House Committee. Actually, McMaster was paraphrasing
the minority report of that Committee.[23] His loose handling of
material both in and outside of quotation marks is amusingly cli-
maxed by the instance in which McMaster attributed to a single
"German Socialist" the inaccurately quoted statements of three different men, none of whom is identified in the source as a Socialist
and one of whom was named Franconi.[24]

While McMaster was working on Volume II, he had a conversation with George Bancroft about the way to footnote a history.

"I see, sir [the patriarch told the young man] that you have many foot
notes in your book. That is a mistake. At the cost of great labor you have
unearthed certain facts and you tell your readers where they may find
them. Some of them will use them and give you no credit." I [Mc-
Master] replied that, since I was an unknown author writing history, it
seemed necessary to give my authority for statements. "You make a
book upon which anyone who chooses may climb," he replied. "All the

[23] See Volume VIII, Section A, pp. 105-06, in Appendix IV.
[24] See Volume VIII, Section A, pp. 104-05, in Appendix IV.

trouble I have ever had with my books came from the notes. I am now revising them, and in the new edition there will be no notes."[25]

Bancroft's advice must have been emphasized by the attitude of McMaster's good friend, the Librarian of the Historical Society of Pennsylvania. When a new volume by McMaster appeared, Stone used to say, "Now we shall soon have something from John Fiske."[26] Yet McMaster did not cut down the number of his footnotes; indeed, proportionately to the number of pages, there are more lines of footnotes in the last than in the first volume of the *History*. As a whole, however, the work is not heavily footnoted— the average being about three lines of footnotes per page.[27]

In the earlier volumes, these footnotes are frequently inaccurate and completely inconsistent in form. In the sections of Volumes I and II that were analyzed, more than forty per cent of the footnotes are inaccurate in some way—either by not exactly supporting the text and thus being part of the general inaccuracy just described, or by having a misquotation within the footnote itself, or by a slip like S. E. Thomas for E. S. Thomas, footnote three for footnote four, Smyth, p. 346 for Smyth, p. 364, or Madison to Jefferson for Jefferson to Madison.[28] Inconsistency of practice is more frequent than inaccuracy. Some sections of the text were footnoted and some sections, of the same nature, were not;[29] sometimes the footnote

[25] Eric F. Goldman, ed., "The Princeton Period of John Bach McMaster," *Proceedings of the New Jersey Historical Society* (1939), LVII, 229.

[26] Ellis P. Oberholtzer, "John Bach McMaster," *Pennsylvania Magazine of History and Biography* (1933), LVII, 26.

[27] These calculations have been made on the basis of the table in Hutchinson in the *Jernegan Essays*, p. 135.

[28] In this calculation, if the footnote contains a misquotation within itself, it is called inaccurate; if the text misquotes the source cited in the footnote but the footnote itself is accurate, the footnote is called accurate.

[29] For example, *History of the People*, I, "The library" on p. 14 to "the well" on p. 17 (the partially comprehensive footnotes on pp. 13, 14 do not cover this material), and I, "The Legislature" on p. 279 to "and asperity" on p. 280. These un-footnoted pages are no different in nature from surrounding pages which are footnoted.

mark was placed after the sentences it supports and sometimes it was placed elsewhere on the page;[30] page numbers were given or omitted without any discernible reason;[31] the same book or document was cited differently.[32] In Volumes V and VIII, the form is more consistent in the sense that volume and page numbers were usually given, and footnote markers were usually placed after the sentences they support, but inconsistencies in form are still frequent and the percentage of inaccuracies only diminishes. In the last section analyzed in the last volume, more than twenty-five per cent of the footnotes are inaccurate in some way.

A careless technique, a confusing technique—but what does it all mean? Does it mean, as the outraged *Tribune* reviewer said, that this is "little better than the art of the copy-book," that, as the critic strongly implied, McMaster was personally dishonest?[33] So far as the Macaulay-like sentences in Volume I are concerned, McMaster has given his own answer: "That I have gotten some of Macaulay's sentences in the book is most true and most unfortunate. That I knew they were there. That I consciously put them there is false. . . ."[34] In view of McMaster's phenomenal memory and the way in which he had soaked himself in Macaulay's writings, it is as easy to accept as to reject this statement.

[30] For example, in *ibid.*, II, 193, footnote 1 belongs after "severe measures," not "to protect them." In *ibid.*, p. 236, a general footnote (footnote 1) is placed at the beginning of the section it partially supports, but in *ibid.*, p. 244, the same type of footnote (footnote 1) is placed at the end of the section.

[31] For example, of seven footnotes of much the same nature in *ibid.*, I, 10-19, five have page references and two do not. Other variations in the usage of page and volume numbers may be seen in *ibid.*, II, 194-95. In footnote 1 of *ibid.*, II, 237, McMaster used a 1798 ed. of a work; in footnote 2 of *ibid.*, I, 13, McMaster used the 1796 ed. of the same work. The paging of the two editions is different, but in neither case is the edition indicated.

[32] For example, the same work is given the title of *Memoirs of Josiah Quincy* in footnote 1 of *ibid.*, I, 13, and the *Life of Josiah Quincy* in the footnotes of *ibid.*, I, 14, 18. In *ibid.*, II, 199, a reader's letter to the newspaper is cited in the first footnote by the newspaper alone and in the second footnote by the letter and newspaper.

[33] *New York Tribune*, July 1, 1883. See *ante*, pp. 45-47.

[34] "Diary," III, July 2, 1883, MS.

The close paraphrasings from Rives and Quincy were something more than phrases which might have been unconsciously remembered. From McMaster's statement about his Macaulay-like sentences, one would infer that, when forced to think about the question, he believed such paraphrasings from secondary works were improper; the fact that McMaster has no similar passages after the *Tribune* review tends to confirm the inference. Yet if one is to believe that McMaster was trying to deceive his reader in Volume I, one must also believe that McMaster was stupid. Very little ingenuity would have been required to make less obvious the paraphrasings from Quincy and from Rives; Quincy's book is mentioned in two comprehensive footnotes placed near the section of the *History* which closely paraphrases it.[35] What happened, it appears likely, was that McMaster, with his mind on the grand contours of his idea and anxious to get the book in print as soon as possible, scrambled together Volume I without much thought or care about the method he was using.

There is no evidence that McMaster saw anything improper in closely paraphrasing from primary sources or in leaning heavily, without indicating the extent of his leaning, on Rives, *Niles' Register*, and Commons. Usually he plainly cited the primary source from which he was paraphrasing. Once past Volume I, in the cases of *Niles' Register* and Commons, McMaster provided in his own footnotes on specific points a clue to the way the section was constructed. The question is not one of personal integrity but of standards of scholarship. Many years before McMaster started writing, George Bancroft had learned in a German seminar a method which makes his history fit present-day standards more closely, and European-trained scholars like Herbert Adams were teaching this method while McMaster was producing his *History*.[36] McMaster

[35] *History of the People*, I, footnote 1 on p. 13, footnote 1 on p. 14.

[36] Prof. Carl L. Becker testified to Bancroft's scholarship in *Everyman His Own Historian* (New York, 1935), pp. 141-42. Prof. Becker's statements are confirmed by an analysis of Bancroft's first three volumes made by Mr. Alfred Goldberg, a graduate student in the Johns Hopkins University. Mr. Goldberg's paper, "The Technique of George Bancroft," is unpublished.

had no such training and, despite his professorship in the University of Pennsylvania, belonged in no such tradition. His was more the tradition of history where you came upon it and as you wanted it. In John Marshall's day this had meant copying from men who, in turn, had copied from other men.[37] By the time of Macaulay and then, a little later, of McMaster and John Morley, there remained only the casualness about quotation marks and about indications of the exact origins of materials. Morley, in his life of Walpole, leaned upon another work much as McMaster leaned upon Rives.[38] McMaster's close paraphrasings of primary sources is an obvious attempt to imitate the effect created by Macaulay's famous "declamatory disquisitions," and if McMaster's disquisitions differ from the adroit summaries of their model in being virtually copies, the difference is probably one of literary skill.[39] If McMaster could have been shown Appendix IV, he might have replied as Brahms did when told that part of his *First Symphony* closely resembled Beethoven's *Ninth*. *Brahms* said, "Dass kennt jeder Esel!"[40]

Other practices of McMaster place him even more squarely in the tradition of Macaulay. Did McMaster rest his account of an incident on a single book, or on a set of materials which represented but one viewpoint? Macaulay is famous for this. Did McMaster violate the present-day sanctity of quotation marks? Macaulay and Jared Sparks had done this too,[41] and McMaster, in the middle of writing his own *History*, defended Sparks against

[37] William A. Foran, "John Marshall as a Historian," *American Historical Review* (1937), XLIII, 51-64.

[38] "Some of Macaulay's most brilliant portraits and sketches of incident," said George Saintsbury (*Encyclopaedia Britannica*, 14th ed., XIX, 859), "are adapted and sometimes almost literally translated from Saint-Simon." See also "Macaulay," in Saintsbury, *Corrected Impressions* (New York, 1895), pp. 79-97. I am indebted to Dr. Charles A. Beard for pointing out to me John Morley's (*Walpole*, New York, 1889) way of using William Coxe, *Memoirs of the Life and Administration of Sir Robert Walpole . . .* , 4 vols., London, 3d ed., 1816.

[39] On Macaulay's "declamatory disquisitions," see Charles H. Firth, *A Commentary on Macaulay's History of England* (London, 1938), pp. 37-40.

[40] The Brahms anecdote is told in Deems Taylor, *The Well Tempered Listener* (New York, 1940), p. 99.

[41] On Macaulay's use of evidence, see C. H. Firth, *A Commentary on Macaulay's*

... assaults made by later editors on his methods and his texts. . . . The language, the spelling, the felicity of expression, are nothing. The facts and the information the letters contain are everything: and these things the work of Sparks has made accessible to us all.[42]

McMaster's inconsistent and incomplete system of footnoting—if it was modeled after anything—was probably modeled after Macaulay's, which is inconsistent and incomplete in much the same ways.[43] Certainly McMaster did not look upon the footnote as an exact guide to the way a given page of history had been constructed, for he said of Edward Freeman that the English historian's

... chief defect . . . [was] prolixity. His earnest desire to be accurate made him not only say the same thing over and over again, but say it with an unnecessary and useless fullness of detail, and back up his statement with a profusion of notes. . . . These notes are always interesting and always instructive. But the end of a volume is not the place for an exhibition of the doubts and fears that have tormented the historian, for a statement of the reasons which have led him to one conclusion rather than another, nor for the denunciation or reputation [*sic*] of the opinions of his predecessors. When the building is finished, we do not want to see the lumber used as the scaffolding piled in the back yard. . . .[44]

No scaffolding piled in the back yard—this fundamentally literary attitude of Macaulay and McMaster permitted both men their over-sweeping generalizations, their characterizations that approach caricatures, their tendency, at times, to be bright rather than right. There is no evidence that McMaster deliberately altered any fact.

While a selective analysis of McMaster's *History* does not impugn his personal integrity, it does make necessary extreme caution in using his volumes. The inaccuracies in the *History* are

---

History, Chaps. III-V, and John Paget, *The New "Examen"* (Edinburgh, 1861). For Sparks' method of editing, see Bernhard Knollenberg, *Washington and the Revolution* (New York, 1940), especially Chap. XV.

[42] "A Pioneer in Historical Literature," *Atlantic Monthly* (1894), LXXIII, 563.

[43] On Macaulay's footnotes, see C. H. Firth, *A Commentary on Macaulay's History*, pp. 77-79.

[44] "Edward Augustus Freeman," in Charles D. Warner, ed., *Library of the World's Best Literature*, X, 5979-80.

frequent enough to suggest that no fact or quotation should be taken from McMaster without independent corroboration. Such corroboration is often exceedingly tedious because of his system of footnoting.

McMaster's technique made a difference, too, because it gave free rein to his prepossessions. Had he adopted the most meticulous scholarly method, his story of America's past would doubtless have been influenced by his feelings about the present and future. But McMaster's earlier volumes, like their model, Macaulay's *History*, give the effect less of an interpretation than of a tract because of their loose method and unbridled language. The combativeness with which McMaster went at the past is suggested by a letter he wrote shortly after Volume I appeared:

The amount of blackguarding that is in store for me, especially as I get down to slavery times is enough to make you faint. When the next volume comes out every democrat in the country will howl over Jefferson. If ever there was a demagogue, a "straddler," a false friend, and an implacable enemy Jefferson was one, and I mean to show him up.[45]

In Volumes I and II, the men McMaster liked are given intemperate praise and those he disliked are given intemperate damnation. A Hamilton was all good, but a Patrick Henry was all bad, and both were whatever they were in extreme language.[46] The source of McMaster's conceptions of personalities is usually not made plain, but his method is suggested by the fact that the Hamilton-Reynolds affair is described largely from Hamilton's defense of himself.[47] By Volume V, the Macaulay-like vignettes have disappeared from McMaster's *History*, but the Macaulay-like lack of balance has not. Since McMaster's method did not demand sources of varied viewpoints, his prepossessions, or his sources' prepossessions, march undisputed through incidents in the volumes. Part of the pre-Constitutional period described almost exclusively on the

[45] McMaster to Gertrude Stevenson, April 22, 1883, MS.

[46] The vignette of Hamilton is in the *History of the People*, I, 125-26; of Henry, in *ibid.*, I, 488-90.

[47] *Ibid.*, II, 336-39.

basis of a strongly pro-Madison work,[48] an account of a fight between Adams and Jackson men resting solely on materials printed or mentioned in an "Address to the People of Kentucky by the Central Jackson Committee of Kentucky" which was published in a violently pro-Jackson newspaper,[49] a page of Governor Geary's activities resting entirely on a book by Geary's secretary[50]—these are examples of the usage found in Volumes I, V, and VII. Not only the unbalance of McMaster's research but its fragmentary nature could sometimes emphasize an interpretation. McMaster's lengthy discussion of the Carter Beverley letter, which put Clay in an unfavorable position, did not include a fact established in another volume of a source McMaster was using and published in a biography of Clay long before McMaster wrote his volume—the fact that Beverley had later admitted his letter was a fake.[51]

A more sophisticated interpretation, a more reliable text—these advantages certainly would have come from a different technique. Yet there is no reason to believe that the grand outlines of McMaster's *History* would have been changed by a stricter scholarly method. His conception of history was not simply a guide for writing; it was something more personal, more emotional. McMaster's philosophy of history—though he would have never called it that—had been one of his chief motives for writing history and it gave to the man's work a kind of crusader's zeal to correct the limitations of predecessors. McMaster wanted to write not simply political and military history, but social history too, and he

[48] *Ibid.*, I, 272-84, analyzed as Volume I, Section B, in Appendix IV. Rives was a strong partisan of Madison and the Federalists.

[49] *History of the People*, V, 511-13, analyzed as Volume V, Section B, pp. 511-12 to pp. 512-13, in Appendix IV. *The United States Telegraph* was fighting for the election of Jackson.

[50] *History of the People*, VIII, 263-64, analyzed as Volume VIII, Section B, p. 264, in Appendix IV. Gihon's position and sympathies are stated on the title page and in the Preface of his volume. While McMaster cited mostly Geary letters printed in Gihon, he apparently took this whole incident from Geary and the reader gets a different impression of an important detail of it by consulting Leverett W. Spring, *Kansas* (Boston, 1887), p. 197.

[51] *History of the People*, V, 504-08. See Volume V, Section B, p. 505, footnote 1, in Appendix IV.

wanted to write it in a way that would show the "splendid progress" of the United States.[52]

Both of these basic ideas are plainly taken from Macaulay, McMaster's first and lasting inspiration. The influence of science-minded thinkers and of realistic fiction, the connection of politics and economics obvious at the time McMaster was thinking about his first volume, might well have prepared his mind for the Macaulay approach, but we know that McMaster was given his direct impetus by reading Macaulay's famous third chapter, and a comparison of the two men's opening paragraphs removes any doubts about the similarity of conception.[53] Both men were going to write history which, though it would not neglect wars and politics, would also include other phases of human activity—the "history of the people," as both phrased it.[54] In doing this each would have the theme of progress, of what Macaulay called "physical . . . moral, and . . . intellectual improvement" and McMaster phrased as "moral and social advancement."[55] In the face of such progress, Macaulay had challenged, how could men talk of a "golden age" followed by "degeneracy and decay," and the Englishman's flashing then-and-now comparisons emphasized the point.[56] McMaster's thought about the progress of the United States carried the same challenge, sometimes in the same words, and then-and-now comparisons are sprinkled through earlier volume of the *History of the People*.[57] It is in the first two volumes of McMaster's work that

[52] *History of the People*, I, 1-2. The quotation is from p. 1.

[53] For Macaulay as McMaster's first influence, see *ante*, p. 13, and an address McMaster made before Vol. I appeared, *French Society during the Reign of Louis XIV*, pp. 1-3. For the other possible influences on McMaster, see *ante*, Chap. II. McMaster wrote a glowing eulogy of Macaulay ("Thomas Babington Macaulay," in Charles D. Warner, ed., *Library of the World's Best Literature*, XVI, 9381-86), and, while visiting in England, still remembered Macaulay's descriptions of various places. J. B. McMaster to R. B. McMaster, July 20, 1906 (?), MS.

[54] *History of the People*, I, 1; T. B. Macaulay, *History of England*, I, 2.

[55] *History of the People*, I, 2; T. B. Macaulay, *History of England*, I, 2.

[56] T. B. Macaulay, *History of England*, I, 2.

[57] Note how McMaster's Chap. I, beginning with a then-and-now setting (pp. 2-3), moves on to its grand paean to progress at the close. "People know so little

Macaulay's conception is most completely transferred to the American scene, and transferred in a style that is a remarkably good imitation of Macaulay's literary strength and weakness. In the later volumes McMaster wrote more like McMaster—in simple, unfigurative, continuously flowing prose. The then-and-now comparisons almost completely vanish, the progress theme is subdued; while large quantities of social history appear, the arrangement and emphasis are such that Frederick Jackson Turner could say, in discussing Volume IV, that McMaster seemed to be "assimilating his history more to the conventional standards which he rejected in the beginning."[58]

Even when McMaster's volumes most closely resembled their model, the *History of the People* stood on its own feet. If McMaster took over his basic ideas of a history of the people which would show progress, he made the ideas his own, and his own was something different. Macaulay was an English Whig writing about a period before the Industrial Revolution at a time when the Industrial Revolution was just beginning to influence thought about the past. The history of McMaster's country was almost coincident with the history of its Industrial Revolution, and McMaster himself was of a later, more industrial-minded generation in a different, more industrial-minded country. McMaster's social history

about their grandfathers," McMaster wrote to Miss Stevenson (April 22, 1883, MS) shortly after Vol. I appeared, "that they think that one hundred years ago was the golden age when all public men were pure and high minded, and that the men who founded the republic were a little better than ourselves. It is a mistake. . . ." Describing how he believed history should be taught ("The Social Function of United States History," *National Herbart Society, Fourth Yearbook*, 1898, p. 30), McMaster said, "Above all, it should be so taught as to destroy that baneful belief that we have degenerated from our forefathers." See also *French Society during the Reign of Louis XIV*, p. 3, and "Four Centuries of Progress," in *With the Fathers*, p. 321.

[58] For the quantity of social history, see Appendix II. Turner's remark is in "Recent Studies in American History," *Atlantic Monthly* (1896), LXXVII, 840. In reviewing Vol. VIII, Charles H. Levermore, accurately remarked that, "Though the latter [Rhodes] makes no special claim to write the story of the people, the two historians do not differ widely in their selection of subjects or in the incidence of emphasis." *American Historical Review* (1914), XIX, 363-64.

was far more economic history; his people were more consistently inclusive of the whole population; his "progress" had in it far more of votes for everyone, of wages and hours, of railroads, cotton gins, and sewerage pipes. The *History of the People* and the *History of England* are very different books, with very different significances for their respective historiographies.

In American historiography McMaster's major stroke, of course, was the social history he wrote. In his volumes readers could, for the first time, find extensive accounts of everyday life in the cities, on the plantations, and on the farms, of the principal inventions, of the development of transportational facilities, of the westward migration, of educational, literary, and artistic trends in the past United States. The conspicuous emphasis of his *History* is non-political and non-military, and almost one-quarter of its pages are devoted to subjects which nearly everyone would agree are social history.[59] The large amounts of social history which McMaster wrote from newspapers and pamphlets—the technique might have been suggested by Macaulay—not only gave his pages a non-political, everyday tone but made him the American pioneer in this practice.[60] The first volume of the *History of the People*, as Edward Channing said, "marked a revolution in our historical outlook." It brought, as William A. Dunning confessed, a shock:

The multiplicity of occupations and interests that were ascribed to the people of the United States was disconcerting. I had been taught that all their waking hours outside of mealtime were devoted to politics, with

[59] See Appendix II.

[60] For Macaulay's use of such sources, see C. H. Firth, *A Commentary on Macaulay's History*, Chap. V; for previous American uses, see *ante*, p. 32. The importance of McMaster as an American pioneer in the practise is summarized in the well-known remark of William A. Dunning—"To the technique of historiography also he [McMaster] added a significant element. Von Holst was imposing upon the writer of American history for all future time the necessity of searching that useful but unalluring repository of information, the Congressional Record; McMaster added the even more burdensome duty of going through all the newspapers of the day." "A Generation of American Historiography," *Annual Report of the American Historical Association for the Year 1917* (Washington, 1920), p. 350.

a view to save the Constitution of the United States from the ravages of the slavocrats. McMaster showed that the people had found time to clear and cultivate a myriad million acres of land, and to develop thereon the conveniences and comforts of a civilized society.[61]

The conveniences and comforts of a civilized society, developed by and for the people, ordinary people like the boarding-house lady of Ballston Spa or her surveyor grandson—here was the heart of McMaster's interests. "How," he would ask Miss Stevenson, "do the dreary political pages read?"[62] The great men of the battlefield and the forum never had any special appeal to McMaster, "The average man," he was sure, "is good enough [to be President]. . . ."[63] All the volumes of the *History* are tied together more by the movements of masses than of individuals; over a quarter of the men singled out for biographical vignettes are non-political and non-military figures.[64] Eli Whitney emerges as a person,[65] but Jefferson, Jackson, and Lincoln are little more than names that move along with the events. McMaster's attitude toward political figures probably joined with his dislike for talk about degeneration to produce his striking treatments of eighteenth-century political figures. Almost as many were attacked as applauded,[66] and even Washington was not spared deflation:

Time has since dealt gently with his memory [McMaster wrote], and he has come down to us as the greatest of all leaders and the most immaculate of all men. . . . The outlines of his biography are known to every school-boy in the land. Yet his true biography is still to be prepared. General Washington is known to us, and President Washington. But George Washington is an unknown man. When at last he is set before us in his habit as he lived, we shall read less of the

---

[61] Letters of Channing and Dunning, in *Testimonial Dinner to John Bach McMaster . . . Letters Received.*

[62] McMaster to Gertrude Stevenson, March 15, 1885, MS.

[63] "The Third-Term Tradition," in *With the Fathers*, pp. 69-70.

[64] See Appendix III. It is interesting that, of the twenty-nine non-political and non-military vignettes, only three are unfavorable.

[65] *History of the People*, II, 161 ff.

[66] See Appendix III. The eighteenth-century figures were in Vols. I and II.

cherry-tree and more of the man. Naught surely that is heroic will be omitted, but side by side with what is heroic will appear much that is commonplace. . . . We shall respect and honor him for being, not the greatest of generals, not the wisest of statesmen, not the most saintly of his race, but a man with many human frailties and much common sense, who rose in the fullness of time to be the political deliverer of our country.[67]

"Unworthy and cynical," James Ford Rhodes said of this characterization, but Rhodes was not a historian of the people.[68]

The social history in McMaster's work was so striking an innovation that it is easy to exaggerate its rôle in the *History*. McMaster's volumes, like Macaulay's, are set in a conventional political, diplomatic, and military framework. The dividing lines between McMaster's volumes and chapters are often blurred, but where the divisions emerge distinctly, they are nearly always similar in nature to Schouler's or Rhodes'. The first page of the *History* had warned that "in the course of this narrative much, indeed, must be written of wars . . . of presidents, of congresses . . . of treaties. . . ." The much turned out to be most, for almost three-quarters of the volumes are devoted to politics, diplomacy, and war. In the period of the writing of the Constitution, McMaster had explained, politics was particularly important in the life of the people, yet long after his volumes swept past 1789, McMaster gave most of his space to politics and wars. Indeed, his volume on the period from 1783 to 1790 has fewer political and military pages than some of his later ones.[69]

McMaster's handling of materials, social or otherwise, is perplexing. Why did McMaster, who was certainly not lacking in literary sense, so often permit his pages to read like rapidly turning notes?

[67] *History of the People*, II, 452-53. For another example of conscious deflation in McMaster's vignettes, see *ibid.*, I, 369.

[68] Review of Vol. II, *Magazine of Western History* (1885), II, 473. Mentioning some of the politicians McMaster had deflated, Rhodes said, ". . . this volume before us has no hero." *Ibid.*

[69] See Appendix II and *ante.*, p. 31.

Why does a sketch of the Patent Office appear in a chapter entitled "The Struggle for Neutrality," or an account of Unitarianism and a yellow fever epidemic in "The British Treaty of 1794"?[70] Why was so little space given to the Northwest Ordinance—space that omitted mention of the slavery provision—when two pages were devoted to Mason Weems and thirty-three to "Burr's Schemes"?[71] Why did McMaster describe the opinions of the "Angel Gabriel" and not those of Ralph Waldo Emerson, when he believed that Emerson was "the only man of that day whose essays had any real influence on his generation, or have lived down to our own"?[72] In seeking an answer to these questions, the critic's eye is naturally caught by the large number of contemporary materials in McMaster's footnotes, and Professor William T. Hutchinson has suggested that "McMaster was interested only in viewing the American scene from their [the contemporaries'] own level, hedged in by their own limited horizon and unconscious of their place in the flowing pattern of life. Unlike most historians, he refused to subordinate the past to the present."[73] Here Professor Hutchinson is in agreement with an earlier critic, Carl Russell Fish, who also believed that McMaster was writing history as it was seen by contemporaries:

The material . . . is in the main allowed to dictate its own order of arrangement which is the despair of the systematic but in reality one of the chief springs of the work's vitality. The arrangement is neither dramatic, dynamic, nor chronological; the parts are held together by a thin glue of "meantimes" and name tags, but lying in the order in which they were perceived by the popular mind the general effect is one of unity. One of the best examples is that of the first fifty pages of volume II. It begins with a description of the South, followed by one of business conditions in the North, Hamilton's proposed excise and bank, conditions in the West, the signing of the bank bill, opposition to the excise in western Pennsylvania, Indian troubles, political divisions, conditions at Philadelphia. Thus within a space that can be grasped as a

[70] History of the People, II, 159-61, 238-45.
[71] Ibid., III, 110-12, I, 230-32, III, 55-88.
[72] Ibid., VII, 94. The "Angel Gabriel" was treated in ibid., VIII, 86-87.
[73] Hutchinson in the Jernegan Essays, p. 133.

single thought conception are placed practically all the conditions surrounding the adoption of Hamilton's financial plan.[74]

There is no doubt that McMaster was intensely interested in contemporary opinion, that he sometimes wrote history by piecing together contemporary documents, that his work often caught the tone of the contemporary market place and forum. Yet it is doubtful whether one can go further and say that he consciously, or at least consistently, was writing history as seen by contemporaries. In the part of Volume II discussed by Fish, in what way were "Amusement, races, etc." or "Washington's anger on hearing of St. Clair's defeat" (two of the topics in the section) "conditions surrounding the adoption of Hamilton's financial plan," or rather, why were they pertinent conditions rather than a score of other things which could have been described? Moreover, the selective analysis of the *History* indicates that McMaster often arrived at his contemporary sources not by thumbing through old newspapers or dipping into piles of documents, but by using the materials as they appeared in *Niles' Register* or Commons. In these instances, at least, McMaster was not seeing events as "they were perceived by the popular mind," and he was certainly not doing it in any of monographic chapters of social history which appear in some of the volumes.[75] Either McMaster did not have the aim that has been attributed to him or he adopted an extraordinarily poor way of achieving it.

It is more likely that McMaster simply started with a political framework and fitted the social history into it without any carefully formulated plan. In determining space allotments, two considerations do seem to have been important. "I am not sure but what John Fiske was wiser," McMaster once plaintively remarked. "I started out to write a chronological history in which a great many periods

[74] "Review of McMaster's History of the People of the United States," *Mississippi Valley Historical Review* (1914), I, 36.
[75] For example, in Vol. V, chapters on "Socialistic and Labor Reforms," "The Negro Problem," "Early Literature," "The Common School in the First Half Century," "Political Ideas in the First Half Century," etc. In the last-mentioned chapter, at the head of six successive pages (pp. 393-403), the dates are in this un-contemporaneous order: 1829, 1775-79, 1784-86, 1786-1805, 1792-95, 1778.

are comparatively uninteresting. Fiske just picked certain interesting periods."[76] At times McMaster seems to have escaped this situation by giving most space to what attracted him most. The American inferiority complex toward England in cultural matters interested McMaster a great deal, for example; there is very little other reason to explain why it received a whole chapter in the *History*.[77] McMaster, a devotee of the concert, the theatre, and illustrated "travel talks," loved the colorful and dramatic, and one of the fascinations of his work is the space given to bizarre incidents.[78] In the second place, McMaster was exceedingly sensitive to the possibility of a charge that he was writing history which had already been written.[79] Bancroft and Hildreth had described the terms of the Northwest Ordinance, and McMaster was casual about them, though he thought they were important and did write a good deal about the conditions surrounding the passage of the Ordinance.[80] Rhodes had treated at length the influence of *Uncle Tom's Cabin*, and McMaster did not mention the book at all, though nothing is more obviously a part of a history of the people.[81] Pulled this way and that by his personal feelings, rarely pausing to ask what was meant by that most intricate conception, social history, McMaster stumbled along with the confidence and confusion of most pioneers.

The *History of the People* was the more pioneering because it

[76] Interview with Dr. R. P. Falkner.

[77] V, Chap. XLVIII. I learned of McMaster's special interest in British-American cultural relations in an interview with Mr. E. W. Mumford.

[78] On McMaster's interests, see Oberholtzer in the *Pennsylvania Magazine of History and Biography*, LVII, 31.

[79] Interview with Mr. E. W. Mumford.

[80] George Bancroft, *History of the Formation of the Constitution of the United States of America* (2 vols., New York, 1882), II, 112-16; Richard Hildreth, *The History of the United States of America* (6 vols., New York, 1856), III, 527-29. McMaster stated the importance of the terms of the Ordinance when he called them "a great stride forward" in "A Century of Struggle for the Rights of Man," *Proceedings of the New York State Historical Association* (1901) I, 68. For the treatment of conditions surrounding the passage of the Ordinance, see *History of the People*, I, 505 ff.

[81] James Ford Rhodes, *History of the United States from the Compromise of 1850* (7 vols., New York, 1893-1906), I, 278-85.

was comparatively national in its focus. Bancroft and Hildreth had stood in New England and looked south; George Tucker had stood in the South and looked north; Turner was standing in the West and looking east. McMaster was the first American to write a large-scale synthesis of his country's history who was a thoroughgoing Middle States man, and if the Middle States have had a regionalism, it has consisted largely of a lack of positive regionalism.[82] McMaster stood in between and looked in all directions—except to Europe.[83] He gave more space to the South than any Northern predecessor, and raised the West to a position of importance in the national past.[84] This Middle States historian even remembered what both Northern and Southern historians had usually forgotten—that a good deal lay between the North and the South. As tart William A. Dunning, of New Jersey and New York, put it:

He [McMaster] brought to notice . . . the neglected fact that on rare occasions a gleam of intelligence had been discernible in other parts of the country than Massachusetts and South Carolina. Even New York and Philadelphia were assigned by him to a humble place in the broad picture of the national development.[85]

In the large *History*, as in the *School History*, McMaster wrote an account in which the Middle States and the West received "more adequate treatment" than they had in books written from an "ultra New England standpoint."[86] Indeed, McMaster's treatment was

[82] This point is developed in Eric F. Goldman, "Middle States Regionalism and American Historiography: A Suggestion," in Goldman, ed., *Historiography and Urbanization, Essays in American History in Honor of W. Stull Holt* (Baltimore, 1941), pp. 211-20.

[83] McMaster's viewpoint was belligerently American—the "our people" one (for example, *History of the People*, V, 289). His sources include documents from Ottawa, London, Paris, and Madrid (Hutchinson in the *Jernegan Essays*, p. 135), but McMaster wrote most of his diplomatic history from exclusively, or almost exclusively American sources. For example, a chapter on "Texas Annexed; Oregon Reoccupied" (*History of the People*, VII, Chap. LXXIX) has only sources obtained in the United States and most of them represent the American viewpoint.

[84] Hutchinson in the *Jernegan Essays*, pp. 138-39.

[85] Dunning's letter, in *Testimonial Dinner to John Bach McMaster . . . Letters Received*.

[86] This is the McMaster letter cited *ante*, p. 79, footnote 3.

not only adequate but more than adequate. His general surveys of the country sometimes give far more space to the Middle States and the West than to the other regions.[87] Perhaps because McMaster did so much of his research in Middle States libraries and in the Library of Congress, he often wrote the history of the United States, as William E. Dodd remarked without too much exaggeration, "in the language of Middle States sources and the Congressional debates."[88]

Living in McMaster's Pennsylvania meant living in one of America's industrial centers in its post-Civil War boom. Bancroft's Boston, Tucker's Charlottesville, were never like this. McMaster not only lived there; he lived with the business bustle, was not repelled by it, as was Henry Adams, was not escaping it, as was Rhodes. An appropriate fellow citizen of Carnegie, McMaster was practical-minded, economic-minded, industrial-minded. When he thought of future generations looking back on his own time, he was sure they would want

to know something of the daily life of a great people who, in one generation, overspread a vast continent, drew to their shores millions of foreigners, fought a civil war and paid for it, produced the most marvellous inventions and discoveries, carried on business ventures upon a gigantic scale, and made enormous fortunes the order of the day. . . .[89]

It is not surprising that a man who was so little romantic in thinking of his own day should deal realistically with economic facts of the past and should be inclined to correlate them with the rest of his cultural pattern.

Generally, McMaster stopped with comparatively realistic but uncorrelated description of political, economic, and other types of facts. In the later volumes, most of the non-political, non-mili-

[87] For example, *History of the People*, V, Chap. XLIV, "State of the Country from 1825 to 1829."
[88] "Profitable Fields of Investigation in American History, 1815-1860," *American Historical Review* (1913), XVIII, 535.
[89] McMaster in the *Pennsylvania Magazine of History and Biography* (1884), VIII, 191.

tary history is even segregated in separate chapters—"The Negro Problem," or "Early Literature," or "The Common School in the First Half Century."[90] Yet McMaster believed that

... real history in which events are brought out in their significant aspects can not be written by following with precision any number of parallel lines. While such special treatment may be of much value, the investigator must remember that even in his choice of facts, as well as in their interpretation, much more must be considered than the changes taking place in one phase of human activity. In the period after the Revolution, for example, all social and industrial conditions had their bearing on constitutional change and on the need of establishing a new political order. The ultimate effect of industrial conditions must affect the choice, arrangement, and presentation of facts.[91]

McMaster's article, "The Social Function of United States History," showed that, at least in his theoretical consideration of large sweeps of history, McMaster could make the mingling of social and political materials a good deal more than putting both of them within the same volume.[92] If the *History*, like the *School History*, did not fulfill the total promise of this article, McMaster did write sections of history that carry within them a certain correlation of political and non-political facts.

Such thinking appears in his handling of three important episodes in the *History of the People*. McMaster's interpretation of the years from 1783 to 1789, when not dominated by Rives, tended to divide the population into the groups described in these striking sentences:

In the first section, decidedly the more respectable, were to be found the merchants and importers of the great towns, the holders of loan certificates, the hard-money men, and that little band of stanch [*sic*] patriots from which in after years came the heads of the Federal party, and the first five Presidents. On the other side was the great body of

[90] *History of the People*, V, Chaps. XLV, XLVII, XLIX.
[91] McMaster's remarks were summarized or paraphrased in the *Ann. Rept. of the A.H.A. for the Year 1904* (Washington, 1905), p. 39. See also his remark in the *History of the People*, I, 2.
[92] *National Herbart Society, Fourth Yearbook*, pp. 26-30.

the middle orders, the farmers, the shopkeepers, the supporters of paper money, all those who clamored for State rights, and all those who found themselves steeped in debts they could not pay. With them were associated many good, brave, and moderate men, who, while they gave an earnest support to the established Government, looked with painful misgiving on every attempt to enlarge its powers as an attack on the independence of the States.[93]

In the introduction to one of McMaster's many rambling sections on the West, published before Turner's famous essay on the frontier, we find,

East of the Alleghanies long-established precedents, time-honored usages, the presence of a ruling class, the thousand hindrances which beset every reform, checked the spread of the new faith [in democratic principles]. West of the Alleghanies no such difficulties were met.[94]

McMaster's sporadic tendency to correlate interests and ideas approached closest to a consistent interpretation in his treatment of the growing divergence between North and South. This, if any, is the theme of the fifth volume:

The effect on the South of the rise of cotton-growing was already apparent [c. 1825]. In every State, from Louisiana to North Carolina, cotton was the great staple. Here, then, was a long belt of States wholly agricultural with identically the same sort of agriculture, carried on by identically the same kind of labor—that of negro slaves. The diversified industry already characteristic of the North was wanting in the South.

The questions of an economic kind which now deeply concerned the North were therefore treated with indifference or viewed as hostile issues by the South. The South had no manufactures; therefore a tariff for the protection of manufactures was unconstitutional. The South had no interstate trade of any consequence; no market to seek in the West; no goods, wares, or merchandise to transport from the seaboard to the Mississippi; therefore the construction of internal improvements, of turnpikes, canals, good roads, or the opening of watercourses by the Federal Government was an exercise of power not granted by the Con-

[93] *History of the People,* I, 201-02.
[94] *Ibid.,* III, 151.

THE HISTORY OF THE PEOPLE

stitution. The South imported heavily from Great Britain; therefore all tariffs must be as low as possible, and to keep them low the expenses of Government must be reduced to a minimum. Thus on the three questions of the hour—the tariff, internal improvements, and the protection of American industries—there was a great gulf fixed between the cotton-growing States on the one hand and the manufacturing and trading States on the other.[95]

Passages like these might suggest that McMaster was a predecessor both of the frontier thesis and of the economic interpretation.

But Turner, the son of Andrew Jackson Turner who could write understandingly of agrarianism, loved the West and was determined to show how much that was good in America had come from its frontier. McMaster had no special enthusiasm for the West.[96] It was a part, and an important part of the Union, and it deserved its description. In this description the interplay of social and political fact sometimes came to the practical eye of McMaster. But from the windows of DeLancey Street the West seemed no more important than any other part of the Union, and no emotional attachment to the frontier led McMaster to correlate frontier life and frontier ideas in a way that would make the West the home of American democracy and nationalism.

Of something that might be called economic interpretation there is much in McMaster, but the economic interpretation is a two-edged sword. The Federalist tradition in American thought, associating the wealthier with the men of good sense and patriotism, had used an economic interpretation to cut against the city poor and small farmers. Charles A. Beard, with his fighting sympathy for the underprivileged, was to stand James Madison on his head and make an economic interpretation cut against the very groups Federalists had glorified.[97] McMaster, industrial-minded Republican that

[95] *Ibid.*, V, 170. See also Chap. XLVI.
[96] The contrast between the two men's approach to the frontier comes out strikingly when one compares any of McMaster's articles on the issues of 1896 with the article Turner published in that year—"The Problem of the West," *Atlantic Monthly*, LXXVIII, 289-97.
[97] How Mr. Beard used the economic thesis of the authors of the *Federalist* is

he was, belonged more in the Federalist tradition. In the *History*, Hamilton is still the great man, the Hamiltonian economic program still the wise and patriotic one.[98] McMaster's harshest biographical vignettes were reserved for the opposition, and he carried out his avowed intention to "show up" Jefferson by putting him down as a man "saturated with democracy in its rankest form," who "remained to the last day of his life a servile worshipper of the people."[99] The whole *History* is favorable to a central bank, to a protective tariff, to the policies and men behind

. . . that splendid line of manufactures which, in the course of two generations, grew rapidly to astonishing proportions, covered her [New England's] streams and rivers with workshops and factories, built up new towns more populous and opulent than the old, and, among many substantial benefits, gave to the world that innumerable host of articles which, under the name of Yankee notions, are now to be found in the markets of every people.[100]

Pre-Constitutional arguments against inflation, McMaster paused to point out, "might be perused with profit by those mischievous schemers who in our own time, under the name of Greenbackers, advocate a money policy as vicious and absurd as that which, ninety-eight years ago, was vainly combated by our ancestors."[101]

It is not surprising, then, that whatever economic interpretation McMaster wrote into his treatment of the Constitutional Period

---

suggested by reading *An Economic Interpretation of the Constitution* (New York, 1913), especially Chap. VI, against the background of the influence of the book as described by Vernon L. Parrington, *Main Currents in American Thought* (3 vols., New York, 1927-30), III, 408 ff.

[98] Though McMaster did sometimes criticize the Federalists on political grounds —for example, *History of the People*, II, 397, 515-17, 628-31.

[99] *History of the People*, II, 51. Of the thirteen political and diplomatic figures given unfavorable vignettes in the *History* (see Appendix III), ten were men opposed to Federalist-Whig policy.

[100] *History of the People*, I, 295. On a central bank and a protective tariff, see *ibid.*, II, 28-32, III, 379-91, 495-509. For an interesting comment of a Democratic Congressman from West Virginia on McMaster's "ultra Federalism," see James A. Barnes, *John G. Carlisle* (New York, 1931), p. 149.

[101] *History of the People*, I, 282.

cut one way—against the Jeffersonian opposition. The Federalists were not only an economic group but "decidedly the more respectable," the men of "close reasoning" and "careful statements."[102] The opposition was not simply an economic group but men given to arguments that were "a singular mingling of appeals to God and the American spirit, with such reasons for hating the Constitution as were every night hiccoughed out in the taverns. . . ."[103]

Yet McMaster was a Republican, not a Federalist, and the creed of industry and commerce had changed with the times. The Civil War had been fought, and in a man like McMaster his industrial-mindedness joined with his Yankee feeling to make him strongly anti-Southern. The South was not only, as Hamilton might have pointed out, an agricultural country without a "thrifty, industrious middle class"; it was narrowly educated, its moral sense was undeveloped, it had based its economy on an inhumane system of labor.[104] "That financial integrity which flourishes best among merchants and traders," McMaster was sure, "was unknown to the landed gentry of Virginia."[105] McMaster may have given comparatively large space to the South, he certainly revealed a greater understanding of the Southern problem than did most of his Northern—and perhaps Southern—contemporaries, but the *History's* interpretation is consistently Republican and Yankee.[106] Here, again, loose use of sources made McMaster's prepossessions the more glaring.[107]

Not only had the Civil War been fought; democracy and the rights of man had become the terminology of almost every important school of American thought. There was a group who were

[102] *Ibid.*, I, 201, 490.

[103] *Ibid.*, pp. 490, 201. See also *ibid.*, pp. 476-77.

[104] The quotation is in *ibid.*, V, 228. For typical treatments of the South, see *ibid.*, I, 26-27, II, 4-20, VII, Chap. LXXVI.

[105] *Ibid.*, II, 12.

[106] For example, the treatment of the Missouri Compromise (*ibid.*, IV, Chap. XXXIX), and of the Compromise of 1850. *Ibid.*, VIII, Chap. LXXXVI.

[107] Edward McCrady, "Colonial Education in South Carolina," in Herbert B. Adams, ed., *Contributions to American Educational History* (Washington, 1887), I, Appendix II.

ready to dismiss the rights of man as "glittering and sounding generalities," but McMaster belonged to the more common type of conservatism which accepted the terminology and wrote its own meaning into it.[108] The underlying thesis of the *History* became explicit in McMaster's little book, *The Acquisition of Political Social and Industrial Rights of Man,* which is an offshoot of, and almost a summary of the first five volumes. The Fathers had proclaimed the rights of man and then not written them into state constitutions:

Yet it would be the height of injustice to accuse the fathers of inconsistency. To have suddenly produced such a social condition as they had in mind, to have recklessly removed from the statute books every law, to have ruthlessly broken down every custom or usage at variance with the new principles they had announced, would have been acts of disorganization of the worst kind. But they were in no sense disorganizers or anarchists. With a steadfast belief in the truth of their principles, they waited but for a chance to apply them decently and in order, and when that chance came they were applied, and the rights of man were steadily extended.[109]

The extension in the meaning and in the application of the rights of man is a major theme in McMaster's *History,* for this extension, together with industrial achievement, was the heart of McMaster's "splendid progress." He gloried in the enfranchisement of the whole population, the increasingly humane treatment of criminals and of the insane, the abolition of imprisonment for debts, the movement for the freeing of slaves, the improved conditions for workingmen. It was probably McMaster's full discussion of these things, particularly of the undemocratic nature of the early state constitutions and of the struggle for industrial rights, that caused the reform-minded colleague of Parrington, J. Allen Smith, to send

---

[108] The phrase is the famous one of Rufus Choate, quoted in V. L. Parrington, *Main Currents in American Thought,* II, 152. McMaster specifically objected to the "glittering generalities" interpretation. *The Acquisition of Political, Social and Industrial Rights of Man in America,* pp. 13-14.

[109] *Ibid.,* pp. 40-41.

his students to McMaster's writings and made one lady think of McMaster as a "master socialist."[110]

The lady misunderstood. McMaster's new Federalism accepted political democracy and those economic and humanitarian changes which had long since been made, and it stopped there. New proposals for extending the meaning of the rights of man, old proposals that had carried over into McMaster's day and offended his conservatism, were "radical . . . extreme measures . . . folly."[111] Abolishing imprisonment for debt was good, but inflationary movements to lift the burden of debt, like the Bryanism of the nineties, were bad.[112] Agitation for better wages or working conditions in the first half of the century was acceptable, but union rules then, like the demands of "social agitators" in McMaster's time, were usually "unjust" or "most tyrannical."[113] Giving the vote to everyone in the early eighteen hundreds was "democracy," but the movement for the direct election of United States senators was disgusting.[114] McMaster's history is permeated with the assurance that the necessary reforms had been made. When Van Buren issued his proclamation calling for the ten-hour day, to take an extreme instance, "the struggle for shorter hours was practically over."[115] The good fight had been fought and won. McMaster was satisfied with his America.

The same attitude is discernible in McMaster's handling of his central concept, "the people." No American historian, not even Ban-

[110] Herman Rensing to McMaster, Aug. 9, 1910; [?] Tinney to McMaster, May 14, 1917, MSS. The quotation is from the second letter. "Your books," wrote a man from Lowndesboro, Alabama (S. M. Dinkins to McMaster, Dec. 29, 1910, MS), are beginning to attract more and more the attention of the laboring classes. . . ."

[111] The adjectives are taken from McMaster's discussion of inflationary measures in "Is Sound Finance Possible under Popular Government?" in *With the Fathers*, pp. 239, 251, 252.

[112] *History of the People*, I, 98, 282.

[113] The quotations are respectively in *ibid.*, II, 616, VI, 369, and *The Acquisition of . . . Rights of Man*, p. 59. For McMaster on the early general reform movements, see *History of the People*, V, Chap. XLIII.

[114] *Ibid.*, III, Chap. XVII, "The Spread of Democracy"; *New York Herald-Tribune*, June 22, 1930.

[115] *The Acquisition of . . . Rights of Man*, p. 110.

croft, has ever glorified the people more. McMaster's people were "that great tribunal . . . before which in our country all public issues sooner or later must be tried."[116] They were not only powerful; they used their power wisely: "The appeal was to the honesty, the hard sense, and the deliberate judgment of the plain people, and, as has always been the case whenever such appeals have been made, the right triumphed."[117] This conception of the people made the Jacksonian movement for McMaster the most interesting episode in American history.[118] It was not Jackson's personality, which McMaster dismissed with little attention, not the machine politics surrounding Jackson, which McMaster found repellent, certainly not Jackson's economic policy, with which McMaster disagreed.[119] It was rather that Jackson's election was "a great uprising of the people, a triumph of democracy. . . ." "The People in Control," shouted McMaster's chapter head.[120]

But in its actual execution, McMaster's conception of the people came close to being a democratic way of avoiding completely democratic thinking. Sections of the American people had done many things McMaster intensely disliked, and when the historian came to these episodes the people ceased to be the people and became a group classified in oppobrious language. The Jeffersonian Republicans in 1797 were not the people but "the party of violence, of disorder, of mob rule";[121] the men of Shay's and the Whiskey Rebellion were not the people but "malcontents," "the mob," "easy dupes."[122] Immigrants of the Middle Period were not the people but the un-American:

Though the newcomers speedily became naturalized, they did not by any means become Americanized. Our institutions they did not understand.

[116] *History of the People*, V, 426.
[117] *Ibid.*, p. 165.
[118] Interview with Dr. Herbert Friedenwald.
[119] For McMaster on machine politics, see *History of the People*, V, 521-22.
[120] *Ibid.*, V, Chap. LII. The quotation in the previous sentence is from *ibid.*, p. 518.
[121] *Ibid.*, II, 310.
[122] *Ibid.*, II, 192 ,197.

. . . The Declaration and the Constitution, the Fourth of July and the twenty-second of February, Bunker Hill and Saratoga, Yorktown and New Orleans, were instruments, days, and events of which they knew nothing, and for which they cared nothing. They . . . looked upon their new home as "the land of liberty," understanding by liberty the right to do as they pleased. In the wild scenes of turbulence, lawlessness, mob rule and riot that disgraced our countrymen for thirty years to come, the naturalized citizen . . . was always conspicuous.[123]

The men and women whom McMaster actually glorified in his concept of the people were the "great middle class" of Anglo-Saxons, "the most persevering, the most energetic, the most thrifty of races," the kind of persons who could conduct even the American Revolution "with the sobriety, with the dignity, with the love of law and order that has ever marked the national uprisings of the Saxon race."[124] McMaster's "people" was the one important element that he had taken over from the Romantic school of American historians. It was Bancroft's "democracy" brought up to date, this time helping to make a history vote for McKinley instead of for Jackson.[125]

That the history voted for McKinley was important for McMaster and for American historiography. After all, the country was voting for McKinley too, and it was probably the conservative tone and interpretation of McMaster's volumes which permitted them to win so large an audience and yet to be, like the *School History*, a transitional work. Whatever the author's bias, somewhere in the *History of the People* were most of the elements that another generation of historians was to develop and reinterpret for its own purposes, and they were in a form palatable to contemporaries who were teaching that next generation. McMaster hailed the people without hailing all popular action. He discarded the bloody

<hr>

[123] *Ibid.*, VI, 84.

[124] *Ibid.*, I, 56, 151, 2; II, 309. For proof that McMaster meant "the Saxon Race" in the second of the quotations, see McMaster to Gertrude Stevenson, Sept. 16, 1882, MS.

[125] This point is developed more fully in Eric F. Goldman, "Democratic Bi-Focalism: A Romantic Idea and American Historiography," in George Boas, ed., *Romanticism in America* (Baltimore, 1940), pp. 1-11.

shirt without being un-Republican. He recognized the West while assailing Bryanism. He emphasized economic factors and gave attention to the struggle between capital and labor without allying himself with "social agitators." The thousands who were voting for McKinley would and did read a book like this. From it they learned that America's past was a good deal more than politicians and warriors, taught it to their classes, put it into their speeches, wrote it into their editorials. *The History of the People* can be criticized on hundreds of minor points and on the major charge that McMaster was not sure where he was going and did not know where he was when he got there. Neither did Columbus. Columbus discovered America; McMaster discovered the American social past.

CHAPTER VIII

The Patriarch

THE *History of the People* finished, McMaster did not know what to do with himself. For more than three decades he had labored on the *History*, always with another volume to finish, always with a dozen other things that had to be done. Now there was nothing that had to be done and McMaster suffered the occupational disease of overworked men. He was too weary to do anything and too restless to do nothing.[1]

What better time for adventure with the family? "The Big Four" had taken trips before, but always with the *History* hanging over them. Now the earth was the limit. In May 1914, Mr. and Mrs. McMaster sailed for Europe, to be followed shortly by Bach and Philip. The day the children joined their parents in London, the newspapers announced the assassination of Archduke Franz Ferdinand; their first hours in Germany were spent amid war stirrings. The historian of the American people in so many of their crises was watching the European people on the verge of their tremendous crisis.

While the countries mobilized, McMaster told in his "Memoirs,"

. . . we were going quietly about town [Freiburg] seeing the sights and noting what happened. Every afternoon aeroplanes flew over the city in the direction of Colmar. They were training, the proprietor of the hotel said, and did so in the afternoon when the wind was mildest. Every day numbers of sun-browned men landed at the station, went to one or [the] other of the two barracks and in time, uniformed and equipped, marched back to the station and entrained. During the late afternoons the main street would be crowded with students in their brightly colored caps, and with townsfolk walking up and down or standing [in] groups apparently discussing events. The war feeling was high. Opinion as

[1] "Second Memoirs," p. 99, MS.

explained to us by the hotel proprietor was that war with Russia was sure to come. She was no friend of Germany, had been crowding her for years. Sooner or later Germany must fight her and now that the widening of the Kiel Canal was finished and large warships could go through, it was as good a time as any to have it out with her. In the evenings Phil took us to some restaurant where the student clubs dined. On one such occasion when our table was up in the gallery where we went to get a good view, we were witnesses to an interesting occurrence. One of the diners on the floor below was reading a French newspaper which so excited a German officer that he marched up to the diner and snatched his paper. For a moment it seemed as if there would be trouble. But matters were quieted down, the offender was ejected, the newspaper taken to the rostrum on which the band sat and burned, while the crowd standing sang "Die Wacht am Rhein."

About five o'clock on the afternoon of August 3, a Saturday, Gertrude and I walked up to the Main Street and found it densely crowded with men and women, so crowded that both sidewalks and roadway were covered. Noticing a dense gathering in front of the office of the newspaper, we stopped to see what would happen. The wait was long, but about six o'clock a notice was posted setting forth that war had been declared and that mobilization would begin the next day. No demonstration was made; students and men thus called to the colors fled in every direction and the crowd silently melted away. "Es kommt," said an old man to his wife as they passed.

At the hotel we found all help, porters, waiters gone. Dinner that night was served to the few guests by the proprietor and his wife who in all probability had cooked it. Dinner over, we were informed that the hotel had been commandeered for the use of officers, that we must go the next morning and the only train that would carry civilians would leave about eight o'clock. The porter then appeared in full uniform to say good-bye to the proprietor and incidentally collect tips. Having paid mine and asked some questions, he told me that once each year he was required to send to his barracks the measure of his chest and of his waist and tracings of his feet, so that, when called into service, shoes and uniform would fit him.

About dusk, notices printed on three different colored papers were posted about town. One was an official notice of a state of war. Another was the notice of mobilization covering thirteen days, the third was a long list of "don'ts" and "musts." No one was to go within 500 feet of a barrack; not more than three people could stand together in a street, talking; every owner of an auto must keep a certain number of litres of petrol in the tank, and must not leave town without permission from the police; wheeled vehicles and horses must be surrendered to the government; children above twelve years of age must work in the fields until the harvest was gathered.

While Gertrude and I packed our trunks, Bach went with Phil to his lodgings and carried his trunk to the hotel. Next morning, having borrowed a push cart, the boys took all trunks to the station. There our hand satchels were taken from us. Such was Gertrude's dismay that Bach suggested that if Phil would go down to the end of the counter and engage the one official in the room in conversation, he would reach over the counter and "swipe" his mother's satchel, which he did. All the way to Cologne signs of war were everywhere. In the fields were children hard at work; along the roads were trains of farm wagons hitched together with several [*undecipherable*] horses tied to the end of the last; at the stations where we stopped were crowds bidding good-bye to relatives off to the front; at Cologne-Dentz the bridge was guarded; pedestrians were held up until a large party was formed when it was taken across under military escort. Automobiles were detained and made to cross in detachments of five or six with a soldier on the running boards of the first and last. When our train stopped in the station at Cologne, there was a soldier at each car who ordered the windows shut and the blinds drawn down. Presently we were ordered out; and while walking up and down the platform saw a huge pile of hand satchels thrown together in disorder. By-and-by we were ordered into another train and started for nobody knew where. Our hoped-for destination was Holland; but we had long since ceased to care where we went so long as we were going. An hour or more riding brought us to a little town, I think it was Herbesthal on the Belgian frontier, where we were once more put out of the train. No conveyance of any kind was in sight so following the crowd we set off for Belgium. Along the way through the town the entire population seemed to be gathered on their front steps to see the band of fugitives go by. At the frontier line a *douanier* ransacked the one poor satchel as never before or since. Its contents were dumped on the ground and every article examined by candle light, and then left for us to replace in the satchel. Gertrude could not walk as fast as many others, so when the Belgian station was reached a crowd was packed about the train gate, and when, at last, the gate was opened, rushed for the cars in a manner that would have done credit to a New York subway mob in the rush hours. Gertrude therefore had no seat, but sat on the upturned end of her satchel in the corridor.

Long after midnight the train drew up in the station of Brussels, and all were ordered out. Towards morning the keeper of the restaurant opened his doors and sold us coffee and rolls. Our breakfast over, we were put into a train going possibly to Paris, as some thought, but somewhere. As it jogged along a bright light appeared in the sky. Could it be that the Germans had invaded Belgium and were burning some town? It must be for the light was too large to be made by a burning house. Some early riser finally suggested that it might be made by the rising sun, as it was. Passing through Ghent and Bruges we knew of course we were bound for Ostend where we arrived early in the morning. While waiting for the boat, a crowd of tourists from northern France and elsewhere began to assemble, and grew in numbers as the hours passed. But the pressing question was the purchase of our tickets. Our money was German paper and some 300 marks in gold, and fifty dollars in American gold for use on our arrival home. Unless the ticket man would take German money we could not take the boat. To test the matter, Bach took place in the long queue before the booking office and while standing there was asked by an old lady to buy her ticket to London, handing him German money as she made the request. When asked if German money would be received, she said, "Yes," and it was. We now had tickets to London. . . .

With no clothes save those on our backs, with no English money in our pockets, and no possibility of getting any, for the moratorium had still several days to run, we reached London and began a search for lodgings in some unpretentious hotel. To find such a place proved to be no easy matter. Again and again we were turned away until Gertrude remembered a small hotel in some street off Oxford Street, not far from the marble arch, and there we found lodgings. When I told the young woman at the desk that we were fugitives from Germany, had no luggage, no money, and that she would have to pay the cabbie, she said, "I have been many years in this hotel, during that time hundreds of American have come and gone, and only one 'did' us."

Having thus been housed, the most pressing matters were clothes and money. For linen we went to Selfridge's great department shop where Bach and I interviewed the proprietor. After listening to our tale of woe, he said, "In England bills are paid quarterly, not monthly as in America. I will give you an order on the bookkeeper for a quarter's credit and you may pay any time." To get money was more difficult. The American Express Company had given notice that it would each day cash one ten dollar check for each holder of its checks. I had some; but on reaching its office on Haymarket Street, we beheld two queues of waiting people stretching from the paying teller's wicket out of the building and far down the Street. No money was obtained that day, but at six o'clock the next morning, Phil took his place at the end of a much shorter line; at eight o'clock Bach took his place, and when I replaced him the office had been opened for business, the line much shortened and in time I secured ten dollars worth of English money. After the moratorium was lifted and the banks were open, I went to Brown, Shipley & Company and was amazed to find they were asking seven dollars and a half for a pound sterling. It was a scandalous charge, and months afterwards the excess over the usual $4.83 was returned to me by Brown Brothers & Company, the branch of the house in Philadelphia.

Our financial troubles were not over yet. We intended to come home from Hamburg and had paid for passage and berths on a Hamburg-American steamer. The war put all German lines out of commission and our passage home must be paid for all over again. Our clothes, our trunks, our wraps, our hand satchels were gone and must be replaced at heavy expense. In our pockets was a hundred dollars in German money, utterly useless for no one would touch it. To these losses of passage home, clothing, and money was added the uncertainty of our stay and the cost thereof, for it was then impossible to get a berth on any British or American liner sailing from an English port. More money it was certain must be had, and to get it I wrote to the Provost of the University requesting that the Treasurer be authorized to send me $500 should I need it, and to D. Appleton & Company to allow their London agent to pay me $500 to be deducted from royalties, and from him obtained that sum.

While we were busy with our own affairs, Americans by thousands, fugitives from Holland and France, had been pouring into London. The first comers met and organized at the Waldorf-Astoria Hotel but soon moved to the Savoy where the great ball-room and other rooms made useless by the war were placed at their disposal. Money was raised, some $30,000 to aid Americans made destitute by the loss of their German Travellers Checks. A committee of American women resident in London took charge of stranded American women, school teachers and what-not, found them proper boarding places and paid their board until berths were secured for them on returning steamers. Liners out of England ceased to carry steerage passengers. Steerage quarters were cleaned and painted; berths were put in steerage dining rooms, and all passengers were first class with the run of the ship. A registration bureau was opened and before we left in October more than 90,000 men and women had registered.

Unable to get transportation, we passed our time seeing London preparing for war. When Gertrude and I landed at Plymouth in May the suffragettes were rampant and it seemed as if all public buildings were closed to women. The National Portrait Gallery was shut to them, and the British Museum save to such as were workers and known. When in Gloucester Cathedral, we asked to be shown the crypt, the request was refused. "Is that," said Gertrude, "because I am a woman?" "I am sorry to say, Madam," was the reply, "it is." "My husband and I," said Gertrude, "are Americans. I am not a suffragette, and will do no damage." Our guide then opened a door, called a workman, and placing himself in the lead, and the workman behind us, we were escorted into the crypt. In London, in June, we were rudely refused admittance into the Temple Church and a morning newspaper which Gertrude held, rolled, in her hand was snatched from her. Riding by [undecipherable] one morning and seeing a crowd about one of the gates we got down from the bus, and were informed that the King, Queen and the Princess Mary would come through the gate in a few minutes. As they passed, I noticed that the King wore a high grey hat in the side of which was a deep dent. The evening newspapers announced that as the Royal party was passing along Constitution Hill, a band of suffragettes pelted the royal party with bundles of suffragette literature, wrecked the Queen's parasol and knocked off the King's hat; hence the dent. On another day we beheld at one of the entrances to the Parliament House, some one lying on a mattress attended by two trained nurses, and were told the person was Mrs. Pankhurst, the great leader of the suffragettes. The lady was engaged in a hunger fest, and was to stay at the door until she died unless Lloyd George or Mr. Asquith or someone would receive a delegation from her party. The afternoon newspapers announced that the Government had yielded, that the delegation would be received, and that Mrs. Pankhurst had been taken home.

Now all was changed; the suffragettes had ceased their militant outrages; the British Museum and the Portrait Gallery were open to everyone, and the city presented a gay appearance for on many private and all public buildings were grouped the flags of the allies, Japan, Russia, France, Belgium, Great Britain. But other signs of war were visible. The busses becoming fewer and fewer day by day as hundreds of them were sent to France; the use of women as conductors on many that remained; the appearance of paper money in the form of the ten shilling note; the placards "Business as Usual" posted in the shop windows, the disappearance of German toys and goods, wares and merchandise from the shops for nobody would buy them; the disappearance of German waiters from the hotels, and of German people from the streets, the closing of their little shops and the boarding up of the windows of the offices of the Hamburg-American and North-German Lloyd Steamship Companies; young men in mufti drilling all day long in the little squares in quiet parts of London, the crowds in the offices of the Atlantic lines seeking passage home, and the still greater crowd that each day crowded in the Savoy hotel, were all ever present reminders of a state of war.

Towards the middle of September our luck changed for the better most unexpectedly; our trunks and satchels were recovered. A World Church Peace Conference was to meet at Constance, and on the evening of Saturday, July 31st, an "acquaintance" gathering was held. In the midst of it a distinguished minister rapped for order and announced that war had been declared, that mobilization would begin within a few hours, and that all must go home at once or remain for thirteen days. Then arose the question of money. All sources of supply were of course closed. A proposal was then made that each should rise and tell how much cash was in his pocket. Even when this was done, there was not enough in the pool to pay the cost of transportation, whereupon the proprietors of one of the hotels offered to accept the checks of their guests for board and loan the sum necessary to make up the deficit, and the next morning the American and English peace delegates set off for Holland in cars attached to the end of a train of German soldiers on their way to the front. At Cologne their luggage disappeared just as ours had done, after mobilization. Through the good offices of the American Ambassador at the Hague, Henry Van Dyke, the Americans were permitted to send an agent to Cologne to bring back their baggage. He was Professor B. F. Ballin of Swarthmore College near Philadelphia. He very kindly consented to search for our lost luggage, so Bach went down one evening to his lodgings and give him the bits of numbered papers which did duty as trunk checks. A fortnight passed before he telephoned that our baggage was at the custom-house at Victoria Station. The boys were then on a pleasure trip in the Isle of Wight, so Gertrude and I went to Victoria and found every one of the lost trunks and satchels awaiting us, each with a long tag certifying that it belonged to a delegate to the Church Peace Conference. But our luck did not end there. On our return to America the German-Americans were raising $10,000,000 for the Fatherland. German money was very welcome so the gold marks nobody would take in England were sold for 22 cents each, only two cents less than their value in time of peace; the Hamburg-Amercian Line returned the money paid for the passage it did not provide, and late in the winter the American Express Company which sent a steamer to bring home the baggage left by Americans in Germany returned the steamer rugs and heavy wraps we sent to Hamburg to be put on board the liner on which we intended to sail for home.

Our trunks recovered, nothing remained but to secure passage home. After some delay the boys secured berths in the steerage of the Laconia and departed. Left to ourselves, Gertrude and I hearing that the steamers of the Canadian Pacific Railway were bringing over troops; that they would not be commandeered, for the troops from Canada must be brought over, went to the office of the Company, secured a very comfortable state room, and sailed from Avonmouth, near Bristol, late in September. The Captain's chart showed that we were going direct to the Gulf of St. Lawrence; but the sun and the stars told a different story, and I knew we were heading for Newfoundland to keep out of the way of German cruisers. The voyage was cold, rough, and the days cloudy and foggy. Our landfall was the north point of Newfoundland at the entrance to the Straits of Belle Isle. There we anchored and rolled about for the better part of a day until the fog lifted, and it was safe to enter the Straits. On the way through the Straits, two icebergs not very large, but large enough, were passed.

A week was spent at Quebec before setting out for Mount Washington on the way home. . . .[2]

Having escaped a war, McMaster could not escape his habit of working. Once home, he was soon preparing a biography of Stephen Girard, Philadelphia's merchant adventurer who had made himself a civic institution by establishing the Girard Trust. The biography was to be an official one, and McMaster was free to use over 50,000 manuscripts rich in materials of America's commercial life during the troubled period of the wars with England.[3]

McMaster was so impressed by the value of his materials that he adopted the technique of "joining letter to answer to make Girard and his correspondents tell the story. . . ."[4] For a biography this was, as he later realized, a blunder.[5] "The diligent student of economic history," one of McMaster's devoted pupils wrote, "may use these volumes as a source; but the biographer's reputation as a historian has not been enhanced by them."[6] It was a ghost returning to his old work table. Over a decade before, Ellis P. Oberholtzer, a student and the scholarly heir-apparent of McMaster, had produced a far more impressive business biography in his *Jay Cooke: Financier of the Civil War.*[7]

One gray afternoon in April 1917, while the Girard biography was still a mass of notes, McMaster stood in Independence Square and heard the American declaration of war announced. His students, one of them later remarked, were "rather cynically" entering the army, but there was nothing cynical in McMaster's attitude.[8] The

[2] "Second Memoirs," pp. 100-17, MS.

[3] *Ibid.*, pp. 99-100, 117-19.

[4] *The Life and Times of Stephen Girard*, I, Preface, viii.

[5] "Second Memoirs," pp. 118-19, MS.

[6] Review of Stephen Girard by Frederic L. Paxson, *Mississippi Valley Historical Review* (1919), VI, 120.

[7] Two vols., Philadelphia, 1907. It is ironical to read that the "Girard biography carried on . . . the tradition established by Oberholtzer in his life of Jay Cooke. . . ." Kenneth W. Porter, "Trends in American Business Biography," *Journal of Economic and Business History* (1931-32), IV, 601.

[8] James Monaghan, "John Bach McMaster, Pioneer," p. 25, a manuscript used through the courtesy of the author.

fighting publicist of the Spanish-American War had aroused himself once again. "What are we waiting for?" he demanded of a cheering Philadelphia audience after the *Lusitania* went down.[9] In an address of March 1916, the historian described the "unpreparedness" of the 1812 period in a way that permitted the chairman of the meeting to remark, "I am not so sure that Professor McMaster's indictment of Presidents Jefferson and Madison could not be made with justice in these days against some one whose name we will not mention."[10] Once war came, McMaster's feeling was deep and continuous.

But this was not McMaster's war. He could not volunteer for the Engineers Corps now; younger men, some of them McMaster's students, worked with Creel's Committee on Public Information.[11] The restless McMaster gave most of his time to *The United States and the World War*, a work started at the suggestion of teachers who needed materials for use in their classrooms. Scarcely was the first volume done when the Armistice stifled interest in war books, but McMaster pushed on and took the story down to the American rejection of the Versailles Peace Treaty. The work was not intended to be "history, but a narrative of passing events."[12] The materials, taken largely from newspapers and public official documents, are often held together only by a thin glue of "it was said" or "it was reported," and the reader has a sense of snatching at the next "Extra" being shouted on the streets in 1918.[13] Here, indeed, was history as seen by a contemporary—it is dedicated "To First Lieutenant Philip Duryee McMaster United States Army Medical Corps"—and it has its value as a document of the confusion and

[9] Interview with Mr. E. W. Mumford, who was in the audience. Mr. Mumford did not remember the date of the speech, and I have not been able to locate a report of it in the Philadelphia newspapers.

[10] *Philadelphia Public Ledger*, March 31, 1916.

[11] Among the scholars helping were McMaster's former students, Profs. E. S. Corwin, W. E. Lingelbach, and F. L. Paxson. James R. Mock and Cedric Larson, *Words That Won the War* (Princeton, 1939), pp. 172, 183, 185.

[12] "Second Memoirs," p. 119, MS.

[13] For example, II, 204.

uncertainties of the times. In the backwash of the war, McMaster, like so many conservative Americans, spoke out his conservatism still more bluntly. His last utterance as a publicist was an attack on the popular election of United States Senators—on an extension of "the right of man" which McMaster had glorified most.

The Senator [McMaster complained] is now more than ever the people's man. Stripped of the ancient dignity and glory of his office, nominated at a primary election, he must take the stump, subject himself to the abuse and vilification characteristic of our popular elections, and be more than ever a politician with a record which appeals to the crowd, which cares nothing for statesmanship, culture, wide experience in world affairs.[14]

While the outside world rushed past McMaster, his personal universe crumbled. Death was shattering "The Big Four." A few months before his graduation from the University of Pennsylvania Law School, just when his literary talent was emerging, John Bach, Jr., died of pneumonia. The stricken father could only collect some of his boy's writings in a sad little volume—for "the promise they give of greater things that might have followed . . . as a tribute to the memory of a lost son and lifelong companion."[15] And then death took from McMaster his wife, the charming Minnie of his miserable Princeton days, the companionable Gertrude of his years of drudgery, the gracious Mrs. McMaster of his triumphs. "God give you every consolation, dear friend," Jameson wrote, and McMaster needed every consolation.[16]

Only work could give solace. For a long time William Appleton had urged McMaster to add another volume to the *History of the People*. It was a mistake, Appleton urged, to take the story of national development up to 1861 and then to stop when the very survival of the nation was in question. Going on had little appeal

---

[14] *NewYork Herald-Tribune,* June 22, 1930.

[15] McMaster, ed., John Bach McMaster, Jr., *The Kidder and Other Tales,* Introduction, p. 6. John Bach, Jr. died on March 1, 1915.

[16] J. Franklin Jameson to McMaster, July 10, 1922, MS. Mrs. McMaster died of a heart attack on June 30, 1922.

to McMaster. He had fulfilled the promise he made to himself and the world in the brave days when he turned out Volume I. "Why not stop?" he asked himself. But, with time dragging, Mc-Master found stopping harder than going on, and the Lincoln volume appeared in 1927.[17] It was a decided anticlimax, a continuation of the *History of the People* long after the merits of the earlier work had been improved upon and many of its faults had become conspicuous faults indeed.[18] Now McMaster knew it was time to stop. Seven years before the Lincoln volume appeared, he had reached the age of retirement at the University of Pennsylvania.[19] His textbooks sold so little that further revisions were not demanded.[20] Walter Hines Page was long since dead, and new editors did not beseech McMaster for an opinion at his earliest convenience. "There, I have come up to you," McMaster said as he handed a copy of the Lincoln book to Oberholtzer, whose opening volumes on the period since the Civil War had already appeared. "It is for you to go on."[21]

McMaster was seventy-five now, a patriarch of his profession in years and in distinction. He had long since served his term as president of the American Historical Association, long since received his share of honorary degrees and honorary memberships, long since been able to say proudly "Historians . . . have found out that the invention of a labor saving machine, the discovery of a cure for some dread disease, may really be a more important event in the history of a nation than any battle its generals ever won, or

[17] "Second Memoirs," pp. 99, 120, MS. The quotation is from p. 99.

[18] For an interesting example of a later generation's attitude toward McMaster's handling of the Civil War, see Charles W. Ramsdell's review in the *American Historical Review* (1927), XXXIII, 156-58.

[19] "Minutes of the Board of Trustees of the University of Pennsylvania" (April 12, 1920), XVIII, 52, MS, University of Pennsylvania Archives.

[20] The year the Lincoln volume was published, only 914 copies of the *School History*, 1,607 copies of the *Brief History*, and 4,272 copies of the *Primary History* were sold. The sales reports are among the McMaster Papers.

[21] Ellis P. Oberholtzer, "John Bach McMaster," *Pennsylvania Magazine of History and Biography* (1933), LVII, 19.

any treaty its statesmen ever concluded."[22] McMaster even looked the patriarch—a solid little man with a twinkling eye and a Madonna-like smile that gave a touch of inscrutability to the massive head. "One thinks of an historian," an interviewer noted, "as a quiet, scholarly person who sits back placidly and lets the world roll by—while he figures out just what it's all about—and that is exactly what John B. McMaster is."[23] The calm was disturbed only by the patriarch's irritation at "debunked" history and the "interpretation of history," at what he and William R. Thayer joined in denouncing as "mere historical grinds."[24] Thayer and McMaster had been the majority of a Pulitzer Prize Committee which gave the award to *Victory at Sea* by Rear Admiral Sims, a man of the generation of '98, of McMaster's generation.[25] But the next year the prize went to James Truslow Adams' *The Founding of New England*, a book rooted in the work of historical grinds, deeply influenced by Turner's frontier interpretation, and not un-

[22] "The Present State of Historical Writing in America," *Proceedings of the American Antiquarian Society*, 1910, new series, XX, 426. McMaster was president of the A.H.A. in 1905. His honorary degrees were: The College of the City of New York (1892), Ph.D.; University of Pennsylvania (1894), Princeton University (1925), Litt.D.; Washington and Jefferson College (Pa., 1901), University of Toronto (1907), LL.D. He had also been elected a member of the American Philosophical Society and of the National Institute of Arts and Letters, and an honorary member of many state and religious historical societies.

[23] Unsigned interview in the *Boardwalk Illustrated News*, May 21, 1923. McMaster was interviewed while vacationing in Atlantic City.

[24] "Second Memoirs," p. 74; William R. Thayer to McMaster, May 11, 1921, MSS. See also Oberholtzer in the *Pennsylvania Magazine of History and Biography*, LVII, 27-30.

[25] William S. Sims (in collaboration with Burton J. Hendrick), *The Victory at Sea*, New York, 1920. The third member of the 1921 committee was Worthington C. Ford, who favored Frederick Jackson Turner, *The Frontier in American History*, New York, 1920. "I agree with you," Thayer wrote McMaster (April 25, 1921, MS.), "that Turner's book—tho excellent in substance—does not come within the definition, or intent of Pulitzer's gift. It isn't a consecutive or symmetrical 'history.' Mr. Ford held the other opinion so strongly, that I wrote to Columbia for information: the people there agree with me. So do five or six of our best men here [Harvard], whom I asked for an informal opinion. So Turner's book is not in the running."

touched by Charles A. Beard's economic thesis.[26] New men, new ideas had risen in the historical firmament. "The youngsters," Mc-Master sighed, "are all enthusiastic about things we discovered were fallacious a half century ago."[27] McMaster, still alive, had become historiography.

All the old man had left were his son, Philip, a few friends, and his memories. Even the table at the Franklin Inn Club was often denied him by a heart that would "suddenly lay down on part of its job" and leave him panting.[28] Philip, now married, had established himself at the Rockefeller Institute for Medical Research, and McMaster's last faltering winter was whiled away at his son's place in Connecticut.[29] Here, under the persistent persuasion of his daughter-in-law, the patriarch began putting his memories on paper.[30] "Time was plentiful . . ." begins the sentence cut off in 1932 by heart attack, and time, indeed, was too plentiful.[31] With justified pride, the "Memoirs" told the story of a career—almost eighty years of it—which had no place for inactivity. McMaster had gone a long way since the day in 1883 when the public, startled by the *History of the People*, wanted to know who John Bach McMaster was. He had come from the people to be a leader among them. He had taught American historians a new American past. He had educated thousands of school children in this past while influencing their parents about public affairs of the present. When the coffin was lowered into Philadelphia soil on a mild spring day, his countrymen had learned full well who John Bach McMaster was.[32]

[26] Boston, 1921.

[27] Interview with Mr. E. W. Mumford.

[28] McMaster to George Gibbs, Nov. 24, 1931, a manuscript in the archives of the Franklin Inn Club.

[29] On Oct. 13, 1923, Dr. Philip D. McMaster married Miss Elizabeth P. Dwight. Dr. McMaster had been appointed a Fellow of the Rockefeller Institute in 1919 and he has remained there, in rising capacities, ever since.

[30] Letter from Dr. P. D. McMaster to the author, April 22, 1938.

[31] "Second Memoirs," p. 120, MS. McMaster died on May 24, 1932, in his son's home in Darien, Conn.

[32] The funeral was described in the *Philadelphia Public Ledger*, May 28, 1932.

Appendix I

THE BOOKS analyzed are those identified in Chapter VI, note 73. Social history here means history that is plainly not political or military, and pages that are doubtful according to this criterion have not been counted. For obvious reasons, pages of teaching devices have been included in approximating the space devoted to various periods of history but not in approximating the space given to various types of history and to the West and the Middle States. "Space given to the West and to the Middle States" means space given to them as regions and not space used to describe events of general importance which occurred in these regions; "Middle States" does not include Maryland. All numbers are percentages.

Author	Space given to								
	−1783	1783–Civil War	Civil War	1865–	Political History	Social History	Military History	West	Middle States
McMaster	31	47	9	9	49	25	24	7	2
Eggleston	51	27	13	6	37	18	41	4	1
Johnston	32	38	15	13	55	17	25	1	1
Thomas	31	34	13	16	61	11	26	3	1

Appendix II

HERE the types of history are distinguished in the way described in Appendix I. Since McMaster's terminal dates are usually indefinite, the "Years Covered" refers to the main body of material in the volume.

Vol.	Years Covered	% of Volume Given to History That is		
		Pol. & Dipl.	Social	Military
I	1783–90	79	20	0
II	1790–1803	70	26	2
III	1803–12	79	13	5
IV	1812–21	41	20	35
V	1821–29	64	35	0
VI	1829–41	80	12	2
VII	1841–49	57	31	8
VIII	1849–61	62	26	0

Appendix III

THE NUMBERS below refer to the number of biographical vignettes. In his Table of Contents, McMaster specifically indicates the short biographies in his text. The biographies marked out in this way include practically all of the biographical material in the *History* and have been the only material considered here. "Fav." means enthusiastically favorable; "Unfav.," sharply unfavorable.

Vol.	Pol. & Dipl.				Military				Non-Pol.				Totals			
	Fav.	Unfav.	Non-Com.	Total	Fav.	Unfav.	Non-Com.	Total	Fav.	Unfav.	Non-Com.	Total	Fav.	Unfav.	Non-Com.	Total
I	8	4	3	15	0	0	0	0	1	0	0	1	9	4	3	16
II	4	7	5	16	1	0	1	2	2	0	1	3	7	7	7	21
III	2	2	2	6	0	0	1	1	0	0	1	1	2	2	4	8
IV	1	0	1	2	0	0	2	2	0	0	1	1	1	0	4	5
V	0	0	2	2	0	0	0	0	7	0	2	9	7	0	4	11
VI	0	0	0	0	0	0	0	0	0	0	1	1	0	0	1	1
VII	0	0	3	3	0	0	0	0	0	2	2	4	0	2	5	7
VIII	0	0	4	4	0	0	0	0	0	1	1	2	0	1	5	6

Appendix IV

THIS APPENDIX analyzes certain sections of McMaster's *History of the People*. The volumes chosen are ones which represent major stages in the preparation of the work—the first, the last, and the middle volumes (Vol. V was published 17 years after Vol. I and 13 years before Vol. VIII, but, from the point of view of its time of preparation, it is more accurately the "middle volume" than any other one). From each of these volumes two sections have been chosen, the one of predominantly social history, the other of predominantly political history, and both including as wide a variety as possible of the types of sources McMaster used. Here social history means the same as in Appendix I. One section from Vol. II, similar in nature to the section in Vol. I which provoked the *New York Tribune* charge of plagiarism (see pp. 45-47), has also been analyzed to see if the savage attack had any immediate effect on Mc-Master's technique.

In part the analysis was made by using materials cited in, or suggested by, McMaster's footnotes; in part, by going through materials which, from internal evidence, might have been McMaster's source. Where it was not possible to be virtually certain that a given source was the one actually used, no comment is made. Since McMaster had no consistent form for footnotes, the question of footnote form has been ignored.

It is suggested that this appendix be used along with the appropriate page of the *History*. Points are made in the appendix in the order in which the eye would come to them as it passed down a page of the *History*.

To shorten the appendix, the following symbols have been used:

b.o. —legitimately based on, though McMaster gives no direct reference to the source.

c.p. —closely paraphrased from.

F. —footnote.

F.–a. —footnote accurate, meaning both (1) that, exclusive of form, the footnote refers accurately to the place where the material is, and (2) that the text based on the footnote uses the source properly.

F.–i.—footnote inaccurate, either because the footnote, exclusive of form, is inaccurate within itself, or because the text based on it does not use the material properly.

i.q. —inaccurately quoted within quotation marks. Unless otherwise specified, the inaccuracy is a minor change of words or punctuation and does not seriously alter the meaning.

M. —McMaster.

par. —paragraph. P. 200, par. 1 means the first paragraph which begins on p. 200 and includes the material in that paragraph even if it runs on to the next page.

t.i. —text inaccurate either in the facts it draws from the source or in the implications it makes on the basis of the source.

The obvious abbreviations have been used to refer to the following materials which have been used in reconstructing McMaster's pages:

NEWSPAPERS

American Daily Advertiser (Phila.)
American Museum (Phila.)
The Awl (Lynn, Mass.)
Boston Gazette
Columbian Magazine (Phila.)
Connecticut Courant (Hartford)
Kentucky Reporter (Lexington)
Lancaster (Pa.) *Journal*
Miner's Journal and Schuylkill Coal and Navigation Register (Pottsville, Pa.)
National Intelligencer (Washington, D.C.)
National Journal (Washington, D.C.)
New England Palladium and Commercial Advertiser (Boston)
New York Evening Post
New York Gazette
New York Times
New York Tribune
Niles' Weekly Register
Ohio Monitor (Columbus)
Philadelphia Public Ledger
Pittsburgh Daily Commercial Journal
Richmond Enquirer

Spirit of the Age (New York City)
United States Telegraph (Washington, D.C.)
Washington (D.C.) *Democratic Press*
Washington (D.C.) *Globe*
Washington (D.C.) *Telegraph*
Working Man's Advocate (New York City)

PAMPHLETS AND OFFICIAL DOCUMENTS

An Address of Henry Clay to the Public, containing Certain Testimony in Refutation of the Charges against Him Made by General Andrew Jackson, Washington, 1827.

Baker, Henry, *Two Chapters from Oligarchy and Hierarchy,* Cincinnati, 1856.

Colonel Frémont's Religion. The Calumnies Against Him Exposed by Indisputable Proofs, —— [1856].

Colonel Frémont's Romanism Established, ——, 1856.

Facts for the People, No. 1, New York, 1856.

Field, David D., *Reasons Why Naturalized Citizens Should Vote for Frémont,* a speech delivered at Troy, New York, in 1856.

Fillmore, Millard, speech at Albany, reprinted in *The Great Fraud by which Pennsylvania is Sought to be Abolitionised in October and November*—[1856].

Frémont a Catholic!! ——, 1856.

Journals of the Virginia House of Delegates, 1779, 1781.

Letter of Judge Ephraim Marsh, of New Jersey . . . Giving his Reasons for Supporting Col. J. C. Fremont, New York [1856].

Massachusetts House Document, No. 50, 1845.

Massachusetts House Document, No. 153, 1850.

Register of Debates in Congress, 1825-26.

The Romish Intrigue, ——, 1856.

The Romanism of Frémont as Demonstrated by His Own Acts, ——, 1856.

Speech of Josiah Randall, of Philadelphia, delivered at Chambersburg, August 6, 1856, Saratoga Springs, 1856.

Walker, Robert J., *An Appeal for the Union. Letter from the Hon. Robert J. Walker* [New York, 1856].

OTHER WORKS

Anburey, Thomas, *Travels Through the Interior Parts of America,* London, 1789.

Bancroft, George, *A History of the United States from the Discovery of the Continent*, 10 vols., Boston, 1834-74.

Bayley, Richard, *An Account of the Epidemic Fever which Prevailed in the City of New York During Part of the Summer and Fall of 1795*, New York, 1796.

Brackenridge, Henry M., *History of the Western Insurrection*, Pittsburgh, 1859.

Brackenridge, Hugh H., *Incidents of the Insurrection in the Western Parts of Pennsylvania, in the Year 1794*, Philadelphia, 1795.

Brissot De Warville, J. P., *New Travels in the United States of America*, Boston, 1797.

Brown, Samuel, *The Life of Rufus Choate*, Boston, 2d ed., 1870, and 6th ed., 1898.

Carnahan, James, "The Pennsylvania Insurrection of 1794," *Proceedings of the New Jersey Historical Society* (1852), VI, 115-52.

Commons, John R., *et al.*, eds., *A Documentary History of American Industrial Society*, 10 vols., Cleveland, 1910-11.

Congdon, Charles T., *Reminiscences of a Journalist*, Boston, 1880.

Coxe, William, *Memoirs of the Life and Administration of Sir Robert Walpole, Earl of Oxford*, 4 vols., London, 3d ed., 1816.

Curtis, George T., *Life of James Buchanan*, 2 vols., New York, 1883.

Curtis, George W., *The Duty of the American Scholar to Politics and the Times*, New York, 1856.

Dallas, George M., *Life and Writings of Alexander James Dallas*, 2 vols., Philadelphia, 1871.

De Roos, Frederick F., *Personal Narrative of Travels in the United States and Canada in 1826*, London, 1827.

Drake, Daniel, *Pioneer Life in Kentucky*, Cincinnati, 1870.

Drake, Samuel A., *Old Landmarks and Historic Personages of Boston*, Boston, 1900.

Drayton, John, *Letters Written During a Tour Through the Northern and Eastern States of America*, Charleston, 1794.

Elliot, Jonathan, ed., *Debates on the Adoption of the Federal Constitution . . .* , 5 vols., Philadelphia, 1876.

Findley, William, *History of the Insurrection in the Four Western Counties of Pennsylvania*, Philadelphia, 1796.

Ford, Thomas, *A History of Illinois*, Chicago, 1854.

Frémont, John C., *Narrative of the Exploring Expedition to the Rocky*

Mountains in the Year 1842, and to Oregon and North California in the Years 1843-44, New York, 1846.

Gihon, John H., *Geary and Kansas,* Philadelphia, 1857.

Gilpin, Henry D., ed., *Letters and Other Writings of James Madison . . . ,* 4 vols., Philadelphia, 1865.

Greeley, Horace, *The Life and Public Services of Henry Clay,* New York, 1852.

Hildreth, Richard, *The History of the United States of America,* New York, 6 vols., 1849-52.

Howells, William C., *Recollections of Life in Ohio,* Cincinnati, 1895.

Hunt, Gaillard, ed., *The Writings of James Madison,* 9 vols., New York, 1900-10.

Johnston, Richard M., and Brown, William H., *Life of Alexander H. Stephens,* Philadelphia, 1878.

Longfellow, Samuel, *Life of Longfellow,* 2 vols., Boston, 1886.

Morley, John, *Walpole,* New York, 1889.

Nicolay, John G., and Hay, John, *Abraham Lincoln: A History,* 10 vols., New York, 1890.

Pike, James S., *First Blows of the Civil War,* New York, 1879.

Priest, William, *Travels in the United States of America, Commencing in the Year 1793 and ending in 1797,* London, 1802.

Quincy, Edmund, *Life of Josiah Quincy,* Boston, 1874.

Ramsay, David, *The History of South Carolina,* 2 vols., Charleston, 1809.

Reynolds, John, *My Own Times,* Chicago, 1879.

Richardson, James, *Messages and Papers of the Presidents, 1789-1897,* 10 vols., Washington, 1896-99.

Riedesel, Frederike C. L., *Letters and Memoirs,* New York, 1827.

Rives, William C., *History of the Life and Times of James Madison,* 3 vols., Boston, 2d ed., 1866-68.

Robinson, Charles, *The Kansas Conflict,* New York, 1892.

Smyth, John F., *Tour Through the United States of America,* London, 1784.

Sparks, Jared, ed., *The Works of Benjamin Franklin,* 10 vols., Philadelphia, 1840.

Thomas, Ebenezer S., *Reminiscences of the Last Sixty-Five Years,* 2 vols., Hartford, 1840.

Tyler, Lyon G., *The Letters and Times of the Tylers*, 3 vols., Richmond, 1884-96.

Wansey, Henry, *An Excursion in the United States of North America in the Summer of 1794*, Salisbury, England, 1st ed., 1796, 2d ed., 1798.

Ward, Townsend, "The Insurrection of the Year 1794," *Memoirs of the Historical Society of Pennsylvania* (1858), VI, 117-203.

Warren, Edward, *The Life of John Warren*, Boston, 1874.

VOLUME I
Section *A*, *pp. 10-19*

P.   10.   Reference to Bancroft in F. is a.

P.   11.   F.—a.

P.   12.   F.1—i. Correct name of author is E. S. Thomas, who gives no evidence to support M.'s statement that Thomas "had often been over" the neck. The quotation from Drake is i.

F.2—i. *Boston Gazette* does not mention bridge. *American Museum* does contain ode (*New York Gazette* insufficiently identified to distinguish it from a number of contemporary papers of that name).

F.3—a.

P.   13.   F.1—a.

F.2—a.

"There the houses" to "under the windows"—text slightly inaccurate (see p. 110) and c.p. from Quincy, p. 36, to which there is no reference close by except in a comprehensive footnote (F.1 on p. 13) placed after the previous par. and a partially comprehensive footnote after part of the following par. (F.1 on p. 14) concerning "the interiors of the Boston houses."

P.   14.   F.1—a. Pages used by McMaster: Warren, pp. 310-11, and Quincy, p. 39.

F.2—i. No evidence in Warren that engravings mentioned by M. were "among the most popular."

P.   17.   F.—a.

P.   18.   F.—a.

P.   19.   F.1—i.q. and both sources contain the same paper.

F.2—i. References are Anburey, not Auburey, II, 69-70, and Smyth, II, 364, not 346. Riedesel does not call Yankees "inquisitive and credulous."

VOLUME I
Section B, pp. 272-84

The structure of this section in McMaster—sequence of events, interpretation, and many of the actual words—rests on Rives. Most of the materials cited in McMaster's footnotes could have been taken from Rives. Rives is not mentioned by McMaster in this section. Reference to him is first made in the next chapter, p. 394.

P. 272.   F.—i.q. The letter is quoted in Rives, II, 18.

P. 273.   "The trade of" to "Rappahannock inspection"—t.i. from letters in F.2, which are quoted in Rives I, 547, and in F.1 of Rives, II, 47. The suggestion to turn back to Vol. I of Rives may have come from F.1 in Rives, II, 57, a page McMaster apparently had been using. The sources do not say that Virginia had "no ships or seamen" and say only that "almost all," not "every one" of her merchants had British connections. The sentence beginning "It was only after much higgling" goes beyond the sources in several small ways.

F.1—i.q. from the letter as checked in Hunt, *Madison's Writings*, II, 162. This particular part of the letter has not been found quoted in Rives, Elliot, or Gilpin, the principal collections of Madison's correspondence printed at the time M. was writing this volume. However, a part of this letter is quoted in F.2 of Rives, II, 21, and a footnote of Rives (F.1 in Rives, II, 38) refers to the whole manuscript letter.

Pp. 273-74. "The attention" (p. 273) to "by Americans" (p. 274) —c.p. from petitions quoted in Rives, II, 46-48.

P. 274.   "Under this pressure" to "into consideration"—c.p. from Rives, II, 48.

"A warm and full discussion" to "Declaration of Independence"—b.o. Rives II, 44, and on a letter from Madison to Washington, Nov. 11, 1785, quoted in Rives, II, 52.

Pp. 274-75. Pars. 2 and 3 (p. 274) and par. 1 (p. 275)—virtually copied from Rives, II, 44-45.

P. 275. Par. 2—c.p. from Rives, II, 46. "Thurston" is Thruston.
Par. 3—c.p. from the letter in the first half of F.2, which is quoted in Rives, II, 52-53.

F.1—a. This whole footnote is the same as F.2 in Rives, II, 45.

F.2—The letter from Madison to Washington (quoted in Rives, II, 52-53) supports par. 3 down to, but not including the last sentence, after which it is placed.

P. 276. Par. 1 down to "appeal to arms"—c.p. from Madison's notes on his speech, which are paraphrased in Rives (II, 49-51) and quoted in F.1 of Rives, II, 51.

"When the vote" to "of the whole"—b.o. various materials in Rives, II, 52, 53, 55.

F.1—i.q. The letter is quoted in Rives, II, 56.

Pp. 276-77. "And now" (p. 276) to "thirteen years" (p. 277)—i.q. and t.i. from a letter of Madison to Jefferson, quoted in Rives, II, 56. No evidence in the letter that the basis of the attack was shifted because of the critical storm.

P. 277. "This was" to "in 1786"—c.p. from Rives, II, 66.

Pp. 277-78. Par. 1—c.p. from various materials in Rives, I, 548-52.

P. 278. F.—i. The second letter should be Jefferson to Madison. Both letters are quoted in Rives, I, 549-50.

Pp. 278-79. Par. 1—c.p. from Rives, II, 57-58.

Pp. 279. "The Legislature" to "on the table"—c.p. from Rives, II, 58-60.

Pp. 279-80. "But at last" (p. 279) to "and asperity" (p. 280)—c.p. from various materials in Rives, II, 64-66.

Pp. 280-81. Par. 1 (p. 280)—c.p. from the letter cited in F. on p. 281, which is quoted in Rives, II, 99.

P. 281. F. Rives (II, 98) does not cite the date of the Randolph communication and M. does not.

Pp. 282-83. "Those who had" (p. 282) to "really lamentable" (p. 283)—c.p. from source in F. on p. 283.

P. 284. F. The first letter mentioned supports the text and is quoted

in Rives, II, 143-44. The second letter is i.q. on the basis
of Hunt, *Madison's Writings*, II, 300. It is not in Elliott
or in Gilpin, and has not been found in Rives. The third
letter is i.q. on the basis of Sparks, *Franklin's Writings*,
X, 294, which had been published long before Vol. I of
the *History*.

VOLUME II
Pp. 189-202

P. 189.   F.—a.

Pp. 189-90. Descriptions of violence rest on Carnahan (pp. 120-21),
which is included in the comprehensive F. on pp. 202-03.

Pp. 190-92. "The matter was" (p. 190) to "left to themselves" (p.
192)—the account rests on H. M. Brackenridge (*History*,
pp. 40-48), with an occasional similarity or identity of
phrase. Brackenridge is included in the comprehensive F.
on pp. 202-03, and is also specifically cited where some of
the material apparently taken from him stops.

P. 193.   "As the robbers sat" to "severe measures"—for this M. cites
Carnahan in F.1. Since both M. and H. M. Bracken-
ridge (*History*, p. 82) quote Bradford directly and Carnahan does not, it is likely that M. was really using Brackenridge, who also cites Carnahan with the same page reference that M. gives. If M. was using Brackenridge, his
quotation is i.q.; if M. was using Carnahan, he put quotation marks around part of an indirect quotation.

F.2—The article cited (Ward) is not "Addison's Charge"
but a general article on the Insurrection which quotes a
small part of the charge.

F.3—a. Both H. H. Brackenridge (*Incidents*, p. 40) and
Findley (p. 95) quote the same circular.

P. 194.   F.—a.

P. 195   "That night" to "six thousand souls"—c.p. from source in
F.4.

F.1—i.q. from Ward, pp. 184-85.

F.2—i.q. from *ibid*.

F.3—i.q. from *ibid*.

F.5—a.

P. 196. F.—a.

P. 197. "As the discussion" to "every girl ten"—c.p. from source in F.1.

F.2—a.

Pp. 197-98. "When the drafts" (p. 197) to "flint and powder" (p. 198)—t.i. from source in F.1 on p. 198. No mention in source of march on Frederick or of activities of terror-stricken merchants.

P. 198. "At Middletown"—t.i. from source in F.2. Source does not mention Middletown.

"At Carlisle" to "for disorder"—t.i. from source in F.4. No evidence in source where "larger pole" was placed.

F.3—a.

P. 199. F.1—i. "some" is one person.

F.2—a. This F. and F.1 refer in different ways to the same letter.

F.3—i. "others" is one person; no evidence that "others" is a different person from "some" in the previous sentence of M.'s text.

F.4—a.

P. 200. F.1—i. Source makes no comparison with Hannibal.

F.2—i. No evidence that "they wondered that in such a land," etc.

F.3—is really F.4 and should come after " 'Cowards and Traitors.' "

F.4—is really F.3.

Pp. 201-02. M. seems to have relied far more on H. H. Bracken-ridge's *Incidents* than on any of the other sources mentioned in the comprehensive F. on pp. 202-03.

VOLUME V
Section A, pp. 150-60

P. 151. "I secured" to "room contained"—i.q. from source in F.1. This section follows the source no more closely than does the unquoted section at the bottom of p. 150.

"When you alight" to "the tavern contains"—c.p. and t.i.

from the *Miner's Journal*, Nov. 26, 1825. In F.1, M. cites this as the issue of Nov. 28. The source says "crowding half a dozen or more persons into one bed room. . . ."

P. 153.   Par. 1—b.o. Howells, p. 49.

P. 154.   Par. 1—c.p. from Howells, pp. 78-79.

          F.—i.q. The part of Drake used is p. 107.

P. 155.   Par. 1—b.o. Howells (p. 115) which M. cites here in a pseudo-comprehensive footnote.

          Par. 2—b.o. Howells, pp. 122-24.

          F.—a.

P. 156.   " 'Boys, the Court' " to " 'on the bench' "—i.q. from source in F.2.

          " 'I knew a judge' " to " 'between the parties' "—i.q. from source in F.3.

          F.1—a. "Nicholay" is Nicolay.

Pp. 156-57. " 'Judge,' said the foreman" (p. 156) to "just your notion" (p. 157)—i.q. from Ford, p. 85. Throughout this quotation M. changed frontier dialect to conventional English.

P. 157.   The story from " 'Mr. Green' " to "preparations to hang him" is from Ford, pp. 83-84 and is i.q.

          F.—a.

P. 158.   Par. 1 down to "a personal affront"—b.o. Nicolay and Hay, I, 63-64.

          Interpretation of material based on F. could be questioned; material comes from p. 82 as well as p. 81 of source cited.

P. 159.   " 'these men' " to " 'a merry jig' "—i.q. from source in F.

Pp. 159-60. Discussion of frontier religion—b.o. Nicolay and Hay, I, 54-55.

VOLUME V
Section B, pp. 501-517

This section leans heavily on *Niles' Register*. Most of McMaster's footnotes refer to the *Register* or to material which may be found in it.

Pp. 501-02. "In June" (p. 501) to "republican principles" (p. 502)—c.p. and t.i. from source in F. on p. 502. Meeting was in May, not June.

Pp. 502-04. Par. 3 (p. 502) to " 'of the community' " (p. 504)—
c.p. from source in F.1 on p. 504.

P. 503. The first two direct quotations given by M. are paraphrases
by a second party in the source (F.1, p. 504). Also, some
of the wording is changed.

"There was a billiard table" to "and a half"—t.i. from source
in F.1 on p. 504. In the source the cost of the billiard
table and balls is given as $56.00.

Pp. 503-04. " 'Is it possible' " (p. 503) to " 'of the community' "
(p. 504)—i.q. from source in F.1, p. 504.

P. 504. "But no" to "a denial"—t.i. from source in F.2. The material in the source says that the Chairman of the Committee had not denied the charge at the time of the congressional debate. The Chairman did deny it in a letter he
wrote and permitted to be published before "a year later."

Par. 1—i.q. from source in F.3 and sentences omitted from
quotation without any indication.

P. 505. F.1. In 1842 Beverley repudiated his earlier letter, and
the relevant documents were published in *Niles' National
Register* (1842), LXI, 402-03. In 1852 Greeley's biography of Clay (p. 118) had retold the story of the re-
pudiation.

Fs. 2-4. Quotations from these are i.q. and papers are quoted
in *Niles' Register* (1827), XXXII, 162.

Pp. 505-06. " 'Early in January' " (p. 505) to " 'in favor of Mr.
Adams' " (p. 506)—i.q. from sources in F.1 on p. 506.

P. 506. F.2—a. The letter is quoted in the *Reporter*, and the *Reporter* is quoted in *Niles' Register*.

Pp. 506-07. " 'I rejoice again' " (p. 506) to " 'fearless confidence' "
(p. 507)—i.q. from source in F.1 on p. 507. The quotation comes only from p. 379 of the source M. cited.

F.2—a.

P. 508. " 'I called upon' " to " 'their own weapons' "—i.q. from
source in F.1 in a way that changes the meaning. The
source quotes Buchanan as having said, "Until I saw
general Jackson's letter to Mr. Beverley of the 5th ult.
and at the same time was informed by a letter from the
editor of the United States' Telegraph, that I was the per-

son to whom he alluded, the conception never once entered my mind that he believed me to have been the agent of Mr. Clay or of his friends. . . ." The *Lancaster Journal* is quoted in the *Niles' Register* cited.

P. 510.   F.—a.

P. 511.   F.—i. Pages are 351-52, not 35-52.

Pp. 511-12. "The session" (p. 511) to "utterly false" (p. 512)—c.p. from *United States Telegraph* (March 1, 1828, I, 1-3), to which M. does not refer except in a specific connection in F.2 on p. 512.

P. 512.   Fs.1 and 2. The sources cited in these Fs. are mentioned by full title and discussed in *United States Telegraph*, I, 3, 6, mentioned by M. in an ambiguous way in F.2.

Pp. 512-13. "This 'placed' " (p. 512) to " 'with Mr. Clay' " (p. 513)—i.q. from source in F.1 on p. 513, which is quoted in *United States Telegraph*, I, 1-5.

Pp. 514-15. Charges similar to those M. describes in par. 1 (p. 514) and par. 1 (p. 515) appear in various numbers of *United States Telegraph*, I.

P. 516.   "The party of" to "the tariff"—c.p from source in F.4.

Fs. 1 and 5. The *Ohio Monitor*, April 19, 26, 1828, is not in the American Antiquarian Society or the Ohio State Archaeological and Historical Society, the only two places where, according to the *Union List of Newspapers*, those issues might be found.

Fs. 2 and 3—a.
Fs. 6 and 7—a.

VOLUME VIII
Section *A, pp. 97-106*

The key work to this section is Commons' *Documentary History*, VIII. The order of material in McMaster usually follows the order in Commons, and more than half of McMaster's footnotes cite Commons or material printed in Commons.

P. 97.   F.1—a. This section of Richardson is printed in Commons, p. 85.

F.2. The material comes from "a Pittsburg paper," quoted in the *Washington Globe*.

P. 98. F.1—a.

F.2—i. No evidence that tickets were put in the field "in eight counties."

P. 99. F.1—a.

F.2—*The Working Man's Advocate* is quoting the *Fall River Mechanic* and is itself quoted in Commons, p. 86.

F.3—*The Awl* is quoting the *Boston Daily Bee* and *The Awl* is quoted in Commons, pp. 97 ff. More resolutions were passed than M. indicated in par. 2.

Pp. 99-100. "The New England" (p. 99) to "its own bargains" (p. 100)—t.i. from source in F. on p. 100. M. selects a few instances from among a larger number of varying instances. "some" in line 6 is one petitioner; "others" in line 7 is one petitioner. Another petitioner, not reported by M. but in the source, testified that she "drew $14.66 for five weeks work" (Commons, p. 137). M.'s F. on p. 100 is quoted in Commons, pp. 133-51.

P. 101. "At Manchester" to "requiring more"—c.p. from source in F.2.

F.1—The act cited was printed in the *New York Tribune* which, in turn, is quoted in Commons, p. 190.

Pp. 101-02. "To Horace Greeley" (p. 101) to "of the law" (p. 102) —c.p. from source in F.1 on p. 102. This source is quoted in Commons, pp. 189-91.

P. 102. Par. 3—b.o. *Pittsburgh Daily Commercial Journal*, quoted in Commons, pp. 202-05.

F.2—a. This issue of the *Tribune* is quoted in Commons, pp. 200-01.

P. 103. "A number of printers" to "co-operative plan"—c.p. and t.i. from source in F.3. From the source one cannot be certain that the shop was on the "co-operative plan."

F.1—the source is the *Boston Chronotype*, quoted in *The Spirit of the Age*, quoted in the Commons citation M. gives.

F.2—a.

F.4—a.

P. 104. F.1—a.

F.2—i. In the *New York Herald* cited by M., the only mention of German workers is a dispatch from the *Buffalo Commercial* which says nothing except that German tailors were striking—and in Buffalo, not New York.

Pp. 104-05. " 'Many of us' " (p. 104) to " 'to the work' " (p. 105) —i.q. and t.i. from source in F.1 on p. 105. The German is not a "Socialist" in the source. The words attributed to him by M. are actually the words of three different men, one of whom was named Franconi.

P. 105. Fs. 2-4—a. These papers are quoted in Commons, pp. 326-27, 331-32, 333-34, 315-26.

Pp. 105-06. "In Massachusetts" (p. 105) to "not passed" (p. 106) —t.i. What M. describes as the "committee" report was actually the minority report of the committee. The source in F.1 on p. 106 is House Doc. No. 153, not 133, and is quoted in Commons, pp. 151-86.

VOLUME VIII
Section B, pp. 263-76

P. 263. F.1—a.

P. 264. "A large body" to "at their peril"—t.i. from source in F.1. M. gives only one of the two reasons mentioned by the Governor for disbanding volunteer militia.

"The orders" to "hurried to Lawrence"—b.o. Gihon, pp. 149-53.

Par. 1—i.q. from source in F.3, which is quoted in Gihon, p. 264.

F.2—a.

P. 265. "The resolution" to "restoring peace"—c.p. from source in F.2.

F.1—i. Letter cited is in Gihon (p. 264) and contains nothing about a recommendation for postponement of the Whig convention.

P. 266. Fs. 1 and 2—a.

Pp. 267-68. "You have come" (p. 267) to "holding for freedom" (p. 268)—c.p. and t.i. from source in F. on p. 268. The burden of Field's remarks (Field, pp. 7-8) did not concern immigrants already in the United States but rather immigrants who would come in the future.

Pp. 268-69. " 'We see' " (p. 268) to " 'precious inheritance' " (p. 269)—i.q. from source in F.1 on p. 269. Pp. 2-3 of the source were used by M.

P. 269. "Toombs believed" to " 'not before' "—i.q. from the letter of Toombs cited in F.3.

F.2—a.

F.3—i. The letter of Toombs is quoted both in *Oligarchy and Hierarchy* and in the *Tribune,* but in the *Tribune* of Aug. 16, not Aug. 18.

Pp. 269-70. "The Republican party" (p. 269) to "our Southern brethren" (p. 270)—c.p. from p. 3 of source in F.1 on p. 270.

P. 270. "In Georgia" to " 'Southern Republic' "—i.q. and t.i. from source in F.2. In the source there is evidence only that the Atchison City toast was made on July 4th. All three toasts have minor mistakes in transcriptions, and the second toast should read, "Gen. Atchison—hoping that he may live to see Kansas a slave state, *in the Union or out of the Union.*"

"The Richmond *Enquirer*" to " 'immediate disunion' "—i.q. from source in F.3.

Fs. 4-6—a.

Pp. 270-71. " 'To the fifteen' " (p. 270) to " 'Declaration of Independence' " (p. 271)—i.q. from source in F.1 on p. 271. In the 2d and 6th eds. of Brown (the only eds. in the Library of Congress), this quotation is found respectively on pp. 306 and 326.

P. 271. "Tyler declared" to "or Black Republican"—t.i. from source in Fs. 2 and 3. While Tyler thought a Republican victory meant disunion, he looked "to no such result of the election" (Tyler, II, 532). Wise, "somehow or other," had "an abiding confidence in the success of our party" (*ibid.,* p. 533). M.'s statements, therefore, are misleading in their implication.

"Longfellow" to "Fremont"—t.i. from source in F.6. Longfellow's plain implication is that a knee injury was the primary cause of canceling the trip.

Fs. 4 and 5—a.

P. 272. Fs. 1-4—a.

P. 273. F.1—i. Date of paper is Sept. 22.

F.2—i. The source should be simply *Facts for the People*, No. 1, p. 3, and not the *Letters of Judge Ephraim Marsh*. *Facts for the People* consisted of a quotation from one pro-Frémont paper and was hardly, as McMaster says in the first part of par. 1, "as the politicians saw the situation."

Pp. 273-74. " 'How could' " (p. 273) to " 'the Capitol?' " (p. 274) —i.q. from source in F.1 on p. 274. The part of the speech outside the quotation marks follows the original almost as closely.

P. 274. Fs. 2-6—a.

Pp. 274-75. "and Greeley that" (p. 274) to "utterly miserable" (p. 275)—c.p. from source in F.1. The phrase within quotation marks is no more similar to the language of the source than most of the rest of the passage.

P. 275. F.1. The Greeley letter is in the book by Pike, which M. cites in the second half of the F.

F.2—a.

F.3—i. No mention of "up to January 1, 1857" in source cited.

P. 276. Par. 1—t.i. from source in F.4. Geary says nothing of expecting prosperity.

F.1—i. Material used by M. not in *Tribune*, Nov. 18. Information comes from a letter, of Nov. 20, in *Tribune*, Nov. 24.

F.2—a.

F.3—a.

List of McMaster's Printed Writings and Speeches

"The Abolition of Slavery in the United States," *Chautauquan* (1892), XV, 24-29.

The Acquisition of Political Social and Industrial Rights of Man in America, Cleveland, 1903.

Address at the formal opening of the new building of the Historical Society of Pennsylvania, *Pennsylvania Magazine of History and Biography* (1910), XXXIV, 299-301.

Address before the Netherlands Society of Philadelphia, *The Netherlands Society of Philadelphia, Fourteenth Annual Banquet . . . 1905,* pp. 40-45.

"The America of 1803," address at Centennial Celebration of the New York Ave. Presbyterian Church, Washington, D.C., printed in part in *Washington Post,* Nov. 17, 1903.

"Annexation and Universal Suffrage," *Forum* (1898), XXVI, 393-402.

Article attacking popular election of United States Senators, *New York Herald-Tribune,* June 22, 1930.

"The 'Bad Lands' of Wyoming and Their Fossil Remains," *Bulletin of the American Geographical Society* (1880), XII, 109-30.

Benjamin Franklin as a Man of Letters, Boston, 1887.

Bridge and Tunnel Centres, New York, 1875.

A Brief History of the United States, New York, 1907.

A Brief History of the United States. Adapted for Use in the California Schools ("California State Series"), Sacramento, 1909.

"A Century of Constitutional Interpretation," *Century Illustrated Monthly Magazine* (1889), XXXVII, 866-78.

"A Century of Social Betterment," *Atlantic Monthly* (1897), LXXIX, 20-27.

"A Century of Struggle for the Rights of Man," *Proceedings of the New York State Historical Association* (1901), I, 65-79.

"A Century's Struggle for Silver," *Forum* (1893), XVI, 1-10.

"Cheaper Currency," *New York Herald,* Oct. 25, 1896.

"Commerce, Expansion, and Slavery, 1828-1850," in *Cambridge Modern History* (13 volumes, New York, 1902-13), VII, 378-404.

Compendio de historia de los Estados Unidos, tr. y. adaptación por Marcos Moré del Solar, New York, 1902.

"Contrasts in History," *New York World,* Jan. 1, 1899.

Daniel Webster, New York, 1902.

"The Delivery of Louisiana to the United States," *Independent* (1903), LV, 2987-92.

"The Dread of Expansion," *Outlook* (1899), XLI, 161-65.

"Early Financial Efforts," *Alumni Register, University of Pennsylvania* (1917), XIX, 293-99.

"Edward Augustus Freeman," in Charles D. Warner, ed., *Library of the World's Best Literature, Ancient and Modern* (30 volumes, New York, 1896-97), X, 5977-81.

"The Election of the President," *Atlantic Monthly* (1896), LXXVIII, 328-37.

Foreword to Anna P. Hannum, ed., *A Quaker Forty-Niner, The Adventures of Charles Edward Pancoast on the American Frontier,* Philadelphia, 1930, pp. ix-xi.

"The Foundations of American Nationality," in *The Booklovers Reading Club Hand-Book,* Philadelphia, 1901.

"The Framers and the Framing of the Constitution," *Century Illustrated Monthly Magazine* (1887), XXXIV, 746-59.

"Franklin in France," *Atlantic Monthly* (1887), LX, 318-26.

"A Free Press in the Middle Colonies," *New Princeton Review* (1886), I, 78-90.

French Society during the Reign of Louis XIV, a paper read before Phi Beta Kappa at the College of the City of New York, Jan. 27, 1882 [New York, 1882].

"General Grant's Life," *Philadelphia Press,* July 24, 1885. Reprinted with additions (of which, apparently, some were not McMaster's) in *The Life, Memoirs, Military Career and Death of General U. S. Grant. With War Anecdotes and Freely Drawn Extracts from His Autobiography,* Philadelphia, 1885 [the copyright date, 1884, must certainly be a mistake].

"Geometry of Position Applied to Surveying," in George J. Specht, McMaster, *et al., Topographical Surveying,* New York, 1884.

"The Government of Foreigners," summarized in *Annual Report of* the *American Historical Association for the Year 1899* (2 volumes, Washington), 1900, I, 20-21.

"The Growth of the Nation," in *Cambridge Modern History* (1903), VII, 349-377.

High Masonry Dams, New York, 1876.

A History of the People of the United States during Lincoln's Administration, New York, 1927.

A History of the People of the United States, from the Revolution to the Civil War, 8 volumes, New York, 1883-1913.

"How the British Left New York," *New York Press*, Nov. 26, 1893.

"How to Deal with a Filibustering Minority," *Forum* (1893), XVI, 470-77.

"The Influence of Geographical Position on the Civilization of Egypt and Greece," *National Quarterly Review* (1876), XXIV, 29-52.

"Is Sound Finance Possible under Popular Government?" *Forum* (1895), XIX, 159-68.

"James Abram Garfield," in *Encyclopaedia Britannica* (10th ed., London, 1902-03), XXVIII, 585-86.

"The Johnstown Flood," *Pennsylvania Magazine of History and Biography* (1933), LVII, 209-43, 316-54.

The Kidder and Other Tales by John Bach McMaster, Jr. (editor), Philadelphia, 1915.

"Liberty Loans of the Revolution," *University of Pennsylvania University Lectures, 1918-19* (Philadelphia, 1919), VI, 233-56.

"The Louisiana Purchase," in *History of the Expedition under the Command of Captains Lewis and Clark* . . . (3 volumes, New York, 1904), I, vii-xvi.

The Life and Times of Stephen Girard, Mariner and Merchant, 2 volumes, Philadelphia, 1918.

"Making a Government," *Philadelphia Press*, Sept. 17, 1887.

Modern Development of the New World, Philadelphia, 1902. Written in collaboration with John Fiske.

"National Expansion," *New York Herald*, Dec. 11, 1898.

New Grammar School History of the United States, compiled by the State Text-Book Committee and Approved by the State Board of Education of California, Sacramento, 1903.

"The North in the War," *Chautauquan* (1892), XV, 152-57.

"Old Standards of Public Morals," in *Annual Report of the American*

Historical Association for the Year 1905 (2 volumes, Washington, 1906), I, 55-70.

"One Year of Cleveland; The Record It Has Made," *New York Press,* March 4, 1894.

" 'Open Door' Policy," *Boston Herald,* Dec. 11, 1898.

The Origin, Meaning, and Application of the Monroe Doctrine, Philadelphia, 1896.

Osborn, Henry F., *A Memoir upon Loxolophodon and Uintatherium . . . Accompanied by a Stratigraphical Report of the Bridger Beds by John Bach McMaster* ("Contributions to the E. M. Museum of Geology and Archaeology of the College of New Jersey" [Princeton, 1881], I, no. 1).

Outline of a Course of Lectures on the Political and Economic History of the United States, delivered at the College of New Jersey, 1893, Lancaster, 1893.

Outline of the Lectures on the Constitutional History of the United States (1789-1889), delivered before the Senior Class, Wharton School, University of Pennsylvania, 1888-89, Philadelphia, 1889.

"A Pioneer in Historical Literature," *Atlantic Monthly* (1894), LXXIII, 559-63.

Pennsylvania and the Federal Constitution, 1787-1788 . . . edited in collaboration with Frederick D. Stone, Lancaster, 1888.

Political History of the United States.—Outline of the Lectures Delivered before the Junior Class, Wharton School, Philadelphia, 1890.

Political History of the United States.—Outline of the Lectures Delivered before the Senior Class, Wharton School, Philadelphia, 1891.

"Political Organization of the United States," in Nathaniel S. Shaler, ed., *The United States of America* (2 volumes, New York, 1894), I, 475-502.

"The Present State of Historical Writing in America," *Proceedings of the American Antiquarian Society,* new series, 1911, XX, 420-26.

A Primary History of the United States, New York, 1901.

"Progress of a Century," in James W. Garner and Henry C. Lodge, eds., *The History of the United States* (4 volumes, Philadelphia, 1906), IV, 1728-1748.

Remarks on a plan for an economic history of the United States, summarized in *Annual Report of the American Historical Association for the Year 1904* (Washington, 1905), p. 39.

Remarks on offering the toast, "History, Like Charity, Begins at Home," in *Pennsylvania Magazine of History and Biography* (1910), XXXIV, 299-301.

"The Riotous Career of the Know-Nothings," *Forum* (1894), XVII, 524-36.

A School History of the United States, New York, 1897.

"A Short History of American Politics," in Karl Baedeker, ed., *The United States With an Excursion into Mexico* (New York, 1893), pp. xxxii-xlv.

"The Social Function of United States History," *National Herbart Society, Fourth Yearbook* (Chicago, 1898), pp. 26-30.

"The Struggle for Commercial Independence," in *Cambridge Modern History* (13 volumes, New York, 1902-13), VII, 305-34.

"The Struggle for the West," *Lippincott's Monthly Magazine* (1892), XLIX, 758-71.

"Syllabus of a Course of Six Lectures on Six American State Papers," *University Extension Lectures under the Auspices of the American Society for the Extension of University Teaching* (Philadelphia, 1896), Series F, No. 16.

"Syllabus of a Course of Six Lectures on the Economic Condition of the People of the United States," *University Extension Lectures under the Auspices of the American Society for the Extension of University Teaching* (Philadelphia, c. 1891), Series A, No. 18.

"Syllabus of a Course of Six Lectures on First Quarter of the Nineteenth Century in the United States," *University Extension Lectures under the Auspices of the American Society for the Extension of University Teaching* (Philadelphia, c. 1894), Series D, No. 7.

"The Teaching of History," *Annual Report of the American Historical Association for the Year 1896* (2 volumes, Washington, 1897, I, 258-63.

"The Third Term Tradition," *Forum* (1895), XX, 257-65.

"Thomas Babington Macaulay," in Charles D. Warner, ed., *Library of the World's Best Literature, Ancient and Modern* (30 volumes, New York, 1896-97), XVI, 9381-86.

"The Tradition against the Third Term," *Atlantic Monthly* (1927), CXL, 374-81.

Trail Makers (editor), 9 volumes, New York, 1902-05.

"The Underground Railway, New York City," *Scientific American*, new series, 1874, XXXI, 307-08, 323, 338-39.

The United States in the World War, 2 volumes, New York, 1918-20.

The University of Pennsylvania Illustrated with a Sketch of Franklin Field by H. Lausatt Geyelin, Philadelphia, 1897.

The Venezuela Dispute, New York, 1896.

"Washington and the French Craze of '93," *Harper's* (1897), XCIV, 659-73.

"Washington's Farewell Address and a Century of American History," *Outlook* (1899), LXI, 448-51.

"Washington's Inauguration," *Harper's* (1889), LXXVIII, 671-86.

"Where the Constitutional Convention Met," *Pennsylvania Magazine of History and Biography* (1887), XI, 81.

With the Fathers: Studies in the History of the United States, New York, 1896.

"Wildcat Banking in the Teens," *Atlantic Monthly* (1893), LXXII, 331-43.

The X.Y.Z. Letters, edited with Herman V. Ames ("Translations and Reprints from the Original Sources of European History" [Philadelphia, 1899], VI, no. 2).

Bibliography

THIS BIBLIOGRAPHY includes only manuscripts, collections of newspaper clippings, and interviews and letters about McMaster. Other sources have been identified in the footnotes.

I. THE McMASTER PAPERS

This correspondence is the property of the historian's son, Dr. Philip D. McMaster, of the Rockefeller Center for Medical Research. It consists of the following categories of materials:

1. Letters to McMaster. Over 5,000 unclassified letters, ranging in time from 1873 to the end of McMaster's life.

2. Two letterbooks containing copies of letters sent to McMaster. The first letterbook runs from April 6, 1889, to April 5, 1893; the second, from May 21, 1894, to March 17, 1897. Most of these letters are brief business notes.

3. The McMaster autobiographies. There are two drafts of the McMaster memoirs, the one covering only his family and boyhood (referred to as "First Memoirs"), the other covering the later as well as the earlier years (referred to as "Second Memoirs"). The memoirs were hastily written in McMaster's last years at the urging of Mrs. Philip D. McMaster. Sections of the memoirs have been published as follows: "Young John Bach McMaster: A Boyhood in New York City," *New York History* (1939), XX, 316-24; "Reliving History: John Bach McMaster as an Army Clerk," *Journal of the American Military Institute* (1940), IV, 127-28; "The Princeton Period of John Bach McMaster," *Proceedings of the New Jersey Historical Society* (1939), LVII, 214-30.

4. The diaries. The diaries consist of sporadic entries in three books which jump spaces in time. The first covers part of McMaster's trip west, June 13, 1878, to August 11, 1878; the second has general entries from March 3, 1891, to February 2, 1892; the third has general entries from February 5, 1883, to December 23, 1883.

5. There are many newspaper and magazine clippings preserved

in various forms among the McMaster Papers. These consist of copies of articles McMaster wrote, reviews of his publications, articles concerning him or his statements, etc.

II. McMaster Family Materials

A few letters of various members of the McMaster family or of friends of the family are in the possession of the historian's sister, Mrs. Samuel G. Metcalf, Staten Island, New York.

III. The Century Collection in the New York Public Library

This collection includes twenty-four letters and eleven telegrams from McMaster to various editors of the *Century Magazine* concerning his publications in that journal.

IV. McMaster's Scrapbook

The Historical Society of Pennsylvania has a scrapbook kept by McMaster at some unknown period of his life. It consists of clippings from various publications of poems or prose that apparently appealed to him.

V. The following people have granted me interviews, written me letters, or loaned me manuscript materials about McMaster:

William C. Ackerman	William F. Magie
William H. Allen	James Monaghan
Albert S. Bolles	Edward W. Mumford
Lewis S. Burchard	Albert Cook Myers
Edward P. Cheyney	Roy F. Nichols
Edward S. Corwin	Mrs. Ellis P. Oberholtzer
Henry Crew	Frederic L. Paxson
Roland P. Falkner	Miss Marie L. Rulkotter
E. McClung Fleming	Donald A. Roberts
Herbert Friedenwald	Arthur M. Schlesinger
George Gibbs	William B. Scott
Martin Goldwasser	Samuel Scoville, Jr.
Nathan Goodman	Richard H. Shryock
Morton Gottschall	Ernest Spofford
William E. Lingelbach	James T. Young

Index

Acquisition of Political Social and Industrial Rights of Man, The, 70, 140
Adams, Brooks, quoted, 106
Adams, Charles K., 15n
Adams, Henry, 1, 11, 15n, 134
Adams, Herbert B., 15 and n, 51, 68n, 103, 120; quoted, 14n
Adams, James T., *The Founding of New England,* 157-58
American Antiquarian Society, 33, 57
American Book Co., *see Brief History;* Hinman, R.; *Primary History; School History;* Vail, H. H.
American Geographical Society, 27
American Historical Association, 15n, 107, 156
American history, Centennial gives impetus to, 25; teaching of, by McMaster, 62-66; teaching of, in C.C.N.Y., 11-12; textbooks of, in 1897, 95-101 and 99n; University of Pennsylvania, early professorship of, 52; *see also* Political history, Social history
American Revolution, 143
Amherst, considers Wilson for its presidency, 68n
Anesthetics, discovery of, 44
Anglo-Saxonism, 143
Anthon, Charles E., 11 and n
Appleton and Co., 55, 103, 105, 149, 155; *History of the People* published by, 37-41, 42; plagiarism charges, concern over, 48
Appleton, Daniel, *see* Appleton and Co.
Appleton, William H., *see* Appleton and Co.
Armstrong and Son, 37
Arnold, Matthew, 53
Art, eighteenth-century American, 44

Arthur, Chester A., 54
Atlantic Monthly, 71

Bach family, Julia Anna Matilda, (Mrs. James McMaster) 3, 4; Margaret Cowan (Mrs. Robert Bach), 2; Robert, 2, 4
Bad Lands, *see* Fossil-collecting
Ballston Spa (Saratoga Springs), 3
Bancroft, George, 13, 15, 31, 32, 33, 37, 41, 43, 51, 120, 132, 133, 134, 141-42, 143; quoted, 117-18
Bancroft, Hubert H., 28
Barker, Eugene C., 66
Battle Hymn of the Republic, 9
Battle of Long Island, 93, 94
Beadle and Munro dime novels, 7
Beard, Charles A., 70n, 75, 101, 137, 158
Beard, Charles A. and Mary, 1, 100
Beauregard, Pierre, 4
Benjamin Franklin as a Man of Letters, 55-56, 57-58
Bible, reading of, in New York schools, 6
Blaine, James G., 43
Bok, Edward, 106
Bolles, Albert S., 51-52
Bolton, Herbert E., 66
Boston Evening Transcript, accuses McMaster of plagiarism, 45
Brahms, Johannes, quoted, 121
Brief History of the United States, A, 95, 156, and n
Brooklyn (New York), 2, 4, 93, 94
Bryan, William J., 101
Bryant, William C., 41
Buckle, Henry, 19-20; *see also* Social history
Burr, William H., 22

Carey, C. Ellsworth, quoted, 92n
Carnegie, Andrew, pension trust for academic men, 70-71
Carter Beverley letter, 124
Catholics, reception of *School History*, 93-94
Cedar Creek (Va.), 16
Centennial of 1876, 25
Century Magazine, 42, 80
Channing, Edward, 1, 98; quoted, 106
Chester Republican, 75 and n
Cheyney, Edward P., 66
Chicago, history textbooks in, 80
Chicago Journal, quoted, 84-85
Chicago Post, 83, 84
Children's games, in New York in the fifties, 8
Choate, Rufus, quoted, 140
Civil engineering, teaching of at Princeton, 23-24; see also Surveying
Civil War, in *School History*, 97; New York during, 8-10; see also Grand Army of the Republic, Surveying
Cleveland, Grover, 91; foreign policy, 73-74
College of the City of New York, 15, 50; history courses in, 11-12, 62; student organizations, 10-11
Colonial period, in textbooks, 98-99
Committee on Public Information, 154
Committee on School Histories, G.A.R., see Grand Army of the Republic
Commons, John R., *Documentary History of American Industrial Society*, 108, 120, 131
Cooper, James F., 40-41
Cooper, Peter, 42
"Cordial Balm of Gilead," 2
Corwin, Edward S., 66, 154n
Cowan, Margaret, see Bach family
Crawford, Thomas, 2
"Critical Period," 135-36, 137-39
Cuba, see Expansionism

Daily Northwest News, 74

Dana, Charles A., quoted, 42
Delta Kappa Epsilon, C.C.N.Y., 10
Democratic thought, in McMaster's writings, 139-43
Dennis, Martin R., 34 and n
Des Moines Leader, quoted, 87
Die Wacht Am Rhein, 5, 146
Dodd, William E., quoted, 134
Donald, E. Winchester, quoted, 68n
Draft riots of 1863, 9-10
Draper, John W., 20, 32
Dunning, William A., quoted, 127-28, 127n, 133
Dwight, Elizabeth P., see McMaster family

Economic interpretation, 134-39
Eggleston, Edward, 54; quoted, 21; textbook, 99
Emerson, Ralph Waldo, 130
E. M. Museum, Princeton, 26
Ericsson, Leif, 91-92, 94
Expansionism of 1898, and McMaster, 74-78

Faculty Club (University of Pennsylvania), 67
Federalist tradition, 137-39
Ferrero, Guglielmo, quoted, 106
Field, Stephen J., 43
Fish, Carl Russell, quoted, 130-31
Fiske, John, 29, 80, 118, 131-32
Ford, Worthington C., 157n
Fort Bridger (Wyo.), 26
Forum, 71, 73, 76
Fossil-collecting, in the Bad Lands, 26-29
Franklin Inn Club, 59-60, 158
Freeman, Edward, 122
Friedenwald, Herbert M., 66
Frontier, see Social history; West, the

George, Henry, 37
German scholarship, influence on writing of American history, 14-15

Gibbs, George, 59
Gillespie, George L., 16, 18
Grand Army of the Republic, Committee on School Histories, attacked, 84-85, 87; confers with McMaster, 83; fails to endorse *School History*, 87; reviews *School History* second time, 86-67; sounded out by McMaster, 80-81; states its policy, 81-83; "writing to order" disavowed by McMaster, 87-88; *see also, School History*
Greeley, Horace, *The American Conflict*, 12
Green, John R., *Short History of the English People, A*, 15, 29
Guide to Health, 2
Guyot, Arnold, 26

Hail Columbia, 9
Hamilton, Alexander, 123, 138
Hamiltonianism, in *History of the People*, 137-39; in *School History*, 97
Hanna, Mark, 1
Hart, Albert B., 74n, 98
Hawaii, U. S. and revolution in, 92n
Hearst papers, 71
Heath, Daniel C., 68n
Henry, Patrick, 123
Hildreth, Richard, 13, 15, 31, 32, 41-42, 132, 133
Hinman, Russell, 79, 80, 88n; quoted, 88-90, 92, 93, 94, 95; *see also, School History*
Historical Society of Pennsylvania, 33, 69-70, 105, 108, *see also* Stone, F. D.
History Club, C.C.N.Y., 12
History of the People of the United States, A, Vol. I, first plans and research, 15-16; inspiration for, 13; plagiarism, charge of, 45-47; publication, 41; publisher, search for a, 36-38; research and writing of, 31-36; success of, 42-44; title, struggle over, 39-40; unfavorable criticism, 44-47 Vol. II, publication, 57; writing of 52, 54, 55, 56-57
Vols. III-VIII, Vol. VIII finished, 105; writing of Vols. III-VIII, 69, 105
Vols. I-VIII, economic interpretation, 134-39; footnotes, 117-19; frontier interpretation, 136; general conception of, 124-27; importance, 143-44, inexactitudes, 114-17; methods, explanation of, 119-22; national scope, 132-34; organization, 129-32; "people," the, concept of, 141-43; personalities, treatment of, 128-29; political history, 129, 131; prejudices, combativeness of, 123-24; quotation marks, use of, 108-14; rights of man, treatment of, 139-41; social history, 127-29; South, treatment of, 139; structure partially based on other works, 107-08; *see also* Macaulay, T. B.
History of the People of the United States during Lincoln's Administration, A, 155-56
Holmes, Oliver W., 33
Horsecars, in New York in the fifties, 5-6
Howells, William D., 106; quoted, 21
Hutchinson, William T., quoted, 130

Immigrants, 142-43
Imperialism, *see* Expansionism
Indians, American, 40-41
In My Prison Cell I Sit, 9
Institute of Arts and Letters, 102
Irving, Henry, 54

Jackson, Andrew, 128, 142, 143

Jefferson, Thomas, 91, 123, 128, 138-39, 142, 154
John Brown's Body, 9
John C. Green School of Science (Princeton University), 21-22, *see also* Princeton University
Johns Hopkins University, The, 43, 51; History Seminar, 15n, 103
Johnson, Andrew, 97
Johnson, Emory R., 66
Johnston, Alexander, quoted, 30; textbook, 99n
Journal of Education, 94

Kelly, William D., 54
Kosciusko, 93, 94

Lafayette, Marquis de, 93, 94
Lee, Robert E., 83-84
Library of Congress, 33, 134
Life and Times of Stephen Girard, The, 153
Lincoln, Abraham, 8-9, 10, 102, 128
Lindsay, Samuel M., 65n, 66
Lingelbach, William E., 66, 154n
Lodge, Henry C., quoted, 78
Lusitania, 154

McClellan, George B., 34-35
McClure, S. S., 71; quoted, 72n
McCosh, James, quoted, 24-25, 48-49
McKesson and Robbins, Inc., 2
McKinley, William, 67, 143
McMaster family, Elizabeth P. Dwight (daughter-in-law), 158 and n; Elizabeth Watrous (grandmother), 3; Gertrude Stevenson (wife), 38-39, 40, 43, 44, 48, 49, 52, 54-55, 56-57, 58, 60, 106-07, 128, 145, 146, 147, 148, 150, 152, 155; James (father), 3-5, 11, 14; John Bach, Jr. (son), 58, 145, 147, 149, 152, 155; Julia A. M. Bach (grandmother), 3, 4; Mary (Mrs. Samuel G. Metcalf, sister), 3n, 4n; Philip Duryee (son), 4n, 58, 94, 145, 146, 147, 149, 152, 154, 158;

Robert Bach (brother), 4n, 88, 90; Roland Bach (brother), 4n
McMaster, John Bach, ancestry, 1-4; birth, 4; boyhood in New York City, 4-10; at C.C.N.Y., 10-13; first interest in history, 12-13; lack of historical training, 14-15; fellow in English at C.C.N.Y., 15-16; with surveying party, 16-18; in Chicago, 18-19; free-lance writing, 19-20; influence of science-minded thinkers, 19-21; influence of Victorian realism, 21; appointed instructor in civil engineering at Princeton, 21-22; dislike of Princeton, 23-25; historical impetus from the Centennial, 25; leads fossil-collecting expedition to the West, 26-27; influence of the West, 27-29; returns to Princeton, 30; writes Vol. I of *History of the People*, 31-36; Vol. I accepted for publication, 36-38; romance with Gertrude Stevenson, 38-39, 54-55, 56-57; publication of Vol. I, 41; its success, 41-45; accused of plagiarism, 45-48; appointed professor of history at University of Pennsylvania, 50-52; Vol. II and *Benjamin Franklin*, 54-58; marriage and his family, 58; social life in Philadelphia, 52-54, 58-60; as a teacher, 61-66; as an administrator, 66-68; offers to go elsewhere, 68-69; *Pennsylvania and the Federal Constitution*, 69-70; *Acquisition of Political Social and Industrial Rights of Man*, 70; as a Philadelphia sage, 70-71; as a national publicist, 71-78; *School History of the United States*, Chap. VI, *passim*; *History of the People*, Chap. VII, *passim*; last trip to Europe with his family, 145-53; *Life and Times of Stephen Girard*, 153; role in World War I, 153-55; *United States and the World War*, 154-55;

death of his wife and son, 155; *History of the People during Lincoln's Administration*, 155-56; as a patriarch of the profession, 156-58; death, 158; *see also* Grand Army of the Republic; *History of the People*; Macaulay, T. B.; *School History*

McMillan, Charles, 50.

Macaulay, Thomas B., 16; borrowings from, by McMaster, 45, 48, 109, 119, 121; historical conception, McMaster's similar to, 124-27; historical technique, McMaster's similar to, 121-22, 123, 127; inspires McMaster to write *History of the People*, 13

Madison, James, 137, 154

Marching Through Georgia, 9

Marsh, A. O., 80, 86; quoted, 80-83

Marshall, John, as a historian, 121

Marshall, William I., quoted, 91

Masonic Order, 91

Massachusetts Historical Society, 33

Massachusetts Reform Club, 74, 78

Methodism, in Winchester, Va., 18

Microcosm, The, C.C.N.Y., 12n

Middle States, in *History of the People*, 133-34; in textbooks, 79, 100-01

Military history, in *School History*, 96-97 and 96n

Milner, Duncan C., 83

Mitchell, S. Weir, 59, 105

Monroe Doctrine, 73-74

Morley, John, *Walpole*, borrowings from William Coxe's *Memoirs*, 121 and n

Mumford, Edward W., 65n

Nationalism, in New York schools in the fifties, 9; in *School History*, 96-97 and 96n

Negroes, as slaves on sugar plantation, 4; during New York draft riots, 10; in textbooks, 91, 100n; in Winchester, Va., in the seventies, 17-18

New England viewpoint in writing of history, 79, 100-01, 133

New Jersey Historical Society, 34

New Orleans, 3

Newspapers and pamphlets, use of as sources, 32 and n, 127, 130, 131

New York City, 2, 19; description of, in the fifties, 5-10

New York Free Academy, *see* College of the City of New York

New York Historical Society, 34-35

New York Times, 73-74

New York Tribune, accuses McMaster of plagiarism, 45-47, 119

New York World, 87-88, 103-04

Newry (Ireland), 2

Niles' Register, 108, 120, 131

Northern viewpoint, 41; in *History of the People*, 136-37, 139, 143-44; in *School History*, 97

Northwest Ordinance, 132

Oak Lawn, 4

Oberholtzer, Ellis P., 60, 66, 153, 156

O'Brien, Father T. J., quoted, 93

Opdyke, George, 9

Osborn, Henry F., 27

Page, Walter Hines, 106, 156; quoted, 71-72

Pankhurst, Mrs. Emmeline, 150-51

Parkman, Francis, *La Salle and the Discovery of the Great West*, 12-13; *Old Régime in Canada, The*, 28

Paxson, Frederic L., 154n

Pennsylvania and the Federal Constitution, 69-70

Pennsylvania, State Librarian of, 69

"People," the, in *History of the People*, 139-43

Pepper, William, 51

Perkins, John M., 85

Personalities, in *History of the People*, 128-29, 138

Petroleum refining, 4-5

Phi Beta Kappa, 54; at C.C.N.Y., 11 and n

Philadelphia, controversy over street names, 70-71

Philip, Frederic W., 2

Philosophy of history, McMaster's, 107

Phrenocosmian Society, C.C.N.Y., 10

Plagiarism, McMaster accused of, 45-48, 108-09, 119-21

Political history, domination in U. S. in the seventies, 14-15; in Bancroft and Hildreth, 13; in *History of the People*, 129, 131; *see also* Social history

Presbyterianism, at Princeton, 30

Prescott, William H., 102

Presidential campaign of 1860, in New York City, 8

Presidential campaign of 1896, 71-72 and 72n

Primary History of the United States, A, 95; declining sales, 156, and n

Princeton University, 30, 50, 52, 59, 68 and n; description of, in the seventies, 21-25; *see also* McMaster, J. B.

Progress, theme of, in Macaulay and McMaster, 125-26

Pulaski, 93, 94

Pulitzer Prize Committee of 1921, 157

Putnam, George H., 33

Quincy, Edmund, *Life of Josiah Quincy*, paraphrasing of, 109-10, 120

Reconstruction, 12

Remington, Frederic, 76

Republicanism, 73; in *History of the People*, 137-39, 143-44

Rhodes, James F., 1, 129, 132, 134; quoted, 129

Rights of man, in *History of the People*, 139-43

Ripley, William Z., 102

Rives, William C., *History of the Life*

and Times of James Madison, 108, 135; McMaster accused of plagiarism from, 45-47, 48, 120-21

Robinson, James H., 14n, 101; quoted 106

Rochambeau, Comte de, 93, 94

Rockefeller Institute for Medical Research, 158

Romanticism, in *History of the People*, 143

Roosevelt, Theodore, 19, 28, 61, 106

Root, William T., 66

St. Louis Post Dispatch, quoted, 91

Saturday Club (Philadelphia), 54

Scandinavians in U. S., believe Ericsson discovered America, 91-92

School Gazette, 94; quoted, 97

School History of the United States, A, colonial period, de-emphasis of, 98-99; G.A.R., involvement with, 80-88; importance of, 101; Middle States in, 100-01; military history in, 96-97; nationalism in, 96-97; New England, de-emphasis of, 100-01; organization, 97-98; praise, 94; readability, 95-96; royalties, 88-90; sales, 94-95, 101, 156; social history in, 99-100; unfavorable criticism, 91-94; *see also* Grand Army of the Republic.

School of American History, see University of Pennsylvania

Schools, in New York City in the fifties, 6-7, 9-10

Schouler, James, 1, 102, 129

Scott, Austin, 51, 52

Scott, David B., 6-7

Scott, William B., 27

Shaw, Albert, 103, 106

Shay's Rebellion, 142

Shepherd, William R., 66

Sheridan, Philip H., 16, 18; McMaster's characterization of, 19

Sherman, William T., 26

Sims, William S., *Victory at Sea*, given Pulitzer Prize, 157
Sloane, William M., 37, 50
Smith, J. Allen, 70n, 140-41
Social history, encouraged by frontier conditions, 27-29; encouraged by science-minded writers, 20-21; encouraged by Victorian realism, 21; in *History of the People*, 127-32, 134-35, 144; in McMaster's teaching, 65; in textbooks, 99-100, 100n; *see also* Political history
Socialism, 102-03, 141
Solomon, Samuel, 2
South, McMaster's conception of, 41, 136-37
Southern viewpoint in writing of history, 133
Spanish-American War, *see* Expansionism
Sparks, Jared, 121-22
Specie payment, suspension of, 9
Stamp collecting, 7
Stevens, John A., 35 and n
Stevenson, Gertrude, *see* McMaster family
Stewart, James L., 65n
Stone, Frederick D., 34, 36, 69; quoted, 42, 118; *see also* Historical Society of Pennsylvania
Sugar cane plantation, 4
Surveying, of Civil War battlefields, 16-18; *see also* Civil Engineering; McMaster, J. B.
Sweet, William W., 66

Terry, Ellen, 54
Textbooks, history, royalties on and selling of, 88-90; *see also* Political history; *School History*; Social history
Thayer, William R., 157; quoted, 157n
Thomas, Allen, quoted, 96; textbook, 99
Thompson, Robert E., 67

Thorpe, Frances N., 61-62
Topical method, in *School History*, 98
Truman, James, quoted, 67-68
Tucker, George, 133, 134
Turner, Frederick J., 28, 101, 133, 157 and n; McMaster on frontier and, 136, 137; offered professorship at University of Pennsylvania, 67; quoted, 126
Tyler, Moses C., 15n

Uncle Tom's Cabin, 132
Union Pacific Railroad, 26, 28
United States in the World War, The, 154-55
U. S. Senate, popular election of, 155
University of Illinois, presidency of, 69
University of Michigan, 50
University of Pennsylvania, 60, 69, 75, 101, 121; History Department, 66-67; Law School interested in Woodrow Wilson, 68; McMaster offered professorship in, 51-52; McMaster retires from, 156; School of American History, 61-62; Wharton School, 51-52

Vail, Henry H., quoted, 86-87
Van Buren, Martin, 141
Van Dyke, Henry, 152
Van Nostrand Science Series, 19
Van Tyne, Claude H., 66
Venezuelan dispute, *see* Cleveland, G.
Victorian realism, *see* Social history
Villard, Oswald Garrison, 106
Von Holst, Hermann E., 32, 108n, 127n; quoted, 43

Warner, Charles D., 44, 55
Washington, George, 128-29
Watrous, Elizabeth, *see* McMaster family
Waynesboro (Va.), 16
We Are Coming, Father Abraham, 9
Wendell, Barrett, 106
West, Benjamin, 33

West, the, and writing of American history, 79, 100-01, 133-34, 136, 137, 144

Wharton, Joseph, 51

Wharton School, *see* University of Pennsylvania

Whiskey Rebellion, 142

White, Andrew D., 15n; quoted, 106

"Whitman legend," 91

Whitman, Walt, 54

Whitney, Eli, 128

Willson, Marcius, *Outlines of History*, 11-12

Wilson, Woodrow, 22, 67-68 and 68n, 101, 103, 105; quoted, 106

Winchester (Va.), 16, 17-18

Woman suffragettes (London), 150-51

World Church Peace Conference (London, 1914), 151-52

World War I, outbreak in Europe, 145-53; U. S. enters, 153-55

Wyoming, *see* Fossil collecting

Young, James T., 66